AIR WARS

AIR WARS

BY
SCOTT HAMILTON

THE GLOBAL COMBAT BETWEEN AIRBUS AND BOEING

UNTOLD STORIES REVEAL
THE MAN AND THE STRATEGIES
THAT CHANGED AVIATION

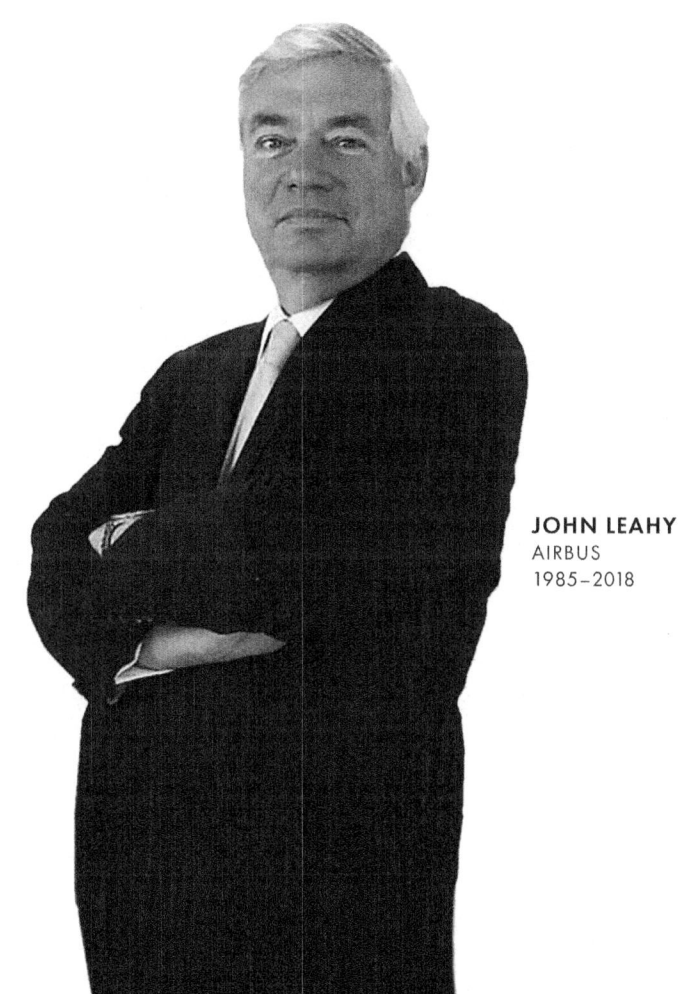

JOHN LEAHY
AIRBUS
1985–2018

TWELVES
PUBLICATIONS

© 2021 by Scott Hamilton

All rights reserved.

No part of this publication may be reproduced, distributed, or transmitted in any form or by any means, including photocopying, recording, or other electronic or mechanical methods, without the prior written permission of the publisher, except in the case of brief quotations embodied in critical reviews and certain other noncommercial uses permitted by copyright law.

ISBN-13: 978-1-73764050-9 (paperback)

Library of Congress Control Number: 2021917443

Edited by Susan O'Meara
Design by Michael Brady Design

Cover photo of airplane courtesy of Wallpaper Cave
Cover photo of John Leahy © Bloomberg/Getty Images
Illustrations of airplanes © Norebbo.com

Contents

	AUTHOR'S NOTE	vii
	FOREWORDS	ix
	CAST OF CHARACTERS	xi
	INTRODUCTION	xiii
1	THE MULTI-BILLION DOLLAR GAMBLE	1
2	FLYING CARGO	10
3	PIPER	15
4	EARLY YEARS AT AIRBUS	20
5	HIGH RISK, HIGH REWARD	29
6	FACING OFF	45
7	THE DEATH OF McDONNELL DOUGLAS	56
8	WAKE-UP CALL	65
9	LAUNCHING THE A380	70
10	MOONSHOT	78
11	TROUBLE IN TOULOUSE	87
12	TRY, TRY AGAIN	93
13	FALLING APART	100
14	LABOR WARS	111
15	UPSTART AND DISRUPTOR	118
16	CREATING NEO	124
17	LAUNCHING MAX	132
18	GROUNDING	138
19	THE X-FACTOR	143

20	**SMASHING A BUG WITH A SLEDGEHAMMER**	152
21	**THE BOEING-EMBRAER JOINT VENTURE**	161
22	**LAST GASP**	168
23	**THE ALPHABET AIRPLANE**	175
24	**GROUNDING**	187
25	**SCANDALS**	203
26	**CORONAVIRUS**	218
27	**RETIREMENT**	227
	ENTRY INTO SERVICE OF MAJOR AIRPLANE MODELS	240
	ACKNOWLEDGMENTS	243
	INDEX	245

Author's Note

THIS BOOK INITIALLY WAS PLANNED to focus on John Leahy's 33 years at Airbus. His hard-driving, take-no-prisoners approach selling airplanes was given the lion's share of the credit, even by his most vociferous critics, for taking Airbus from an 18 percent market share as late as 1995 to 55 percent by his retirement in 2018.

Leahy and I began talking five years before he retired about his writing a book, after retirement, a kind of memoir. We were having dinner in a New York City restaurant. We each perused the wine list. Leahy chose a bottle of fine wine. I couldn't help but remark his choice wasn't the one for $25,000. He didn't miss a beat. Leahy replied he'd order that bottle when I ordered a fleet of airplanes.

Over time, this book evolved into much more than a memoir. The theme became a combination of a Leahy semi-biography and John Newhouse's 1982 book, *The Sporty Game.* That book was the definitive record of the competition between Boeing, McDonnell Douglas Corp. and Airbus, then still in distant third place. Interestingly, Newhouse's book was published two years before Leahy joined Airbus. Eventually, Leahy suggested I write the book. *Air Wars: The Global Combat Between Airbus and Boeing* is the result. It's also about the man, Leahy, and the strategies by Airbus and Boeing that changed aviation as we know it. This is a story about the intense, often bitter rivalry between Airbus and Boeing. Boeing initially blithely dismissed Airbus as just another European jobs program that would produce mediocre airplanes. The views were not without some basis. Boeing assumed it had—and always would have—superior airplanes, and airlines wouldn't be swayed by this government-owned upstart.

Airbus took risks that Boeing didn't think of, dismissed or rejected. Boeing badly misjudged the importance of lessors and, initially, the potential of low-cost carriers. Unlike previous European airplane companies, whether state or privately owned, Airbus officials had the right vision. In addition, with state subsidies and launch aid, they also had adequate resources to produce a family of airplanes to rival Boeing.

Leahy, a brash New Yorker from Queens, was a key to Airbus's growth and success. He had the strong backing of Jean Pierson, an early CEO whose own vision and brashness were critical to Airbus's development and success—and to Leahy's success.

As with any such organization, Leahy's is not the only story. While Leahy is the lead actor in this book, he's hardly the only one responsible for Airbus's successes. Leahy prefers to say he served as the coach of a sales team. Scores of executives played vital roles; thousands of managers and directors implemented decisions. Hundreds of thousands of employees over the decades designed and built the airplanes. So, with apologies to others at Airbus who were crucial parts of the company's success, and to all those who designed and built airplanes, this book focuses on Leahy's years rather than on the larger story.

Interviews principally occurred during 2019 and 2020 at a time when the Boeing 737 MAX was grounded. This unfortunate timing, following the tragic accidents of Lion Air Flight 610 and Ethiopian Airlines Flight 302, caused several people to decline interviews because of their association with the MAX, either at Boeing or as a purchaser of the airplane. The grounding and later the coronavirus pandemic required inclusion of these events as they are so impactful to the story of Airbus and Boeing.

My reporting of Airbus, Boeing and the airline industry began in 1985, the same year Leahy joined Airbus, and continues to this day. Some of this finds its way into the book, reflecting my first-hand knowledge and coverage.

SCOTT HAMILTON
Bainbridge Island, WA
August 2021

Forewords

AIR WARS: THE GLOBAL COMBAT BETWEEN AIRBUS AND BOEING: *Untold Stories Reveal the Man and the Strategies That Changed Aviation* is the story of 35 years of competition between these two global commercial aviation behemoths. Over 33 of these years, John Leahy and his remarkable sales skills took Airbus from No. 3 to No. 1 in global market share. In many ways, he became the face of Airbus--and a thorn in the side of Boeing. Jim Albaugh, the CEO of Boeing Commercial Airplanes (BCA) for several years, later remarked Boeing would have been money ahead to pay Leahy $10 million a year to just go sit in the corner.

Scott Hamilton's chronicle of the global combat between Airbus and Boeing over the last 35 years is filled with insights, rich anecdotes and behind-the-scenes detail from executives, salespeople and engineers at both companies.

Scott covers key sales campaigns won or lost by the companies. *Air Wars* details the critical narrow-body sales campaign at American Airlines, in which Airbus ruptured Boeing's exclusive relationship with American and maneuvered Boeing into launching a re-engined 737, instead of an entirely new airplane program. Then Scott takes us back to John Leahy's beginnings as a New York City taxi driver, and his early days as a pilot and young executive at Piper Aircraft.

Product strategy at both companies provide insider thinking that hasn't been divulged before: development of the A330/A340, the 777, the 787 and A380, as well as the A320neo and 737 MAX. The stillborn development of Boeing's New Midmarket Aircraft—a concept originally intended to replace the 737 but on a smaller scale—also is covered.

Was the Boeing Sonic Cruiser a real idea? Did Boeing, in some Machiavellian move, trick Airbus into producing the A380? How did Airbus maneuver Boeing into launching the re-engining of the 737, the airplane that was named the MAX?

Scott has it all. As a reporter, Scott has covered Airbus and Boeing since 1985. His institutional knowledge, his own reporting and his own archives contribute to *Air Wars*, but his interviews with key executives from both companies provide a history that makes *Air Wars* unmatched.

I saw John Leahy both through the lens of a customer (FedEx) and as his

Airbus colleague. He has a unique sales talent, an encyclopedic knowledge of the industry, an unmatched tenacity and a sharp wit. Thanks to Scott's *Air Wars*, you can experience it all.

ALLAN McARTOR
    Chairman of Airbus Americas 2001–2018
    Former Administrator of the Federal Aviation Administration 1987–1989
    Senior Vice President for Air Operations, FedEx
    Former member USAF Thunderbirds

THE BUSINESS OF DESIGNING AND BUILDING JETLINERS is arguably the world's most exciting industry. The geopolitical and economic consequences of winning and losing in this market, of betting company fortunes on exciting new technologies, and, of course, all the money changing hands and the people employed in hundreds of companies, make for incredible stories to tell.

Air Wars is filled with these fascinating stories. Just after John Newhouse wrote *The Sporty Game*, which gave me my first taste of great aviation industry writing, Scott Hamilton began chronicling the industry. Also, around the same time, John Leahy joined Airbus as a hugely influential salesman and executive. Leahy retired a few years ago, but thankfully Scott is very much hard at work. His book uses Leahy's impact on Airbus and the industry as a useful way of framing a distinct and pivotal era.

Like Scott, I spend my time reacting to events in this industry. For over three decades, I've analyzed the consequences of big and small events, trying to quantify implications and possible outcomes. So do many people. But reacting and analyzing is one thing. It's a big challenge to look back, to try to understand what happened over the years and to construct a compelling narrative of the developments that brought the industry to where it is today.

That's what this book does extremely well. Scott has the experience, and sources, needed to look back through the years and assemble a coherent narrative. The product launches, the big gambles, the commercial triumphs, the scandals, the politics, the tragedies and, of course, the people are all in here.

My hope is that superb books like these inspire newcomers to join our industry, just as *The Sporty Game* inspired me thirtysomething years ago. And if like me you've been watching the industry for some time, I hope *Air Wars* gives you the pleasure I've felt reading stories from three fascinating decades of the greatest industry in the world.

RICHARD ABOULAFIA
    Fellow, Royal Aeronautical Society
    Vice President, The Teal Group Corp.

Cast of Characters

Albaugh, James	Boeing Commercial Airplanes, 2009–2012
Allen, Ron	Chairman, President, CEO, Delta Air Lines, 1987–1997
Alonso, Rafael	President, Airbus Latin America, 2014–2018, EVP 1984–2014
Arpey, Gerard	Chairman, American Airlines, 2004; plus various other executive positions
Barron, Laurence	President, Airbus China, 2004–2014; Chairman 2017
Bellemare, Alain	Chairman, President and CEO Bombardier, 2015–2020
Boyd, Alan	Chairman of Airbus North America, 1982–1992
Bregier, Fabrice	President of Airbus Commercial Aircraft, 2006–2018
Bright, Toby	Various sales positions, Boeing Commercial Airplanes, 1977–2004
Buchholz, Nico	SVP, Bombardier, 2015–2017; EVP, Lufthansa, 2001–2015; Rolls-Royce and Airbus
Calhoun, David	President, CEO, The Boeing Co., 2020–Current; Chairman, 2019–2020; Board Member since 2009
Carson, Scott	President, CEO, Boeing Commercial Aircraft 2006–2009; lifetime Boeing employee
Cherney, Richard	Head of Marketing, Aviation Capital Group, 2001–2010; Managing Director-Fleet, American Airlines, 1994–2001.
Clark, Tim	President, COO, Emirates Airline, 2003–Current
Cleaver, Charles	Treasurer and Sales Finance, and various positions; International Aero Engines, 1988–1996
Conner, Ray	President and CEO, Boeing Commercial Airplanes, 2012–2017; EVP Sales and various other positions; lifetime Boeing employee
Conway, Mike	President, Co-Founder, America West Airlines, 1981–1993
Crandall, Robert	Chairman, CEO, American Airlines, 1985–1998; joined American in 1973 as Senior Financial Vice President
Eccleston, Barry	President, CEO, Airbus Americas, 2005–2018
Enders, Tom	Chairman, CEO Airbus Group (EADS) 2012–2019; President, CEO Airbus Commercial Aircraft, 2007–2012
Faury, Guillaume	CEO, Airbus Group, 2019–Current; COO Airbus Commercial Aircraft, 2018–2019
Feren, John	VP Sales, Boeing and McDonnell Douglas, 1978–2008
Gallois, Louis	CEO, EADS, 2007–2012; CEO, Airbus, 2006–2007

Hazy, Steven	Co-Founder of Air Lease Corp., International Lease Finance Corp.; former CEO of each
Horton, Tom	American Airlines executive 1985–2002; 2006–2010; President 2010–2011; Chairman and CEO, 2011–2014
Krauthamer, Gary	Head hunter who recruited John Leahy for Airbus
Lange, Robert	Senior Vice President, Head of Business Analysis and Market Forecast at Airbus
Leahy, John	Joined Airbus North America in 1985 as a salesman. Named senior vice president and head of sales, 1987, and president in 1990. In 1994, named chief commercial officer at Airbus in Toulouse. In 2005, named chief operating officer-customers. Retired 2018.
Lockhart, Dana	CFO and other positions, Airbus Americas, 1987–2008
McAllister, Kevin	President, CEO, Boeing Commercial Airplanes, 2016–2019; President, CEO of GE Aviation Services, 2014–2016
McNerney, James	Chairman, CEO, The Boeing Co., 2005–2015
Muilenburg, Dennis	Chairman, President, CEO of The Boeing Co., 2015–2019; lifetime Boeing employee
Pierson, Jean	Managing Director, Airbus, 1985–1998
Pilarski, Adam	Economist at McDonnell Douglas Corp., Douglas Aircraft Co. division, to the 1997 merger with Boeing; now an economist with Avitas
Priddy, Robert	Chairman, CEO, ValuJet Airlines
Rao, Kiran	Airbus, 25-year employee and sales executive, including SVP Sales and Strategy
Scherer, Christian	Airbus, currently Chief Commercial Officer
Sinnett, Mike	Boeing, Vice President and General Manager-Product Development
Slattery, John	Former CEO of Embraer Commercial Aircraft; currently CEO of GE Aviation
Stonecipher, Harry	Chairman, CEO, The Boeing Co., 2003–2005; President and COO 1997–2001; President and CEO of McDonnell Douglas Corp., 1994–1997
Streiff, Christian	Short-term CEO of Airbus Commercial Aircraft, three months in 2006
Tomassetti, Nicolas	Executive positions with Airbus, International Aero Engines, Pratt & Whitney and McDonnell Douglas
Vella, Steven	Consultant to airlines working with Airbus and Boeing
Williams, Tom	Airbus, 1999–2018, various positions, including COO Airbus Commercial Aircraft

Introduction

"Airbus has a full family of airplanes. They've improved their product line immensely over the course of time. We're competing head-to-head now. Every single market. We've never had to do that before in our history, and they are dead-set on being the number one producer of commercial airplanes in the world."

—**RAY CONNER,** CEO OF BOEING COMMERCIAL AIRPLANES, IN AN INTERVIEW MAY 13, 2015, WITH DOMINIC GATES OF *THE SEATTLE TIMES*

THE BOEING CO. WAS FORMED IN 1916, early in the infancy of aviation, by William E. Boeing, a logger in the Seattle, Washington, area. Starting with a single-engine biplane on floats, Boeing was an early innovator—and one of the growing number of airplane makers that designed aircraft to carry passengers.

Aviation was a growth business. During the 1920s, even the auto manufacturer, Ford, got into the airliner business. Ford copied the Fokker Tri Motor, a Dutch design, to create the Ford Tri Motor. The visually identical airplanes had one major difference. The Fokker was of wooden construction and the Ford was metal, leading to the affectionate nickname, Tin Goose.

Both were slow, noisy and ungainly. Boeing, which has designed its own wood-and-fabric trimotor, the bi-wing Model 80, in 1933 introduced a revolutionary design, the twin-engine, low-wing Model 247. It was fast, it could stay aloft on one engine and it carried 10 passengers in reasonable comfort. Then part of a conglomerate that included engine-maker Pratt & Whitney (which powered the 247) and United Air Lines (UAL), Boeing had to sell its first 60 aircraft to UAL. Barred from ordering from Boeing for competitive deliveries, the Transcontinental and Western Airline (TWA) turned to the Douglas Aircraft Co., which designed the DC-1. Considered a test airplane, only one was built. The production model became the DC-2, which outclassed the Boeing 247 in every way. It was faster, more powerful, had longer range and carried two more passengers. Soon, the DC-2 was superseded by the legendary DC-3, an even larger model. Boeing was essentially driven from the commercial aviation market.

With World War II, Boeing concentrated on designing and building the B-17 and B-29 bombers, the first and last of the long-range bombers at the start and end of the global conflict. Boeing's only post-war piston airliner was an outgrowth of the B-29, the Stratocruiser. It was an operational nightmare and a commercial failure. But the Stratocruiser's military version, the KC-97 aerial refueling tanker, became the mainstay of aerial refueling for the U.S. Air Force: 888 were built. But the KC-97 was too slow to keep pace with Boeing's new jet bombers, the B-47 and B-52 that were the backbone of the USAF and the new Strategic Air Command. Pilots had to slow the B-47 and B-52 to nearly stalling speed to match the propeller-driven KC-97s. A jet tanker was needed.

Boeing designed the KC-135 jet tanker, whose sibling, the 707, launched the commercial jet age, along with Douglas's DC-8. But Boeing was far more willing to take the riskier approach to create several models of the 707. By the time the first commercial flight, by Pan American World Airways, in October 1958 took place, Boeing surpassed its once-rival, Douglas, in jet sales. Boeing didn't stop there. It soon designed the 727, the first tri-motored aircraft since the Fords and Fokkers. This short- to medium-range jet was versatile, economic and many considered it a pilot's airplane. Douglas responded with the twin-jet DC-9, but it proved not nearly as flexible as the 727. Boeing cemented its lead.

With the 737 following in 1968 and the 747 in 1970, Boeing offered a full family of airplanes while Douglas struggled with the aging DC-8, the popular if limited DC-9 and the new DC-10. In 1967, an ailing Douglas Aircraft Co. merged with the defense contractor, the McDonnell Corp., to form McDonnell Douglas Corp. (MDC). While the merger breathed new life into the Douglas division, McDonnell's heart clearly wasn't in the commercial side of aerospace. In 1982 and 1984, Boeing added to its family of aircraft with the 767 and 757.

But there was trouble brewing in Europe. A group of companies in France, Germany, Spain and the United Kingdom banded together to design and build a new twin-aisle, wide-body 250 passenger airplane, an "airbus," to compete with Boeing and MDC. A French business entity, Airbus Industries, was formed. The A300 was its first airplane.

Boeing, MDC and Lockheed Co. (with only one commercial product, the L-1011), looked the other way. Their executives sniffed that Airbus was nothing more than another European jobs company that stood little chance of success. The view was not without merit, given Europe's dismal record of producing successful airplane programs and instead delivering spectacular commercial failures.

But this time was different. Airbus followed the A300 with the smaller A310. Neither was a particular sales success, reinforcing the jingoistic disdain the U.S. manufacturers had for Airbus. Even when Airbus launched the single-aisle A320 in 1984, which was directly competitive with the Boeing 737 and DC-9, Boeing and MDC didn't take the airplane seriously.

(Lockheed by this time once again withdrew from the commercial airplane market.) But in 1992, Airbus's sales chief, a brash New Yorker named John Leahy, scored a coup when he and his team won a large order from United, which was part of the same company with Boeing back in the prop days, for the A320. Boeing offered the 737-400, a plane that proved to be inferior to the A320. With the loss, Boeing finally understood that Airbus—and Leahy—were a real threat.

Boeing redesigned the 737 into the "Next Generation" aircraft, the 737 NG. The 737-800 overtook the A320 in range and marginally so in economics. The smaller A319 was slightly better than the competing 737-700 and the larger A321 was marginally better than the competing 737-900. But the heart of the market was the A320–737-800 sector, and Boeing was winning this combat.

AIR WARS

1

The Multi-Billion Dollar Gamble

"Boeing could not launch an all-new airplane."
—**KIRAN RAO,** FORMER AIRBUS EXECUTIVE

BY 2010, AIRBUS OFFICIALS had some hard decisions to make. And some in the executive ranks were "terrified" to make it.

The A320 single-aisle family was selling well, with more than 7,000 program orders. The heart and soul of the Airbus, the family consisted of the 125-passenger A319, the 160-passenger A320 and the 190-passenger A321. The A319, once a strong selling airplane, held its own compared with Boeing's 737-700, but sales of both aircraft had fallen off in favor of the larger A320 and Boeing's 737-800. The -800 carried 12 more passengers than the A320, and its larger wing gave it more range. Boeing held a sales advantage between these two airplanes.

Airbus's A321 had a clear market preference over Boeing's 737-900ER. The A321 carried more passengers. The -900ER (for Extended Range) could fly farther. But airlines, especially those catering to leisure markets, preferred capacity to range. The A321 outsold the -900ER by about 3:1.

Airbus and Boeing each were producing about three dozen A320s and 737s a month. But the 737-800, which represented the bulk of the market, was slowly gaining market share against the competing A320. From Airbus's perspective, something eventually needed to be done.

Thanks in no small part to Boeing's miscues with the twin-aisle, wide-body 787 program, Airbus was cleaning up with the rival A330. The 787 was supposed to enter service in May 2008. Design and production delays were so severe that the 787 would not enter service until December 2011.

Sales for the Airbus A350 were on the rise. It was meant to succeed the A330 and compete more effectively with the 787, which was economically superior to the A330. However, orders for the giant A380, Airbus's answer to the 747, languished. The military Airbus A400M remained a technical and financial drag.

Boeing lagged with 737 sales, but the program was immensely profitable, even in the No. 2 position. The 777-300ER passenger wide-body aircraft and 777-200LRF Long Range Freighter were selling exceptionally well. Orders for the 747-400 passenger aircraft were non-existent. Sales of the 747-8F freighter were good, but the 747-8 passenger model sold poorly. Like the 787, the 747-8 program was over budget and delayed, though not nearly as badly as for the 787. Still, the single-aisle sector was the core of Airbus and Boeing. The 737-800 and A320 represented, Boeing declared, "the heart of the market." This is where Airbus and Boeing had their biggest profits—and their fiercest competition.

A sideshow to the Airbus vs. Boeing rivalry was a new airplane being developed by Canada's Bombardier. Up to 2008, the company was known for its successful regional jet, the CRJ, the Dash 8 turboprop, a family of corporate jets and its commuter trains.

The CRJ had become outclassed by the Embraer E-Jets, also serving the regional market. In response, Bombardier developed the C Series. Using new technology materials for the fuselage, a lightweight composite for the wings and tail, as well as new technology engines from P&W, the C Series came in two models: the 110-passenger CS100 and the 130-passenger CS300, when configured for first and coach classes. The CS100 was slightly smaller than the A319 and 737-700. The CS300 was a direct competitor.

The cabin was roomier than the rival Airbus and Boeing aircraft. Configured in a 2x3 seating arrangement vs. 3x3, the C Series window and aisle seats were 18 inches wide, wider than on Boeing and the same as on Airbus. The dreaded middle seat was 19 inches wide, the roomiest of any narrow-body airplane, matching the giant A380's coach seats. The C Series' aisle was wider than the A320 and 737, and the overhead bins were bigger than the rivals at the time.

It was a bold and risky move by Bombardier, but neither Airbus nor Boeing took the effort seriously, though for different reasons. Throughout 2008 and 2009, John Leahy, chief operating officer-customers, and Tom Williams, the executive vice president of programs, colorfully dismissed Bombardier's C Series as a "cute little airplane," or threatened to "carpet bomb" Bombardier in price competitions.

Still, the C Series used the new P&W Geared Turbo Fan (GTF) engine, which offered double-digit fuel savings over the engines then in widespread use on the A320 and 737. Airbus had been testing the GTF on its A340 test airplane and liked what it saw.

Airlines in 2010 were still recovering from the Global Financial Crisis of 2008. Losses were enormous, and some airlines went out of business. Others sought ways to cut costs, and one of the highest costs was fuel. Boeing was flirting with offering a new airplane to replace the 737. It also studied re-engining the 737. Airbus favored a lower-cost solution: re-engining the A320 with the GTF and an engine offered by P&W rival CFM International, called the LEAP.

However, if Airbus went this route, investing up to $2 billion in the process (with about half picked up by the engine manufacturers), would Boe-

CHAPTER 1 **THE MULTI-BILLION DOLLAR GAMBLE**

ing offer the new airplane? If so, Airbus would be forced to follow. Having committed to the re-engined A320, all this money would be down the drain. Airbus would have to develop a new airplane, costing at least $10 billion.

Leahy initially scoffed at re-engining the A320, at least publicly, but he had come around. Supported by Barry Eccleston, the president of Airbus North America, strategist Christian Scherer, his top lieutenant Kiran Rao and others on the Toulouse staff, Leahy now advocated the re-engining route. The family would have more range and substantially lower fuel consumption than the A320 or 737NG (for Next Generation). New engines also meant lower fuel emissions. Activists in Europe were gaining ground in targeting commercial aviation as a polluter. Airbus was ramping up its "green aviation" efforts.

Leahy wanted the GTF offered through International Aero Engines (IAE), one of the incumbent suppliers on the A320. He also was adamant, unlike some at Airbus, that two engine choices must be provided. Leahy would not support re-engining if it was sole-sourced. Tom Enders, the CEO of Airbus, was skeptical. What if Airbus committed to the re-engining, and Boeing went with a new airplane? What if Airbus got it wrong? It was a multi-billion dollar gamble.

Unbeknown to Airbus, officials worried about the wrong airplane. Airbus believed Boeing was going to offer a new single-aisle design. To be sure, Boeing had shown concepts of such a plane to customers, and no firm decision had been made internally by Boeing what direction it would go. But some within Boeing were pushing hard for a new twin-aisle concept called the New Light Twin. Those within Boeing at the time said, years later, this was the favored solution.

This twin-aisle airplane concept carried 180 to 225 passengers with a range of up to 4,500nm. It was a composite with a novel elliptical or ovoid shape. This airplane would rely on ground-breaking production techniques, which in many respects was key to the entire business plan. It would have single-aisle economics. What's more, a key benefit to the airlines was that twin aisles allowed a rapid turnaround at airport gates. It was a family for three airplanes.

Instead, Airbus was focused on a single-aisle 737 replacement concept. The stakes were even higher than Airbus realized. Leahy was convinced Airbus could force Boeing's hand into forgoing the new airplane and instead decide to re-engine the 737. Leahy and his strategic team believed a re-engined 737 would be inferior to the re-engined A320. They believed an A320RE (re-engine) would at long last give Airbus a clear advantage over the 737NG and a 737RE. For a lot of technical reasons, they were convinced a 737RE could not be competitive with the A320RE.

Leahy now had to persuade Enders and the executive board. He said that what was needed was a significant order from a key Boeing customer to shock Boeing into making this move. The dynamics in the U.S. at the time were stacked against Airbus, however. American, Delta, Southwest and United were all key Boeing customers. Each had large 737 fleets. American had signed a deal in the mid-1990s to buy exclusively from Boeing. Airbus was not welcome at American, a holdover from the A300 days when relations soured from a mix of commercial disputes and the November 2001 crash of an A300-600R after take-off from New York's JFK Airport.

Southwest owed its very existence to Boeing. When Southwest was a three- or four-airplane operator facing financial calamity, Boeing helped the airline stay in business. The odds of Southwest buying from Airbus were virtually nil.

Delta and United flew A320s, but Delta, like American, had been an exclusive Boeing customer. Its Airbuses came into the fleet after it acquired Northwest Airlines. With the merger came Northwest's management, who eventually took over at Delta. They liked Airbus but did not like becoming launch customers of new technology engines. It was a view that, in retrospect, would prove prescient.

United's A320 fleet was ordered by a long-gone management team. Although the merged airline was branded United, in reality, Continental was the surviving carrier. The remaining executive team mostly came from Continental. It was the third U.S. airline to become an exclusive Boeing customer by contract. The Continental management, now in control at United, wasn't receptive to Airbus.

The question was how and with whom could Airbus get an A320RE order to force Boeing's hand. In December 2010, Airbus launched the airplane, by now called the A320neo (new engine option). Boeing predictably sniffed that the neo was merely a catch-up to the 737NG. "Boeing couldn't build a new airplane," Rao said confidently. But it wasn't a sure thing and, more importantly, Leahy believed that Boeing could and eventually would. During the next six months, Boeing talked down the prospect of a 737RE and up the possibility of a new airplane. Airbus's leaders had their work cut out for them.

TARGETING AMERICAN

American's predicament presented just the kind of opportunity that Leahy relished. By 2011, American was in a dire financial condition. It also had one of the oldest fleets of any carrier. It had some 300 aging Boeing MD-80s, purchased initially from McDonnell Douglas, beginning in the 1980s when MDC was an independent yet struggling commercial airplane manufacturer.

The MD-80 was the first of a new generation of airplanes when introduced in 1980 (hence the root of its name), but by 2011, it had been eclipsed by the A320 (1988) and the 737NG (1994). Following the 1991 Gulf War, terror attacks in New York and Washington, D.C., in 2001 and the Global Financial Crisis of 2008, fuel prices spiked dramatically. The MD-80 became economically obsolete.

American was the only one of the old U.S. "legacy" carriers to avoid bankruptcy throughout two decades of turmoil. It couldn't afford to renew its fleet as its competitors had. Continental, Delta, Northwest, United and US Airways had each gone through bankruptcies, some of them twice, to shed debt and cut wages.

American's CEO, Gerard Arpey, philosophically opposed bankruptcy for the harm it would do to creditors, shareholders and employees. The result was an ancient fleet that guzzled fuel and was becoming more and more costly to maintain. The campaign to sell American hundreds of A320s began in early 2011, but Leahy initially was nowhere to be seen by American.

On November 12, 2001, when American was still reeling from the hijacking of two of its airplanes used in the 9/11 attacks, an Airbus A300-600R took off from New York's JFK Airport. It flew through the wake turbulence of a Boeing 747 that departed just ahead of AA 587. Suddenly, the vertical fin separated from the airplane. In the dive toward Queens, where JFK is located, the engines also separated. Flight 587 crashed, killing 260 on board and five on the ground.

Given that only two months had passed since the horrific 9/11 attacks—and the fact that New York and American were involved again—first suspicions were of yet another terrorist event. Flight data and cockpit voice recorders (FDR and CVR) soon pointed to operational, not terrorism, factors. Airbus pointed directly at the co-pilot, who was flying the plane, and American's training procedures. The co-pilot, the National Transportation Safety Board (NTSB) ultimately concluded, overreacted with rudder controls to fly through the 747's wake turbulence. The co-pilot over-corrected to the point that the stresses caused the vertical fin to snap off. The NTSB also pointed to issues with the composite tail and composite lugs, used with titanium lugs, to attach the tail. The composite lugs failed; the titanium lugs didn't.

The finger-pointing between Airbus and American soured American toward Airbus. The A300s were the only Airbuses in the American fleet. Eccleston said Leahy and Airbus weren't welcome at American, at least at the working level. Once or twice a year, Leahy met socially with Arpey and a few other senior executives at industry associations. Eccleston, though, happened to be friends with Arpey and Tom Horton, the president.

"There was no relationship between American and Airbus," Eccleston recalled in 2019. "It stemmed back to the unfortunate A300 event on Long Island. Their relationships deteriorated badly before my time, but when I came on board [in 2005], that was still a hangover, whereby Airbus found it very difficult to make any headway into American."

However, a former American official who was there at the time, Richard Cherney, said the animosity American held toward Airbus predated the A300 accident. It went to commercial maintenance guarantees Airbus made for the A300 when American ordered the airplane. The guarantees fell short by amounts Cherney didn't recall decades later. But American sued Airbus. According to Cherney, Bob Crandall, then American's irascible CEO, wasn't a fan of Leahy, but Crandall only had praise for Leahy in a 2019 interview for this book.

"I had known and done deals with Gerard Arpey and some other American folks in my other careers in the past, mostly at Rolls-Royce," Eccleston recalled. "I got to know Gerard really well, and I was quite close to him and his wife, personally. I used my relationship with Gerard and with Tom [Horton] to at least initiate a debate. That debate mostly involved having nice dinners at the Mansion at Turtle Creek [a posh Dallas restaurant and hotel] once every quarter or so to sort of stay in touch."

In early 2011, Eccleston's conversations with American heated up. By then, he could show officials the neo's specifications, performance, economics and engine options. Arpey was, at the time, still pretty much sitting on the fence. He left the discussion to Horton, Eccleston said. "It got to the point where it became so serious, we decided we've got to set up a camp in Dallas. We went to the Ritz Carlton in downtown Dallas and set up a mini-Airbus office there. From then on, most of the discussions took place down there."

Eccleston recalled it became apparent that American was nervous about Boeing getting to know too much about this discussion.[1] Talks progressed to the point of nearing a deal by the spring. It was time for Leahy to become personally involved. A confidential lunch meeting was arranged in Ft. Lauderdale in March with Horton and a few key staff members. Eccleston agreed with a restaurant to open privately for lunch to be sure it remained confidential. By the end of the meal, Leahy concluded American was serious, and a deal could possibly be done. It was a blockbuster, too: more than 400 ceos and neos.

As spring melted into summer (literally and figuratively—temperatures in Dallas were above 100 degrees for 10 days running), some crucial meetings shifted to other locations. "The discussion was pretty hot as well," Eccleston stated. "It became apparent to us that there was a deal to be done and that Horton would be able to convince Gerard to set aside his concerns

---

1. Boeing wasn't in the dark as much as Eccleston thought. In May 2011, Horton filled in Ray Conner, at the time the head of BCA's supply chain management, during a golf outing. Conner passed the information on to sales, but the warning went unheeded.

about working with Airbus. This was going to be a great airplane, and it was going to be a great deal. It would transform American's future. They would show a lot of confidence in the future by placing an order of around 200 airplanes." An equal number of options would be part of the package.

But then a big wrinkle appeared. "Suddenly, one day, American called up," according to Eccleston. "Horton says, 'So, how would Airbus feel if we ordered Airbus and Boeing, and we took both?' Why would American say that?" Eccleston asked of Horton in wonderment.

"You remember when we had this agreement back in 1997 about exclusivity [with Boeing], and we were one of the three airlines?" Horton said.

"Yes, I'm aware of that, but that went away when Boeing bought Douglas and the European Union said that's dead. So, as far as I'm concerned, Tom, you don't have to worry about that."

Horton replied that there were some people in the room at the time with Crandall and Ron Woodard[2] when the exclusive agreement was signed. "They feel it's kind of a commitment to Boeing, and they're nervous about walking away from that."

It was clear that American was very concerned that, if they just bought an Airbus, then Boeing was going to get really, really upset, Eccleston recalled. Horton pressed Eccleston about the Airbus reaction if American also ordered the 737.

Although Eccleston and his team were initially devastated that their firm aircraft order was reduced, Leahy quickly agreed. What he needed from a major Boeing customer was a commitment for at least 100 A320neo aircraft, firmly ordered. American wanted the same terms and conditions agreed for 400 aircraft. Leahy agreed to this as well, a tactic he'd used in previous deals. He was sure American would eventually buy that many.

Eccleston's assessment that Boeing would be "really, really upset" was on the mark. "The next thing was, and this is really weird, I had a call from Horton saying, 'Boeing said if American bought Airbus with or without Boeing, Boeing was going to sue American for breaching the exclusivity.' We would like to ask Airbus if you would indemnify us against that,' Horton said."

Leahy quickly rejected the suggestion. "Why would we want to do that? That's entirely your issue. It's your problem," Eccleston told Horton. "We're happy if you want to buy our airplane. If you don't, fine. But no, we're not going to indemnify you if Boeing sues."

The next thing Eccleston heard was that Boeing showed up in American's headquarters in Dallas with half a dozen people, most of whom were lawyers, to prove how serious Boeing was about suing them. "It really up-

---

2. Ron Woodard was then president of BCA.

set American. It really upset Tom. It kind of upset Gerard, who is a very mild-mannered man and doesn't upset easily," Eccleston recalled.[3]

In the end, the deal included Airbus and Boeing. But for the latter, it was a near thing. Had it not been for Arpey's call, Boeing would have missed out on a huge American order.

ASLEEP AT THE SWITCH

Why did American open the door to Airbus with the exclusive Boeing deal in place? "Boeing was asleep at the switch," recalled an American official, still with the carrier in 2020. American had been asking Boeing for an upgrade to the 737NG in response to the A320neo. Boeing didn't believe American would leave the exclusive agreement.[4] Thus, the opportunity for Airbus. "It caught a lot of people by surprise. Boeing was pressed into doing something," an American insider said years later. "Some didn't want to have their hands tied to the 737RE."

Southwest also had been asking Boeing for a re-engined 737. But, while Boeing had a design, officials simply weren't all that interested, preferring a brand-new airplane.

American's precarious financial condition was also a factor for Boeing, recalled a Boeing insider. Airbus and Boeing agreed to backstop the financing of 230 airplanes. "There was a lot of debate if we should even be doing the deal because of their financial condition," this insider recalled. Indeed, on November 29, just five months after the record-setting $40 billion order, American filed for Chapter 11 bankruptcy. The filing eliminated the financing commitment if the purchase contracts were later "assumed," a legal term that means the orders survived the bankruptcy. American assumed both contracts.

American fleet planners found the neo economics compelling, especially compared with the aging MD-80 fleet, said the American insider. But Boeing, he relayed, was confident American would not order from Airbus, and it didn't up its game, offering only more 737-800s and a batch of -900ERs. American simply had no interest in the latter airplane.

Arpey was the bearer of bad news in 1994 when he called Leahy about

---

3. Throughout this tale, the author requested interviews with Horton and Arpey. Both declined. The research for this book occurred, in large part, during the grounding of the 737 MAX. Given American's role in the launch of the MAX, Horton and Arpey made it known through a middleman tht they weren't giving interviews, even on topics unrelated to the MAX-neo.

4. The attitude by Boeing's Albaugh and others that the 737NG was better than the A320neo may have been a factor, too.

CHAPTER 1 THE MULTI-BILLION DOLLAR GAMBLE

the looming, exclusive Boeing deal. Now he called Marlin Dailey, Boeing's vice president of sales-commercial airplanes, to tell him Leahy was at American's headquarters ready to sign a deal for 400 aircraft, a former Boeing employee recalled seven years later. If Boeing wanted a piece of this deal, Arpey said, Boeing needed to get on an airplane and get down to the airline's Ft. Worth, Texas, headquarters, per the former employee.

This was on a Tuesday. Boeing salesmen spent all day and night Wednesday coming up with a re-engined 737 program, and terms and conditions. Jim McNerney, then the CEO of The Boeing Co., stepped in and decided to launch the re-engined 737, killing Albaugh's dream—and that of many others—of an entirely new airplane.[5]

On July 20, 2011, American announced the dual orders at the newly opened Admirals Club at the Dallas/Ft. Worth Airport. Arpey, Horton, Airbus CEO Enders and BCA's CEO Albaugh were present. Leahy, Eccleston and a host of others from Airbus, Boeing and American were there as well.

Airbus succeeded in forcing Boeing to re-engine the 737. Leahy had his deal from a major Boeing customer; the future for the A320neo was now secure. The prospect of Boeing launching a new airplane was dead, for now. For Boeing, the decision to drop a new airplane in favor of the 737RE would prove to be a fateful one because the 737RE would eventually become known as the 737 MAX

---

5. The American order reportedly angered Southwest's CEO Gary Kelly, who had been urging Boeing for months to proceed with the re-engined 737. Southwest had launched the 737-300, -500 and -700, and Kelly was keen to launch the MAX. Reportedly, he refused to take Boeing's calls for weeks after the American order. Kelly, always the gentleman, never confirmed this story, which was shared by others with knowledge of the situation. Immersed in the MAX grounding and coronavirus crisis, Kelly declined a request for an interview. However, Southwest became the launch operator when American made it clear that, despite being the first customer, it didn't want to be the first operator.

2

Flying Cargo

"I never used the relief tube."

—**JOHN LEAHY,** TALKING ABOUT HIS DAYS FLYING CARGO

LEAHY'S STRATEGY AND TEAMWORK PAID OFF. Landing an exclusive 737 customer forced Boeing's hand to re-engine the airplane, not launch a brand-new design. Staying in the background, letting Eccleston take the lead to open the doors at American, also was a strategic play. Throughout his career, Leahy often let the local Airbus leaders or sales force press the deal. He stayed behind the scenes, giving guidance, making recommendations and decisions, and showing up at crucial points.

In winning the American order, Airbus won its multi-billion dollar gamble to force Boeing's hand. The neo program got a huge boost. Winning a big order from a blue-chip airline like American, and cracking the Boeing exclusivity in the process, would pay dividends of incalculable proportions.

For Leahy, it was payback for having been blindsided by the American-Boeing exclusive deal. And, up to then, it was clearly the high point of his career at Airbus. At the time, Leahy had spent a quarter of a century as Airbus's chief salesman, leading them from being a small manufacturer to the market leader, outperforming Boeing in commercial aircraft sales.

Leahy joined Airbus in January 1985 from Piper Aircraft as a salesman in the small U.S. office, which was located at Rockefeller Center in New York City. It was then called Airbus North America. As the name indicated, the office covered the U.S. and Canada. Mexico is part of North America, but this Latin country was the responsibility of Airbus headquarters in Toulouse. Within two years, Leahy was named head of sales for the U.S. and Canada. When he joined Airbus, he had no previous experience selling airliners. In fact, Leahy didn't sell airplanes at Piper. He was in charge of marketing and dealer training in finance and business development during his tenure there.

Leahy, like many in the aviation industry, became interested in airplanes in his youth. Born and raised in Queens, New York, not far from LaGuardia Airport, his family moved while he was in the eighth grade to Springfield, Massachusetts. He became president of the aeronautical society in high school. Students would occasionally rent Cessna 172s with a pilot. They weren't rated; they'd just go flying and navigating.

Leahy went to Fordham University in New York City at the Rose Hill Campus in the Bronx. He took on two majors: philosophy and communications. To make some money, Leahy took on a part-time job as a taxicab driver in Manhattan. Even then, private universities were expensive, and his family was not in a position to help financially. "I was always looking for some extra money to pay my way through," Leahy recalled. "I had scholarships, loans and student work-study programs. I was running the campus center. In the summer, when I was off from school, I had gotten a job driving a Checker cab."

Leahy drove at night because it was easier moving around the city. "I started about four in the afternoon from JFK, waiting in the taxi line to get a fare, hopefully into Manhattan. Then I'd cruise up and down the East Side picking people up from the bars and taking them to a nice restaurant. After, I'd go to LaGuardia, pick up some fares there, come back into the city, and end around midnight." Leahy got half the meter plus tips.

In 1969, he met "the woman of my life," Grace, whom he married in 1973. Although Leahy didn't say, she must have been one of the world's most patient women. (Leahy would spend about half of the year on the road once he joined Airbus.) He graduated in 1972 and went to work for Columbia University in New York, managing some of their real estate in Manhattan. "It was student and faculty housing," Leahy said. He had 40 to 50 people working for him. "I did some MBA work on the side but commuting up to Syracuse University on weekends was getting to be a drag."

Grace had gone to Syracuse to study for her PhD. In 1976, Leahy followed, transferring from Columbia, which was one of the top business schools in the U.S. Syracuse was good, but it wasn't the same ranking. "When I filled in my application, the dean asked to see me. He said usually people don't transfer from places like Columbia," Leahy said.

"I'm curious, why do you want to come here?" the dean asked.

Leahy replied, "Well, I don't want to continue to be part-time at Columbia. My wife is up here. I want to go straight through, get an MBA in about a year, a year and a half, and get on with my life."

"Well, that's pretty reasonable," the dean said. "I'll tell you what. Would you like a teaching assistantship? It will take you about twice as long. You get to teach some courses. We pay you, and, of course, the tuition is free. Or do you want a full scholarship, go straight through as fast as you want, and we pay everything?" The ambitious Leahy said he'd take the fastest option.

He had begun taking flying lessons while visiting Grace on the weekends in Syracuse, soloing during their honeymoon. Leahy built up his time, earning a commercial license and becoming an instrument flight instructor. He also was rated on multi-engine aircraft—all by the time he was 26.

Despite Leahy's multi-engine rating, most of his flying was single-engine time. "I found it very frustrating to be constantly building time in a single-engine airplane, going around the traffic pattern and out to the practice area, teaching people to get their private or commercial license," Leahy said. "I kept pestering the chief pilot. They had a charter department; I wanted to fly charter. He said every flight instructor wants to fly charter, and you'd have to start in the right seat as a co-pilot. We had Navajos and Aztecs and that sort of thing."

The chief pilot told Leahy that he'd have to wait another year before he could get into the cockpit flying charter, lacking enough seniority. "I hope in another year, I'll have graduated, and I'll be off doing something else," Leahy replied. The chief pilot advised him to check out another company, Stagecoach Airlines, at the airport flying a twin-engine Beech 18 converted turboprop on cargo runs four times a week between Syracuse and Chicago O'Hare airports. It involved night flying, leaving Syracuse about 8:30 p.m. and returning about 5 or 6 the next morning—some nine or 10 hours of flying time.

"I got there the first night and went over to the FBO[6] where they parked their airplane," Leahy said. "We were standing around. This big burly guy comes up to me and says, 'You must be the new co-pilot.'" He was the pilot. "We chatted for awhile, and he asked about my flying background. I told him that I was a flight instructor across the field and everything that he wanted to know about how much multi-engine time I had. I said, 'Not a lot at this point.' Multi-engine rating, obviously, was a commercial pilot's license, but that's why I was looking forward to building multi-engine and turbine time."

The captain, whose name Leahy has long since forgotten, observed that as a student, Leahy would get back from Chicago and want to go to classes. Sleep was going to be an issue. "What we'll do is, you fly for about an hour, an hour and a half, and then you can sleep. I fly for an hour and a half, and then I sleep. It goes back and forth so that we will actually get, if we do this right, to have at least half the flying time sleeping."

"That's not a bad idea!"

"But there's a rule about doing this." The pilot warned Leahy that should both of them fall asleep at the same time, the airplane would wake them up. There was no autopilot. "You'll hear it," the pilot said. "The airplane will fall off on a wing and start into a spiral dive, and you'll hear it."

"The whole idea," Leahy said, "was you're supposed to wake up fast, get it back straight and level without disturbing your partner. I actually got quite good at it."

The Beech required two pilots. The plane was unpressurized. It had no radar or auto-pilot. At least it had de-icing boots. And it had a contract with

---

6. FBO, or Fixed Base Operator.

Burlington Northern, which at the time ran a railroad. "If we don't deliver the freight, we don't get paid," the captain said.

Leahy asked what happened if the flight ran into bad weather or other problems. "Well, as captain, I've got a credit card, and we go up to the line of thunderstorms. We decide if we want to turn left or right, and we keep going until we see a break. If we run low on fuel, we stop and buy fuel, and we just keep going until we get to our destination."

Leahy flew from the autumn of 1976 into the spring the following year. The job paid "just about nothing," but it was great experience. "I was able to build nighttime in my logbook, multi-engine time, IFR [Instrument Flight Rules] time and icing conditions," he recalled. "Almost every night, we were filing IFR. The weather was usually horrendous."

There were a few incidents. "We took off once, and the No. 1 Pratt and Whitney turbine temperatures were starting to get high. The power was starting to go down, and I can remember by the time we got it all the way back to Syracuse, there was almost no power left in that engine. But, of course, everybody wants to get home, so we would just keep flying and just watching the power go down. Nothing dramatic, but we essentially landed on one engine."

The operations were rather loose, to say the least. "I'm standing there drinking coffee, and the captain said, 'Well, let's get going.' I'd been looking out the window, and I saw that there were two pallets of freight that were sitting out there, and I said, 'We can't go yet. They haven't loaded the freight.' The pilot responded, 'They don't load the freight in Syracuse. We load the freight. They just drop it off there.'"

Leahy learned then and there that part of the job was loading freight, not just flying it. He also got a quick lesson about unions on his first flight to O'Hare. "I learned you don't touch the freight in O'Hare. The union guys will break your arm. That's their job out there, and it pays very well," he said.

One flight gave Leahy an important lesson about weights and balances. One day, there were some Caterpillar steel tracks to ship. They were on a pallet. Taking off, the Beech had trouble becoming airborne. "We go charging down the runway, and this thing doesn't want to get into the air," Leahy said. "We pull it off into ground effect. Both engines turning at full power, and slowly it starts climbing. I said, 'Gee, that was really odd.'"

The pilots looked at the engine instruments. The thrust was right, and the temperatures were okay. When they got to O'Hare, they checked the manifest and discovered the problem. The tracks were listed at 2,000 pounds. "We thought it was 2,000 pounds for the pallet," Leahy said. "It was 2,000 pounds for each one of the tracks. We were 2,000 pounds overweight. Two thousand pounds overweight was enormous on that airplane. If we'd lost an engine, we would have just gone straight down, slowly perhaps, but down."

It was a fun job hand flying the aircraft. "I fell asleep more times than I can count, but I got very good at just hearing the slight change in pitch as the airplane would fall off on a wing and then snap awake, get the aircraft level and not even wake the guy sleeping next to me."

Leahy also learned the art of "holding it." The Beech 18 didn't have a toilet. "If you have to pee, not to worry, there's a relief tube. You just pee into it," said the captain. "You know, I don't think it's been cleaned since 1958."

"I never once used the relief tube," Leahy recalled.

3

Piper

"We decided to go with someone more familiar with our corporate culture."
—**AMERICAN AIRLINES,** REJECTING CANDIDATE JOHN LEAHY FOR A JOB

LEAHY GRADUATED IN MAY 1977 with his MBA in finance and transportation management. It was time to get a real job. He wanted to be a pilot, but he needed glasses and he wasn't ex-military, so airline flying was out. Leahy missed getting straight A's because of one B, but his academic standing was right at the top of his class. He sent a resume to American, which was then still headquartered in New York. The finance department invited him in for an interview. American sent him a round-trip, first-class ticket from Syracuse. Leahy bought a three-piece suit and a briefcase, figuring he needed to look the part going to see American. In those days, it was all white shirts, buttoned-down collars and short hair.

"I get up in the morning, go there, bright-eyed and bushy-tailed, for a 9 a.m. meeting with these guys," Leahy said. "I walk in, and the secretary brings me up. They have an open floor plan with a bunch of guys sitting there in finance, treasury or whatever. Up against the walls are some of the executive offices. I knew things weren't going to go well because my hair came down to my shoulders. My beard was pretty full, and everyone sitting there had a crew cut, a 1977 ex-military crew cut. I said, Oh, shit!

"I don't think I ever met the CFO. They very nicely spent the whole day, bought me lunch, told me about the position. They said how much they liked the interview. About two weeks later, I get this nice American Airlines letter and it says, 'John, it was a tough decision. Your qualifications are excellent, and we enjoyed the interview with you but, in the end, we decided to go with someone more familiar with our corporate culture.'"

Crandall, the future CEO of American, hearing this story for the first time in 2019, laughed. "That would not have worked with me. He was a smart young man, even then."

Leahy went home and chopped his hair to 1977 business standards and cut off his beard. "My wife got home. When I first started dating her, I had a beard in college," Leahy said. "She's never seen me without a beard, she starts crying."

"Oh my God, this is not right, you can't do this," Grace exclaimed. "Do you want to starve? In this industry, I can't have a big bushy beard, and

I can't have long hair," Leahy replied. He began sending resumes to the general aviation aircraft industry. He wrote Cessna, Beech and Piper. Leahy was offered interviews with the first two within a week. Piper trailed but sent an airplane to pick him up.

Piper headquarters in Lock Haven, Pennsylvania, was an hour's flight from Syracuse. Dressed in his three-piece suit, armed with his briefcase and, this time, clean shaven with short hair, Piper told Leahy he was a perfect fit. "We've got a new opening, and we're looking for your exact profile," a Piper executive told Leahy. "We have a dealer distributor network. We think these guys are good old boys. They are pilots. They're almost like flying car dealers. They need to understand taxes, depreciation and how to sell our planes in a very competitive market, how to set up leasebacks. Give a guy who wants to have a Navajo the tax and business reasons to make the Navajo work for him. We're going to have a business management department in marketing. Maybe we'll get one or two other people into it. You're going to help teach our dealers and distributors all about the business of aviation, not just how to demo our airplanes."

Leahy said great. The salary was okay for the time. It was small, but everything was small then. A benefit, an important one to Leahy, was the fact that Piper offered him the use of its new airplanes. Leahy could take an aircraft off the flight line for business or personal use. Piper would give him a credit card, buy fuel and pay for the tie-down. Leahy needed a minimum number of hours to keep his IFR current. And Piper wanted its senior executives to be current and familiar with its product line. On weekends, Leahy could take a new plane to fly out to the beach with Grace and the children. He could fly to Maine to buy lobsters for a Saturday barbeque. How could Leahy say no? At 27, it was a hell of a job.

During the seven years at Piper, Leahy organized seminars for dealers to cover sales training, interviewing and sales techniques, tax breaks and benefits, financing, cash flow analysis and how to run a dealership. Leahy designed the courses and helped teach them. He and his team also engaged in role-playing with the Piper dealers.

"We took them through the airplanes showing the strengths and the weaknesses of the Piper airplane," Leahy said. "Then I'd be the salesman for Cessna, and my partner would be the salesman for Beechcraft. The dealers would talk as potential clients and ask us about the airplane. We'd even do a demo flight in the Piper, as well as in the competing models from Beech and Cessna. It was fun."

Leahy and his team went to Australia, Europe, across the U.S. and Canada. They also went to South Africa. During this trip, Leahy took a low pass at 200 mph down one township street. He pulled up and fell off on the wing. His host asked, "What are you doing?"

"Well, I'm coming back to do it again."

"You know it's Sunday morning? They've all got hangovers, you probably woke everybody in the township up, and they've all got guns. Do you really want to do another low pass down Main Street?"

"Okay, what do we do next?"

At the next stop at Kruger National Park, near Mozambique, Leahy was refueling his plane, an Aerostar 602P, adjacent to a chain-link fence. He was concentrating on his task when a lion roared. Leahy nearly jumped out of his skin. The lion was just on the other side of the fence, which was short enough that the the big cat could probably jump over it if it really wanted to. Leahy turned the refueling over to a local and climbed into the cockpit to "file his flight plan."

Leahy never sold an airplane for Piper. That was the job of dealers and distributors. After focusing on finance and dealer training, he took over marketing and advertising. He used the same advertising agency that FedEx used in its early days, Ally and Gargano. Carl Ally personally handled the Piper account. "I learned a lot about advertising just listening to Carl Ally talk, and he really could talk. How you need to target your audience, focus your advert, make it memorable, and that sort of thing," Leahy said. In those days, the package carrier had humorous TV ads with a fast-talking face and the 80-year-old chairman character marveling that using FedEx was "so easy, even the chairman of the board can do it."

General Aviation (GA) took off in 1978–79, spurred by investment tax credits and other tax breaks, which Leahy discussed with Piper's distributors. The other GA manufacturers benefitted as well. Sales peaked in 1978 with 17,811 airplanes sold by all GA Original Equipment Manufacturers (OEMs). Sales dipped slightly in 1979, then went down to 11,877 in 1980.

"Then it just went right off the edge of the cliff," Leahy said. "By the time I left at the end of '84, they produced about 2,500 airplanes. It was an absolute collapse of the light aircraft industry." Leahy attributed the collapse to over-selling, over-estimating the popularity of flying clubs and a recession. The manufacturers weren't updating the airplanes much, either.

Lawyers and the product liability laws also hurt the GA industry. A "Sunday flier," the visual flight rules [VFR] pilot out for a ride with his family, might take off into an approaching storm. Despite receiving a weather warning and being told it was IFR flying, the plane might crash, and the manufacturer got sued.

"How are we supposed to design airplanes that can fly at 150 miles an hour into the side of a mountain?" Leahy said. "It's carrying 100 gallons of high-octane fuel. How can you not burn up? Cessna was losing lawsuits. Beechcraft was also losing lawsuits. Finally, it took another 10 or 15 years until Congress got involved and changed the laws to say, 'There's got to be a limit on some of this liability.' I don't think the industry has recovered from it to this day."

Time came for Leahy to move on from Piper's headquarters. Piper had moved them from Pennsylvania to Vero Beach, Florida. Leahy could move there, continuing as director of marketing, but he wanted to get into sales, and he wanted to go overseas. Piper had an office in Geneva, Switzerland. It agreed to transfer Leahy there as sales director for Europe, the Middle East and Asia. His business card actually read, "Director, Eastern Hemisphere."

Grace was teaching at Pennsylvania State and wanted to work if they moved to Switzerland. Piper helped find a possible position with the European Organization for Nuclear Research, or CERN as it was known. But Leahy was having trouble arranging a work permit. "There was no problem bringing your wife over, but they weren't too keen on wives working," he said.

Leahy and Piper were still working through the logistics of the transfer to Geneva and finding a job for Grace when a headhunter, Gary Krauthamer, approached him in November 1984. They met at the Admirals Club at LaGuardia Airport. "Why don't you get some international experience working in America for an international company?" Krauthamer asked Leahy. "We're going to try to revitalize the Airbus operations in the U.S." Leahy would work out of the offices at Rockefeller Center.

Leahy, of course, was a New Yorker. Grace's family lived there. Leahy's brother and uncle were on Long Island. "They were looking for people who didn't just come in with a bunch of brochures as a salesman," Leahy said.

Krauthamer said, "To sell an airplane you need to really know the economics of the airplane. We don't expect you to go in and talk to the pilots. They're not going to make the final decision about which airplane to buy anyway. You've got to go talk to the finance people, the planning people, and convince them that going with our airplane is better than staying with the Boeing airplane."

Airbus even offered to train Leahy to achieve a type rating on its aircraft if he wanted. As it turns out, he never took this offer up. It would take at least eight weeks to obtain a type rating he would never use. It would have been fun, but family time came first.

Airbus was planning on hiring four or five salesmen, all with MBAs, Leahy among them, but Leahy shot higher. He told Alan Boyd, chairman of Airbus North America and formerly the first Secretary of the U.S. Department of Transportation, that he should hire him as the sales manager. "I made a big pitch for that," Leahy recalled. "I remember Alan Boyd just looking at me and saying, 'Well, John, there is zero chance we're going to do that. I hope you come along with us as a salesman. If you're as good as you think you are, a year from now, you'll probably be the sales manager. We're not hiring you as a sales manager now. We're hiring all five guys individually, reporting directly to the CEO of the North American company.'"

But in two years, Leahy had the job he sought. Steve Udvar-Hazy, one of commercial aviation's giants who co-founded two of the industry's leading leasing companies, recalled Leahy at the time. "He was kind of a salesman, ferry pilot, kind of a jack-of-all-trades at Piper," Hazy said in a 2019 interview. "He was hired as almost like a young marketing apprentice at Airbus in North America. He didn't know anything about large commercial aircraft. He learned very quickly."

Actually, Leahy was director of marketing at Piper with a team of 40 people when Airbus approached him. They offered to double Leahy's salary. He could move to New York. He would have international travel, flying first class, including the Concorde. And he'd be working for a European company.

The first reference Krauthamer checked when verifying Leahy's was Chuck Yeager, the legendary test pilot who was doing promotional work for Piper at the time. Needless to say, Yeager gave Leahy a strong endorsement. Krauthamer moved to close the deal.

"A lot of people go over and live in Europe," Krauthamer said. "A lot of military guys say, 'I spent three, four years, five years in Europe. I know the European system.' No, they don't. You're in your own little American enclave. You're working for an American company or the military, and then you come back. Maybe you didn't have to go as far to see the Eiffel Tower, but you don't know the French at all. You've got to work for the French to really know the French."

Although initially assigned to North America, Leahy would nevertheless be working for a French company with all the politics this entailed. There was a lot of logic to that, Leahy said, intrigued with that whole idea. He accepted.

4

Early Years at Airbus

"They are pregnant with 10 airplanes."
—**JOHN LEAHY,** SELLING AIRBUS ON NORTHWEST AIRLINES A320 DEAL

LEAHY WAS JUST 34 WHEN HE JOINED AIRBUS. His initial assignments were Pan Am, Northwest and Piedmont Airlines. Pan Am was a basket case by 1984–85. The unofficial flag carrier of the U.S. since before World War II, Pan Am pioneered transoceanic flying, inventing technology in the 1930s to support communications and airplanes capable of transiting vast distances. Flying boats built by Sikorsky, Martin and Boeing became legendary and were the epitome of luxury, especially the latter two. Pan Am was often viewed and criticized as acting as its own State Department to get foreign operating rights. Legend has it that Pan Am toppled foreign governments when necessary.

Juan Trippe, Pan Am's founder, was one of the most influential figures in U.S. aviation and in Washington, D.C. In addition to launching the Martin 130 and Boeing 314 flying boats, Trippe launched the U.S. jet age with simultaneous orders for the Boeing 707 and Douglas DC-8. He also launched the Boeing 747, starting an entirely new era of air travel and the jumbo jet.

Yet for all Trippe's power and influence, he was stymied at every turn on how to make Pan Am the official flag carrier of the U.S., the "Chosen Instrument." Just as other governments designated one airline to fly overseas, like Britain's BOAC and France's Air France (both government owned), he wanted Pan Am to be the sole beneficiary of U.S. routes to foreign lands. Pan Am tried to acquire airlines to access the vast U.S. market, unsuccessfully. Then Trippe retired.

The 747 entered service in January 1970, after nearly bankrupting Boeing in the process. There is general agreement that the big order also set the stage to send Pan Am on its own financial spiral into eventual dissolution.

By the end of the 1970s, airline deregulation began to emerge. Pan Am could enter the U.S. markets on its own but building up a network would take decades and billions of dollars. Instead, Pan Am got into a bidding war with Frank Lorenzo's Texas Air Corp. (TAC) to buy National Airlines. Eastern also bid for National.

Pan Am won, spending $437 million.[7] It was generally agreed Pan Am overpaid and the debt burden, coupled with that of the 747s and on top of operating losses through the 1970s, became the death knell. By 1984, Pan Am was a sick airline. But at that point the airline's reputation internationally was much higher than it was in the U.S., where it was considered a failing carrier. Everyone could see the handwriting on the wall. It couldn't afford to pay for new airplanes, so creative financing was necessary. Airbus needed to place a bunch of white-tail A300B4s and make further inroads into the U.S. Additionally, given Pan Am's still good international stature, an Airbus order would be seen as an endorsement.

"I didn't realize when I was hired that Airbus was sitting on about 20 white tails," Leahy said. "Not white tails in an order book. They had built about 20 wide-body A300-B4s that were parked in Toulouse."[8] The airplanes were produced without customers to keep the production line flowing. "Airbus was losing a lot of money. It was the shareholders that were still willing to write off a little bit to keep this project alive because they were getting jobs out of building wings and cockpits and fuselages."

Jobs. Boeing, Lockheed and Douglas seemed vindicated. They dismissed Airbus in the 1970s when it was formed as merely another European jobs program. So far, this seemed to be the case, but finding a home for the airplanes with Pan Am required creativity.

Airbus could do things with finance that Boeing wasn't going to do. Airbus could use its balance sheet (the credit really flowed back to its owner-partners) to do what was called lease-in-lease-out structures. Airbus would sign up for 22 years to 24 years to lease the A300 or A310 from a group of investors. It was Lehman Brothers who put this together first. Leahy called it a flaky idea, given the novelty at the time. Then Airbus would sub-lease the planes to the airline, so it wasn't the Pan Am credit anymore. It was the Airbus credit that was driving the lease. Airbus passed the lease rate through without a profit, although it did over-finance the aircraft resulting in a one-time upside for the partners.

"We'd take the risk of putting it on our balance sheet. Pan Am would get financing at substantially lower rates than they ever could on their own, or even going to Boeing Capital to finance the 767," Leahy said. "Things like that were a price to pay to get into the market."

---

7. Texas Air Corp. (TAC) made a tidy profit on the stock it acquired in its effort to buy National. Thus, Pan Am effectively gave Lorenzo a nice piggy bank that led to TAC's expansion in the following years.

8. It was the financial fiasco of these 20 white tails that led to the appointment of Jean Pierson as CEO of Airbus. Pierson would be the one to bring Leahy to Toulouse.

As part of the wide-body deal, Pan Am also ordered 50 A320s, becoming one of the early launch customers. Pan Am didn't need the A320s and couldn't use them. But Airbus, which wanted the Pan Am name on the order book for the international prestige, talked the airline into it. The 50 A320s were icing on the cake. Airbus desperately wanted that order to claim that Pan Am had bought 50 of the airplanes. The pitch to Pan Am was "Well, this is your contract. If things don't work out, maybe you could sell it to somebody else, get an upside," Leahy said. "Pan Am replied, 'That's an interesting idea. Okay, we'll take 50 of those.'"

When Leahy arrived at Airbus in January 1985, these deals were Letters of Intent (LOI). It took another seven or eight months to firm up the orders. Airbus didn't understand the complexity of U.S. contracts and financings, or the sophistication of Pan Am, and its legal and financial advisors.

Northwest was another early target. It was also a tough one. Airbus was the new entrant. Except for a small fleet of Douglas DC-8s at the start of the jet age and the DC-10-40, Northwest bought only Boeing jets. "We battled the A300-600 to the 767 to a draw, but we didn't get the order. Neither did Boeing. I'm convinced that Northwest wasn't a draw, that we'd won, but they couldn't bring themselves to buy Airbus at that point in time. They said, 'Maybe, we don't have to make this decision right now. We'll think about the widebodies for a while.' Then, a year later, they were looking for single-aisle airplanes."

Northwest firmly ordered 100 A320s in 1986, but it had rights to cancel up to the last 90 in batches of 10 if the aircraft didn't meet their expectations. It was an unusual deal.

Having come close to nabbing Northwest for the A300, only to have it slip away, Leahy got creative. It gave Airbus officials in Toulouse some queasiness. "A deal for 100 A320s had these guys at Northwest tensing up. The numbers favored us, but executives clearly thought, 'Do I want to gamble my whole career and reputation on 100 European airplanes?'" Leahy said.

Mid-level management at Northwest remembered the Caravelle and the other European disasters, like the Mercure.[9] But on the other hand, the A320 was not another Caravelle or Mercure. Airbus might be here to stay, and it certainly had a future around the world. Airbus may not have been Boeing, but it probably was going to end up better than McDonnell Douglas in a three-player game.

---

9. The Caravelle was a reasonable success for its era. The second Western jet after the de Havilland Comet, Sud Aviation sold 282 airplanes—but only 20 were sold into the U.S., to United Airlines. Sud was headquartered in Toulouse. It became an ancestor of Airbus.

Northwest wanted 100 airplanes, but officials were nervous. Leahy suggested that they irrevocably order 10. Even so, Northwest wanted pricing for 100. Leahy was game. It was Toulouse's turn to be nervous. "What's our big risk if we give them the price for 100 for only 10 airplanes? If we were willing to accept it for 100, why not accept it for 10, and give them an out?" Leahy told his bosses.

Leahy basically had to convince only one person, Airbus CEO Jean Pierson. "We can get on a high horse and say it's not fair that they buy 10 for the price of 100, but we just won Northwest Airlines. They pay cash. They are still pregnant with 10 of our airplanes, they're going to be flying them and they'll probably come back," Leahy told Pierson. "If they canceled the 90 because our product support is shitty, when our product support gets better, then I'll come back and I'll sell them, maybe another 20, another 30, and soon we'll be back to 100."

This was the thinking Leahy employed years later with his willingness to price American's deal at 400 airplanes with a reduced order that would be split with Boeing. The risk was that if Airbus didn't do the deal, Northwest would turn to Boeing, and then Airbus would be out for the foreseeable future. "I said we've got to do it. It was very quick decision-making, and we did it," Leahy recalled. In 1987, Northwest finally ordered the wide-bodies it had put off years before. It signed up for 24 A330-300s. In 2001, it upped the order with A340s. And then 9/11 happened, and the entire industry went into a spiral.

While Leahy and Airbus had success with Pan Am and Northwest, two other U.S. targets failed to come through. Alan Boyd knew everybody there was to know in the airline industry. He arranged a dinner with US Air's CEO, Ed Colodny. US Air, formerly known as Allegheny Airlines, operated DC-9s and 737s. It also had BAC-111s, acquired with the 1972 merger of Mohawk Airlines, so it wasn't unfamiliar with European airplanes. But, Leahy said, while the dinner was nice, it was clear Colodny wasn't interested in buying from Airbus. Winning US Air would come years later, long after Colodny was gone.

At Piedmont, Leahy came close to winning a deal for the A310. "I had a real breakthrough getting to know Gordon Bethune personally," Leahy recalled. Bethune was the head of Piedmont's operations at the time. "We ran a big sales campaign with the 310 up against the 767. I think we essentially won it. Then, the CEO at Boeing, Frank Shrontz, heard that they were close to going to go with Airbus. He flew down, asked for a private meeting with the executive committee and basically said, 'What do I have to do to keep you from making this big mistake of going with Airbus?'" Whatever it was, Piedmont bought the 767-200ER instead.

Boeing tried a similar tactic at Northwest, but failed, Leahy said. "That's how I'm pretty sure they eventually got into the mentality of the 20-year exclusivity. They thought, 'We can't keep losing deals to these guys, and then doing whatever it takes to buy them back.'"

But Pan Am became Leahy's inextricable problem. By 1989, the financially ailing airline was in such dire straits that it sold the A320 delivery positions to Braniff Inc., the second iteration of Braniff International Airways. "BI," as the original Braniff was sometimes called, became the first victim of deregulation. Gross overexpansion, coupled with disastrous fuel price hikes when OPEC discovered the power of pricing against the West, along with a sharp drop in passenger traffic due to a recession under President Jimmy Carter, and a huge spike in interest rates all converged to put Braniff into bankruptcy in 1982.

Braniff was reorganized at Braniff Inc., colloquially called Braniff II, as a much smaller company. The Pritzker family of Hyatt Hotel fame financed it, bringing Braniff out of bankruptcy in 1984. By 1988, a group of investors made an offer to buy Braniff from the Pritzkers. The principals were Jeffrey Chodorow, whose company made Alexander dolls; Arthur Cohen, CEO of a Philadelphia-based investment company; and Scot Spencer. Their company was called BIA-COR.

Spencer was an oddity. More of an aviation geek than anything else, he was in his 20s, yet became the driving force to acquire Braniff with Chodorow and Cohen. The group recruited the executive team from Piedmont, now out of work since this carrier was taken over by US Air. The Piedmont executives gave BIA-COR instant credibility.

Braniff sold its terminal at Dallas/Ft. Worth to American, which lent Braniff money in the process. The latter moved its hub from Dallas to Kansas City, a secondary hub of the original Braniff. Later, people within American acknowledged they expected to write off their loan to Braniff, discounting the future viability of the company. But getting a third terminal at Dallas/Ft. Worth and Braniff's Dallas market share more than offset this.

The BIA-COR team acquired Florida Express, a small operator, which used BAC-111s, including some from the original Braniff that had passed through several hands. Braniff moved its headquarters to Orlando, Florida. When Pan Am, desperate for cash, decided to exercise the option to sell its slots for those A320s, Braniff was interested. It bought the Pan Am contract and arranged with the Irish lessor, GPA Group, to execute a purchase/leaseback of the aircraft to Braniff.

Leahy led an Airbus team that spent Christmas to New Year's Eve 1988 in conferences rooms at Airbus's law firm, Simpson Thatcher in New York City, with teams from Braniff, Pan Am, GPA and IAE trying to negotiate the sale/transfer/lease of the 50 A320s. It was finally agreed at midnight on New Year's Eve.

With the deal done, the team went to P.J. Rourke, a tavern on Third Avenue in Manhattan, drinking Guinness until dawn. The celebration was short-lived. As American predicted, Braniff II ran into financial trouble. By October 1989, the situation was critical. Braniff, in conjunction with GPA, arranged to raise just over $100 million. Then, the unexpected happened.

Braniff was a publicly traded stock company, but only 18 percent of the stock traded among the public. BIA-COR owned the rest. With so little float, stock analysts didn't follow the airline, but its financials were filed with the Securities and Exchange Commission or SEC. An editor of the trade magazine *Airfinance Journal*, known as *AFJ*—focusing, as the name suggests, on aviation finance—followed Braniff. The SEC filings, in turn, were quite revealing.

Buried within the 10-K and 10-Q annual and quarterly filings with the SEC, *AFJ* discovered that BIA-COR officials were raking off consulting fees and bumping lease rates, "upstreaming" cash to the principals. There was nothing illegal about this. After all, Frank Lorenzo and his Jet Capital Co., and later TAC, did this routinely with Texas International Airlines, Continental, Eastern and all the little airlines TAC owned. Nor was it secret. Braniff disclosed the upstreaming and consulting fees in its SEC 10-Ks.

AFJ reported the upstreaming in routine reporting. Charles Cleaver, who was with IAE at the time, hired a consultant to review Braniff's finances. The consultant recommended that P&W take a pass. With P&W balking, the entire package collapsed. The deal called for an all-or-none participation. Braniff had taken delivery of a dozen A320s. The company filed for Chapter 11 bankruptcy reorganization; it ceased operations entirely within a matter of months. Now, those dozen airplanes had to come back to GPA. Airbus had agreed to help in remarketing in such an eventuality.

The A320s were new technology, they were available, and GPA and Airbus were anxious to find homes for them. Negotiations included America West president Mike Conway, GPA executives Jim King and Colm Barrington, Leahy and officials from P&W and IAE. P&W was one of the two leading shareholders in IAE, which provided the engines.

A new magazine, *Commercial Aviation Report*, had been formed by the editors of *AFJ*. Publishing bi-weekly instead of monthly like *AFJ*, *CAR* (as the magazine was known in shorthand) aggressively sought to follow deals and potential orders, as well as finance news. *CAR* closely tracked those Pan Am/GPA/Braniff A320s. The magazine reported that America West was in negotiation and had several updated stories.

GPA was unhappy at all the news leaks emerging from the negotiations. King accused Leahy of being their source. After several such episodes, and during a particularly intense meeting, Conway calmly lit a match in the charged atmosphere. In his low-key but biting humor, he asked whether the day's negotiations were completed in time for the *CAR* deadline. King once more accused Leahy of leaking. Leahy, according to Cleaver, virtually leapt over the table at King. Leahy refused to talk to *CAR* for the duration of the negotiations.[10]

When the parties met later in Paris for a celebratory dinner, Conway shipped 10 bottles of supermarket California wine to the upscale French restaurant. Tipping the waiter $100, the wine was served to the assembly without revealing the origin. The party enjoyed the wine. At an opportune time, Conway revealed the joke. The Americans and British laughed uproariously. The French were not amused.

Those Pan Am/Braniff A320s all went to America West. The deal had less to do with thoughtful fleet planning and expansion than it did with financing. Cleaver and Conway each recalled the A320 deal was about the money. America West already was stretched. The cash infusion was critical to its survival. Although the airline entered bankruptcy anyway in 1991, after the first Gulf War and oil price shock, America West successfully reorganized. The airplanes remained at the carrier, and the airline purchased more Airbus aircraft over the coming years.

Reorganizing America West proved fruitful for Airbus in an unexpected way, however. Leahy and Dana Lockhart, Airbus's financial guru in the U.S. office, met with David Bonderman of Texas Pacific Group, a private equity firm, one Sunday evening at a Washington, D.C., restaurant, shortly after America West filed Chapter 11. Lockhart, who worked for Leahy, represented Airbus on the creditors' committee. Bonderman, a leading private equity investor, wanted Airbus support for his attempt to take control and revitalize the airline. He was bringing in a man new to the industry, Bill Franke, to reorganize America West. Leahy arranged for Airbus to support the restructuring. Franke ultimately became one of the biggest purchasers of Airbus aircraft at other airlines he subsequently owned or in which he invested.

But Leahy still wasn't done with Pan Am. By 1991, the storied carrier was on its last legs. Pan Am had closed its domestic operations; it sold off its Pacific route structure to United. Pan Am also sold its European routes and assets to Delta. In the process, the airline was reduced to its Latin American routes, which Pan Am intended to operate with Delta as an investor and partner. It would use A310-300s.

Delta wanted to acquire nine new A310-300s as part of the Pan Am venture, but there was a catch. Delta CEO Ron Allen telephoned Leahy at his home in Virginia. "We really want those Pan Am airplanes. It's key to making this whole thing work. I'm not sure we're even going to go through with taking Pan Am, if I can't have those airplanes," Leahy quoted Allen as saying. "I told him, 'Ron, I'll trip over myself to give you those airplanes. You have no problem whatsoever.'"

---

10. Leahy wasn't the leak.

"But the reason I'm looking for you," Allen said, "is I want you to do what you did for Crandall at American. I need a 30-day walkaway on them, because I don't know if the pilots are going to like them." Leahy ended up with a 90-day walkaway. Sure enough, after about two years, Allen walked. American never did. In retrospect, Leahy thought he got hustled by Allen. "I don't think he ever intended to keep them more than this transition period of a couple years."

In fairness to Allen, he exercised the walkaway during a Delta price-cutting drive called Leadership 7.5. Airlines were still suffering big losses in the years after the Persian Gulf War. Delta, always generous with its employees, was bleeding cash. Leadership 7.5's goal was to reduce Cost Per Available Seat-Mile (CASM) to the same 7.5 level as Southwest, which was America's leading low-cost carrier. It operated only one fleet type, the 737. On-board amenities were limited to soft drinks, alcoholic beverages for sale, and peanuts or pretzels for snacks. There was no first class, only coach.

Given the international route structure, the multiple fleets, multiple classes, food and beverage service, a major frequent flier program and years of paying industry-leading wages, reducing its CASM to 7.5 cents was a tall order. Having a small fleet of nine A310-300s made no sense. Also, the Latin American deal with Pan Am collapsed when losses were far greater than forecast. United moved into many of the former Pan Am markets.

Years later, Leahy explained some of the thinking about the risky Pan Am deal. "Risk management is something we tried hard to work on. We needed to take risks to make deals, but those risks needed to be controlled and limited. You're coming in as the underdog. If all things are even close to equal, the airline stays with Boeing. You start thinking that, like with Pan Am, we've got an interesting airplane with the A310. We could, however, add value by leasing them the airplane or offering an asset value guarantee [AVG] to help them get better financing," Leahy said in 2019. "So, Airbus leased these to Pan Am, as risky a deal as there ever was, but it solved a problem for Pan Am. For Airbus, it provided a foothold—as tenuous as it was—in the U.S. market, and it put the Pan Am brand on Airbus, something of value elsewhere in the world."

At last, Leahy was free of Pan Am. However, Delta was not. Former Pan Am employees sued Delta, alleging it caused Pan Am's 1991 shutdown when it withdrew from the Latin American deal. The lawsuit, filed in federal court, sought $1 billion in damages. Delta duly reported the lawsuit in its quarterly 10-Q SEC filings but almost as a footnote.

At the same time, Texaco had been sued by Pennzoil for interference in a merger. The lawsuit also was in a federal court. Texaco was found liable. Given the size of the claim at $1 billion, a bond was required in federal court equal to the claim in order to appeal. Texaco didn't have a billion dollars in cash (this was 1991, remember), so it filed bankruptcy while the appeal worked its way through the court.

CAR wrote up the Pan Am employee lawsuit for a story and noted Delta pretty much blithely dismissed the risk. *CAR* also noted the Texaco case and compared it with Delta's situation. Some airline analysts picked up the story and reported it in research notes to clients. It was the first time in Delta's history that "Delta" and "bankruptcy" were mentioned in the same sentence. Delta's corporate communications department was not pleased. However, the next 10-Q noted that if Delta lost the lawsuit, it could result in a "material adverse affect" on the airline, a euphemism for a possible Chapter 11.

As part of Allen's Leadership 7.5 drive, across-the-board cost cutting for non-union labor was implemented. However, the unionized pilot group had to agree to any concessions, unlike the non-union work force that otherwise dominated Delta. Delta ALPA (DALPA) resisted any concessions. In the meantime, Delta filed an 8-K, an SEC document for an unscheduled event. The board of directors had given Allen a $100,000 raise, from $400,000 to $500,000, even as he sent a letter to DALPA explaining why cost cutting for Leadership 7.5 was required. *CAR* obtained a copy of the letter. In the next "News Brief" section of *CAR*, most of the letter was quoted. The very next item, one sentence long, was a report of the 8-K citing Allen's raise. DALPA saw the two items. Allen's raise was rescinded.

5

High Risk, High Reward

"The whole idea was to get your foot in the door."
—**JOHN LEAHY,** ON ONE OF HIS HIGH-RISK DEALS

LEAHY'S EARLY U.S. DEALS showed that he, and Airbus, were willing to take high risks for high rewards. Pierson backed Leahy's moves. Pierson's leadership and support of Leahy can't be understated. Pierson became managing director of Airbus in April 1985. He charged Leahy with bringing a higher level of professionalism to the North American operation and, after bringing Leahy to Toulouse in 1994, instilling the same philosophy in Airbus worldwide. Without Pierson's strong backing at key points, neither Leahy nor Airbus would have made the strides they did against Boeing and McDonnell Douglas.

Pierson's vision for Airbus demanded a full family of airplanes to compete with the Americans. After the twin-aisle A300/310, Airbus's first airplanes, and the launch of the single-aisle A320, which "made" the company, Airbus tackled the need for a successor to the original wide-body twins. Neither the A300 nor the A310 were good, long-haul airplanes. Airbus needed a modern medium-range airliner *and* a long-haul airplane.

Pierson's vision evolved into the twin-airplane program, the A330 and A340; both are twin-aisle aircraft. In the coming decades, the A330 became one of the best-selling twin-aisle airplanes, right alongside the Boeing 767, 777 and even the later technology 787. The A340, however, ended up a sales dud when an engine maker killed the engine designed for the airplane.

The A330 and A340 were essentially the same airplane. They had the same cockpit, the same wing, the same systems and the same fuselage. The basic difference: The 330 was a twin-engine airplane for medium-distance routes, and the A340 was a four-engine airplane for long-range service. A key decision that enhanced the family of airplanes was to give the new wide-body airplanes the same cockpit as the single-aisle A320 family.

Development costs for the A330/A340 were estimated at a combined $3.5 billion in the early 1990s, compared with $3 billion for a single model. In those early days, Airbus had an 18 percent global market share but much less in the U.S. With some funding provided by France, Germany, Spain and, indirectly, the U.K., Airbus could afford to take some financial risks.

(Boeing would, for decades, point to "illegal" subsidies as the reason for Airbus's success.)

The Northwest deal—10 firm single-aisle A320s priced for 100—really wasn't too much of a risk. It was highly doubtful the airlines would stop at 10. In this respect, it wasn't dissimilar to the move made by McDonnell Douglas with American for the MD-80, which was nothing more than a modernized DC-9 with a stretch and new engines. With an entry into service (EIS) in 1980, the original name was the DC-9 Super 80. The plane was rebranded MD-80 to reflect the McDonnell Douglas corporate name.

Sales of the MD-80 had stalled. American needed a big fleet of new airplanes to replace the gas-guzzling 707s of the 1950s design. American then had little in the way of international routes. There were a few to Canada and Mexico, but those 707s were sucking American dry in domestic service. The oil price shock during the presidency of Jimmy Carter made the 707 (and the competing Douglas DC-8) uneconomical on U.S. domestic routes. American had way too many 707s flying within the continental U.S.

MDC offered American a five-year walkaway deal for 20 MD-80s. If, for specified reasons, American decided after five years it didn't want the MD-80s, it could simply return them to MDC. The price, while never revealed, was widely reported to be a screaming bargain. American didn't return the airplanes. Including those acquired from the mergers with TWA and Reno Air, American eventually operated 360 MD-80s. The last was retired from service in 2019.

Leahy's gamble with Northwest was a success. On the other hand, the gambles with Pan Am were headaches for years to come, but even this worked out in the end for those A320s. These airplanes landed at America West and, over time, the carrier stopped buying from Boeing. It eventually relied on Airbus for its single-aisle aircraft. America West's management also relied on Airbus for long-haul aircraft after merging with US Airways.

The Delta A310 deal, however, turned out to be a bad risk. So why did Leahy do it? "I intended to sell them more, so the whole idea was to get your foot in the door and expand that fleet. The A310-300 was going to be much better for Delta's international travel," Leahy said, alluding to the longer range of the airplane and its wider fuselage. Clearly Boeing and ultimately Delta disagreed. Delta was flying 767s at the time. The airlines eventually dumped the A310s and relied on the 767 in various models for its growing international routes.

"Ron Allen had stood eyeball to eyeball with Jean Pierson and said that 'these walkaways are just window dressing for my accountants.' Then, of course, they pulled the ripcord on those," recalled Dana Lockhart, who was head of Airbus North America finance through much of Leahy's time there. Airbus previously had done a walkaway lease deal for 25 two-engine, widebody A300-600Rs with American. American did a similar walkaway deal with Boeing for 767s at the same time, breaking precedent and ordering both types, instead of going with one or the other—much to Boeing's annoyance. In fact, Boeing only did the walkaway with American because Crandall had led them to believe that they were blocking the Airbus deal by doing so. But Crandall took both.

For Leahy, getting into American was another "Good Housekeeping Seal of Approval." But like Northwest, he didn't consider the risk factor all that high. "When Crandall took the walkaway, he intended to keep the airplanes, he really did," Leahy said. "He was using it more as a way to get it past his board, to show his balance sheet as having less risk. They also bought 10 more with no walkaways."

"We were going to buy 25 of one, and we bought 25 of each, as it turned out, because each of the manufacturers made us a deal that we thought was extraordinarily attractive," Crandall recalled in 2019. American isolated the A300s to its Caribbean operations, where the larger cargo capacity was a plus compared to the 767s.

"In the late '80s and the early '90s, it was a period of deal after deal after deal, but we were also getting into the early stages of airline bankruptcies, which turned a lot of deals from wins to losses," Lockhart said. Leahy also sold A330s to Northwest, TWA and Continental, as well as A340s to Continental and Northwest, both twin-aisle, wide-body aircraft. Only Northwest took delivery of the A330s. All three airlines went into bankruptcy, with TWA and Continental rejecting the contracts. Northwest kept the A330 order.

"We had some big accomplishments on paper, but by those early '90s, we were living with Eastern having gone into bankruptcy and, in 1989, America West was in there, Braniff was in there, TWA ultimately was in there," Lockhart recalled. Airbus lent money to some of the bankrupt carriers as part of their reorganization, either as bridge funding or incentives to place orders. Boeing would selectively do the same in future years, but for Airbus during the late 1980s and 1990s, it seemed commonplace.

Providing secured debtor-in-possession financing also put Airbus at the head of the line in case of liquidation. It wasn't as high risk as some thought at the time. Airbus actually made a profit from it. "But John's mission, undoubtedly conveyed to him by management above, in particular, by Jean Pierson, was build a presence, build mass, build market share," Lockhart said.

The U.S. Chapter 11 bankruptcy code in those days was foreign to Europeans. (It was unprecedented for U.S. airlines, too, until 1982–1983 with the Chapter 11 filings of Braniff and then Continental.) Chapter 11 allows for *reorganization* of the debtor company. Sometimes, it turned out to be a staying action leading to Chapter 7 liquidation. In Europe, an airline went bankrupt and into receivership. It was wound up, and it disappeared.

In the U.S., contracts could be rejected, leases could be assumed or not assumed, debt restructured, often for pennies on the dollar, and airlines could be resurrected. Creditors sit on a creditors' committee and help them rehabilitate.

Airbus North America had good bankruptcy lawyers, and it had a team of people who became expert and adept in bankruptcy situations. "Dana Lockhart was one of the best," said Leahy. "He became not only our expert in airline bankruptcy but also a respected name among bankruptcy attorneys—and airline finance departments as well."

When Pan Am filed for Chapter 11 in 1991, Airbus saw it coming. A few weeks before, Lockhart's team terminated leases on 21 aircraft. Pan Am was seriously in default. Lockhart proposed to Leahy that Airbus terminate the leases. Leahy asked, "What are we going to do with all those airplanes? We can't take those airplanes back." Lockhart replied that Pan Am would most likely keep the airplanes: "They desperately need them. The first thing they'll want to do is negotiate a way to keep the airplanes."

When Airbus terminated the leases on a Friday afternoon, Leahy immediately got a raging call from Pan Am's chief financial officer, David Davies. The next day, Lockhart, Leahy and a few others were in Pan Am's offices in Manhattan, negotiating a new short-term lease for those same airplanes. The 21 aircraft never left Pan Am's service. The leases were changed from being long-term to basically week-to-week leases, which completely defeated Section 1110, the bankruptcy provision governing control and return of aircraft in Chapter 11.

Airbus faxed Davies A310 lease terminations so many times that Davies' fax machine was turned off in a futile attempt to stop the terminations. Each A310 lease required its own termination notice. Airbus's law firm was forced to deliver the required legal notices and demands by courier. At that point, the aircraft were immediately grounded. The international flights from JFK were canceled that evening, unfortunately leaving many stranded passengers.

Airbus was able to raise the rent on the planes over the course of the bankruptcy by tens of thousands of dollars a month. "The rest of the creditors were freaking out over that," Lockhart said. "They said, 'How can you do that?' We said, 'Well, these are critical for the operation. They were at low market rates before the bankruptcy. We're simply adjusting them to market rates, and we can do it because they are short-term leases. They are not subject to 1110.'"

This performance helped the stature of Airbus North America in Toulouse, especially for Leahy, Lockhart and the bankruptcy team. "We were trying to demonstrate to Toulouse that we could do deals within an airline bankruptcy," Lockhart said. "John was our leader, with the help of all of us worker bees, but we were also trying to show we can manage these critical situations. That's why, as a philosophy, we got up close and personal with Chapter 11s and sat on as many creditors' committees as we did, much to the chagrin and the wonderment of Boeing."

LIVING WITH THE CUSTOMERS

Lockhart said Airbus was successful because it was a lot more flexible, and its sales force "lived" with the customer. "I don't know whether Boeing just flew in and flew out, but we put a whole team of people there, and we stayed there until we got things done. We were willing to make deals of course. Some of the walkaway leases and things like that have one way or another attracted attention over the years," Lockhart said.

Leahy's appetite for risk-reward showed up throughout his 33 years at Airbus, but it wasn't limited to financially ailing airlines. He recognized the potential in selling speculative orders to leasing companies and the up-and-coming wave of low-cost carriers. Lessors offered a way for Airbus to expand the airline customer base. Lessors, of course, had to place the airplanes. Not only would they market them to existing customers; they sought new customers. These were across their established base of legacy airlines, as well as new entrants. New entrants almost always turned to lessors for equipment, albeit usually older, cheaper aircraft than new A320s or 737s. But this, too, began to change. For Airbus, the lessors became an unofficial extension of Leahy's sales and marketing, and the lessors were financing airplanes that Airbus, or the airlines, didn't have to or couldn't.

In the early years of the single-aisle, narrow-body A320 program, Airbus sold a large number of airplanes to lessors. In the late 1980s and early 1990s, the market reaction was that Airbus must be doing this because it wasn't having success selling to airlines directly. Leasing then didn't represent the broad market share it does today. Lessors weren't viewed as quality customers, but Leahy saw an opportunity. Lessors now account for up to 40 percent of new orders and finance about 50 percent of the airplanes operated by airlines.

One up-and-coming lessor was International Lease Finance Corp., referred to as ILFC. It was founded in 1973 by Leslie and Lou Gonda, father and son, and Steve Udvar-Hazy. The Gondas and Hazy were Hungarian immigrants. John Plueger was an early member of the team and would eventually become president to Hazy's CEO after the Gondas retired.

Hazy would become one of Leahy's best friends in the industry, and ILFC became one of Airbus's largest customers. The first deal between Airbus and ILFC was in 1988 for a single A310 for lease to Kenya Airways. ILFC was acquired by the insurance conglomerate AIG in 1990, a seminal moment for the lessor. This gave ILFC deep, deep pockets and a halo effect that helped ILFC's debt ratings, which were investment grade.

By 1992, ILFC had placed some speculative orders with Boeing. "It was about that time that we were really contemplating our first significant order with Airbus on a speculative nature," recalled Plueger. "We'd already been ordering from Boeing, but it was really then [1992] that we started with the success of Airbus globally with the A320 family."

"It was not 'till after the merger with AIG in August of '90 that we began to really accelerate our Airbus relationship," Hazy said. "Leahy also recognized, very smartly, that even though we were not focused on the U.S. airlines, we could really enhance the customer base for the A320, the A330 and A340 in a large way by seeding a lot of airlines all over the world."

"John realized that the merger with AIG gave us additional capital and effectively a big wallet, bigger than we had before. Leahy was the one who probably recognized that the first," Plueger said. "So, he started making trips to California where ILFC was headquartered." Plueger also said Leahy had the right grand vision, wanting to penetrate the large North American carriers, including those in Canada. But he knew that for Airbus to achieve 50 percent or greater market share overall, and especially in the single-aisle business, Airbus needed to pull out all the stops and source aircraft globally. ILFC and the leasing platform added value.

If a carrier hadn't operated a particular aircraft before, a lessor placing this aircraft with a carrier would, two times out of three, lead to that carrier ordering directly from Airbus or Boeing, according to Plueger. Leahy had to explore all these alternatives. "I think he also knew that there was a limitation to how much Airbus could finance or how much the export credit agencies could finance. Leasing was the only way. When you look at it, in historical hindsight, he was right," added Plueger.

The Irish leasing company GPA, which had aggressively over-expanded, collapsed. GE Capital Aviation Services (GECAS) acquired GPA's portfolio, but ILFC effectively became the only alternative to the giant lessor when it came to new, speculative orders. "We and GECAS, in the later 1990s, were really the guys that were doing Boeings," Hazy stated. "Before John Leahy was on the scene at Airbus, we ordered 130 Boeing planes: the 737, 757, 767 and 747. Airbus was not at that time really in the picture in a big way." By the late 1990s and the early 2000s, Airbus's push to the lessors overtook Boeing's penetration into the leasing community. Boeing has a different view toward lessors. Boeing generally views its relationship with lessors as a necessary evil.

To this day, lessors frequently complain that Boeing doesn't really want to sell speculative orders to lessors because these conflict with Boeing's own direct sales. Lessors complain that having sold airplanes to lessors, Boeing's sales force nevertheless will attempt direct sales to the very carriers pursued by lessors. Direct pricing is also sometimes lower than what lessors get, meaning Boeing can offer airlines cheaper deals (if it chooses) than lessors.

CHAPTER 5 HIGH RISK, HIGH REWARD

Ray Conner was a career Boeing employee who started on the production line and worked his way up through sales and other positions to become CEO of BCA. He agrees that Pierson and Leahy were willing to take more risks than Boeing. Part of it was because Airbus was the upstart, Conner said. But there was more to it than that.

"I don't think Boeing at the time recognized the competitive threat," Conner said in 2020. "I would say that we viewed that we could demand a premium or a significant premium for our products. I think in some cases, that is true. In some cases, it wasn't as true. I think Airbus was willing to be more aggressive than we were. I think that evolved over time, and I think Boeing became equally as aggressive as Airbus."

But Boeing faced another problem that customers, observers and competitors frequently mentioned. Boeing was viewed as complacent and arrogant. This hurt Boeing in many sales campaigns. Conner agreed. So did its top salesman in 2003, Toby Bright. As the upstart, Airbus had to take risks where Boeing or McDonnell Douglas were entrenched.

CHINA

China was a target with huge potential, even in the 1980s and 1990s. The world's largest Communist country had been a closed society after the revolution in 1949 brought Mao Zedong to power. Over the next several decades, the U.S. isolated China politically and economically. Mao allied with the Soviet Union and relied on it for military and civil airplanes.

As a U.S. senator and vice president, Richard Nixon was an avowed anti-communist and anti-China politician (as well as anti-Soviet). As a presidential candidate in 1960 and again in 1968, his views never wavered. Nixon lost the presidency in 1960 but won in 1968. His public views didn't change but behind the scenes, Nixon's outreach to China and later the Soviet Union leaders paid off. In 1972, Nixon announced a new initiative to China. With it came a breakthrough for Boeing.

Nixon's Air Force One was a Boeing 707. The supporting staff and press planes were also 707s, operated by Pan Am and TWA. During Nixon's ground-breaking trip to China, he authorized negotiations for Boeing to begin talks with China to order the 707.[11,12] Within two months of Nixon's visit, Boeing had an order for 10 707s.

P&W also received a one-for-one order for spare engines. The Chinese, used to the unreliable Soviet engines, now had 40 spare JT3Ds. P&W tried

---

11. For a short narrative from a Boeing representative in the negotiations, see https://www.boeing.com/boeing100/stories/2015/july/707s-for-china-07-15.page

12. https://macropolo.org/analysis/boeing-us-china-relations-history/

to talk the Chinese out of it. In December 1988, some of these spare engines were said to still be in their original packing crates.[13]

McDonnell Douglas struck a deal to assemble MD-80s (and later, MD-90s) in Shanghai, but this program was commercially unsuccessful. The assembly line was primitive, and the airplanes were essentially hand-built. In December 1988, only a few years into the project, Shanghai was far less advanced than it is today. The local government created electrical brownouts to divert power to the Final Assembly Line (FAL). Boeing shut down the operation after acquiring MDC in 1997.

The first Airbus aircraft delivered was an A310 to CAAC (the Civil Aviation Administration of China) Shanghai division in 1985. "When I made my first trip to China in 1994, one could count the number of Airbus aircraft on your fingers and toes," said Leahy. Pierson wanted to repeat the North American success in China. So, he arranged for land near the Beijing airport to build an office, training center and spares facility. Leahy hired local salesmen and trained locals as marketing analysts. Significant orders eventually followed.

Leahy remembers speaking with a vice minister of CAAC in 1996, during which he pressed for a 50 percent market share in China. The vice minister smiled, "But Airbus only has 18 percent market share worldwide," he said, "and if my briefing is correct, that's similar to your new order market share in China."

Boeing had a large installed base. By 2003, Airbus had a 20 percent share of the Chinese installed market, even as it was approaching 50 percent of the new orders. Leahy set a sales goal of achieving a 50 percent market share of the installed fleet by 2015. Airbus reached this point two years ahead of schedule.

How did Airbus achieve this? It goes straight to a difference in the risk-reward strategies of Airbus and Boeing. "Our message to the Chinese was we'd like to have 50 percent of the in-service market," recalled Laurence Barron, who served as president of Airbus China from 2004-2012 and chairman until 2017. China's response, he said, was what would become a familiar refrain: How much industrial participation did China have in Airbus manufacturing compared with Boeing? That was always the key to the Chinese market.

At the time, it was very little, Barron said. While China didn't participate much in Boeing's airplane supply and industrial chain, it was still four times the share in Airbus in 2003. In response, Airbus set a goal to match Boeing's industrial footprint by 2007. "Before getting there, our target was doubled,"

---

13. The Chinese made the cliché-ridden Chinese copy of a 707, the Y10, purportedly reverse engineering one of the 707s. Four of the 40 spare P&W engines were hung on the airplane. It never entered service.

CHAPTER 5   HIGH RISK, HIGH REWARD

Barron said. "We subcontracted more work to AVIC [Aviation Industry Corporation of China]. The major procurement was the wing for A320."

Airbus took other initiatives as well. It gave the design of A350 rudder, elevators and the belly fairing to the new Airbus Beijing Engineering Centre (ABEC), a joint venture (JV) with AVIC established in 2010. A composites manufacturing center was established in Harbin for the A320 and expanded to the A350. Composite structures, also known as carbon fiber, weren't new to airplanes. Some had been used on Boeing 727s, called fairings, that formed aerodynamic mating between the wings and fuselage. But Airbus expanded its use with the vertical tail on the wide-body A300-600. Boeing's big bet with composites came with the all-carbon fiber fuselage, wings and tail of the 787. Airbus followed with the all-composite A350. For China, with its own aerospace ambitions, gaining access to this technology was an important step.

Most visible was the decision to establish an A320 FAL in Tianjin. The FAL opened in 2008, and the first delivery was in 2009. Since then, more than 500 A320 family members have been delivered. The Chinese asked Boeing to establish a FAL for the 737. Boeing declined, although opposition was less from Boeing management than it was from its tough labor union, the International Association of Machinists (IAM) District 751. Boeing asked District 751 leadership if it would agree to an offshore 737 FAL—all 737s were assembled at the Renton, Washington, plant—as long as it meant expanded production rather than diverted assembly. The union said no.[14]

Airbus had better luck with its unions over opening the Tianjin plant. The Toulouse and Hamburg facilities were already full, and Tianjin was sold to labor as an expansion. The new FAL, which replicated the Hamburg plant, had capacity to assemble eight airplanes per month. The initial production rate was two per month, and it steadied at four. By 2019, Airbus not only expanded the Hamburg plant—it opened one in Mobile, Alabama, and boosted the rate at Tianjin. Another A320/321 FAL facility may be opened in the space once occupied by the A380 in Toulouse.[15] (The COVID pandemic put this expansion on temporary hold.)

Airbus's decision to open an FAL in Tianjin was not without controversy, however. Even then, China was notorious for allegations of ignoring in-

---

14. Having gone through the 2009 fight to retain all 787 assembly in Everett, Washington, only to see Boeing open a second line in North Charleston, South Carolina, and have Boeing threaten (in 2011) to build the 737 MAX outside Puget Sound, IAM 751 was in no mood to let this camel's nose into the tent. In 2013, Boeing again threatened to move 777 production out of Everett when it came time to select an FAL site for the 777X. Boeing finally announced plans in 2017 to establish a 737 completion center near Shanghai. Airplanes would be assembled in Renton and flown to China for installation of the interior and painting. The center opened in 2018.

15. Production of the A380 ceased in 2021.

tellectual property (IP) rights. Suppliers always worried about technology transfer required by China for the ability to do business there. They said they would make a point of transferring "yesterday's" technology to China while working on "tomorrow's" technology in their home, secure Western markets. What technology wasn't transferred to China voluntarily in JVs or by other commercial means was stolen through cyber-hacking, suppliers complained. So, when Airbus agreed to open a FAL, technology transfer and IP theft were questions raised by observers.

At the 2007 pre-Paris Air Show briefings held by EADS (European Aeronautic Defence and Space Company, then the name of Airbus's parent) and Airbus, Airbus CEO Enders rotated among the dinner tables to chat with media. He was asked about the fear of IP theft. The FAL represented only a small portion of IP in developing an airplane and didn't include any of the technology IP, Enders replied. Besides, there were protections Airbus was putting in place.

Nevertheless, in the first year after the FAL opened, news emerged that more than a half-dozen cyberattacks against Airbus came from within China. (China denied the reports.) In 2019, Enders—by now retired—recalled the decision to open a FAL in Tianjin. "It was pretty easy. The government invited us there. The government calls the shots. There are no aircraft sales or deals in China without government authorization. You could make that calculation rather easily," Enders said. "You could talk about the government and how many aircraft they would take. Not so in the U.S., as we know." Airbus has since opened an A330 completion center at the request of the Chinese. This resulted in additional A330 sales.

Another worry expressed at the time: Wasn't Airbus helping create a new competitor? Boeing's CEO in 2008, Jim McNerney, used China (and Russia and Japan) as a threat to the IAM 751, seeking labor concessions in return for selecting Everett as the site for the second 787 FAL. China, McNerney wrote the union in an email at one point during a particularly contentious moment, was going to be Boeing's next big threat, a new competitor.

Consultant Richard Aboulafia thinks the worries about a Chinese airliner competitor are overblown, but he's in the minority. He correctly points out the COMAC (Commercial Aircraft Corporation of China) ARJ21 is an overweight, uneconomic, old-technology dog, and the COMAC C919 won't be competitive with the 737 and A320. But this is hardly the point. These are planes intended to establish infrastructure and know-how. The proposed CR929 is the next step. It may take a generation for China to establish a commercially viable airliner, but this day will come. Leahy agrees. "China is still 20 years away from being a major player in commercial aviation, but they eventually will be."

Airbus's China president, Laurence Barron, looked back at the era 10 years later, long after he retired. "My personal view is that it's not for technology transfer. They would have done it anyway. They would have found a way to get technology," Barron said. "The A320 was first delivered in 1988. It's not exactly new technology. Copying and reverse engineering doesn't work. They proved that with ARJ21. The only real protection against competition is to invest in R&D. In my view, the person to catch Airbus would be Boeing. They did that with the 787. Thank God, they screwed it up. If they hadn't been late, their advantage in terms of timing would have been enormous. I was always far more worried about Boeing than any other country. That's my personal view." Boeing declined to put any significant 787 work in China, precisely because of the IP and technology transfer worries.

Increasing the industrial footprint was key to Airbus's picking up market share. Sales increased dramatically. The campaigns weren't easy. In the early 1990s, Airbus had a recognition problem in China, despite having sold a few A300s and A310s there. And there was the lost-in-translation issue. Leahy recalls an early meeting with one of the major Chinese airlines. Meetings were in large rooms with chairs set around the wall. The Chinese had a translator and so did the visitors. Meetings broke up precisely on the allotted time.

Leahy and his team explained the structure of Airbus and discussed the Airbus forecast for Chinese aviation. When the meeting ended in exactly 60 minutes, the Chinese airline chairman, through the translator, thanked Leahy for his visit, but said they wouldn't need his product. You see, Leahy was told, the airline was installing jetways and no longer needed buses to move passengers. Even establishing the Tianjin FAL didn't automatically produce results, either.

"Chinese airlines didn't want initially to take airplanes from Tianjin because they thought quality wouldn't be as good," Barron said, a residual memory from the 1980s and 1990s when McDonnell Douglas had an MD-80 and MD-90 FAL in Shanghai. "The MD-80 FAL was a disaster for everybody, I think. I looked at that very carefully, and we decided to do things very differently. MDC subcontracted to a Chinese factory. The Airbus JV maintained total control of the technical side. The objective was to turn out planes identical to Toulouse and Hamburg. The delivery process is in Airbus's hands." Barron also relayed that the first A320 deliveries had 100 percent dispatch reliability, a key metric for an airline. This means the airplane left the gate on time, every time—no mechanical delays.

To this day, the government in China must approve all aircraft orders. Sometimes the airlines announce orders, but more often than not, a government procurement agency announces a deal, and the airplanes are assigned later to the airlines—sometimes whether they want them or not.[16]

---

16. It's common lore that the airlines and lessors that "ordered" the ARJ21 or C919 were often less than enthusiastic.

"You had to sell the airplanes twice, once to the airline and once to the government. The government likes to announce big packages," Barron said.

Politics play a major role in China's aircraft ordering policies. The government plays a central role and likes to announce at big political events. If the politics are wrong, orders are put on ice. Following Donald Trump's election as president in November 2016, during which he campaigned heavily against China's trade practices, his administration started a trade war with China. Tariffs were imposed upon billions of dollars' worth of goods. China retaliated.

It may be a coincidence—but probably not—that China hadn't ordered more than a few Boeing airplanes since 2017, shortly after Trump assumed office. The lack of orders is one reason why Boeing, in late 2019, announced a production rate reduction for the 787 from 14 per month to 12. That also probably contributed to the tepid sales of the 777X.

Airbus has also been on the receiving end of China's governmental political pique, going through droughts if Beijing was unhappy with the French or German governments for some reason. "It's a headache you don't have in most other markets," Barron said, "but it's part of doing business in China."

As the upstart, Airbus had to take risks everywhere, except perhaps in the Airbus home countries. These governments pretty much made sure the flag carriers bought at least a few Airbuses. The exception for years was British Airways, which remained a loyal Boeing customer until after acquiring British Caledonian, an Airbus customer.

LATIN AMERICA

Latin America had largely been a Boeing preserve. Douglas (later McDonnell Douglas) and Lockheed had modest success with the DC-8, DC-9, DC-10 and L-1011. Convair sold a few CV-880s. But Boeing's long-haul airplanes and the 737 by far dominated in the region. Airbus saw this as a ripe market.

In 1984, Rafael Alonso began with Airbus as a salesman for Argentina, Costa Rica and Ecuador. He eventually became president for Latin America. "In 1984, the presence of Airbus in the region was almost zero. We had something like six A300s operating," Alonso recalled. "Latin America was the backyard of North America. 'Just buy American' was the logical thing to do."

Little progress was made by Airbus until 1997. Then, Taca Airlines (TACA) of El Salvador realized that buying airplanes in concert with other carriers would provide great financial benefits. The CEO of TACA was Federico Bloc, one of the most well-known names in Latin American aviation during that era. He was a very dominant, very outspoken person in the airline industry, in general—and in Latin America, in particular.

CHAPTER 5 HIGH RISK, HIGH REWARD

Bloc approached Alonso, who by this time had been put in charge of all Latin America by Leahy. "Rafael, we are fed up. We are buying three, four planes here and there. The fact is that it's very difficult for us to compete with bigger airlines because of the prices that you guys are putting in from the cost," he said.

Alonso replied that Airbus couldn't give TACA the same price for three or four airplanes as it did for a customer who ordered 100. "Does it mean that if I come back to you, and I place an order for 100 planes, you will give me an aggressive price?" Bloc asked. "Of course," Alonso replied. At the time, an order for 100 airplanes was a huge deal. Airlines then were more conservative in placing orders than they were in 2019, when orders of 200 to 300 or more planes were not uncommon.

In 1997, Latin American carriers were especially conservative. Air traffic was still modest at best, and intra-Latin America air service was still small. Nevertheless, Bloc returned to Alonso in July 1997 with a proposal. "Rafael, I have been talking to LAN Chile and I have talked to TAM." (TAM was a Brazilian airline; LAN Chile was owned by the highly regarded Cueto family.) "We have decided that we could join forces and place a big order with Airbus or Boeing," Bloc said. "Be prepared because we are going to issue a request for a proposal. It's going to be for almost 100 planes plus options, and just resharpen your pencil."

TACA already operated the A320; LAN was a 737 operator; and TAM flew Fokker 100s. Airbus called the group the "Three Amigos", and Boeing named them the "Latin Trio." Alonso said, "Negotiations, as you can imagine, were very, very difficult. John Leahy was involved in them. We went back and forth, and we were able to win this contest because I think we had a very good plane. We had the right financing. One of the conditions was to help them on the financing. It was not Airbus doing the financing but just to support and to help them."

John Feren was the Boeing salesman. "This was a fairly seminal campaign that got kicked off right after the merger of Boeing and McDonnell Douglas," recalled Feren, who joined Boeing from MDC. "It was the Latin Trio with LAN Chile, TAM Airlines of Brazil and TACA of El Salvador deciding that they wanted to do a joint buy."

The concept of a joint buy wasn't new. Four European airlines—KLM, SAS, Swissair and UTA—pursued common purchasing for the DC-10. Known collectively as KSSU, the collaboration was broader than purchasing. It included cooperative maintenance work, which reduced costs through volume. It also allowed concentration in expertise. One carrier did the airframe maintenance, another did the engines, and a third airline did the avionics.

"KSSU was the whole deal," Feren said. "The Latin Trio was just a facade in order to get a lower price." The Latin Trio was a straight-up airplane purchase and a first for a broad single-aisle acquisition in Latin America.

"If it hadn't been done previously by KSSU, it would have been very, very unusual and doing it at this scale was equally unusual. I think it was the first of its kind, and it certainly was poised to be the largest sale ever in Latin America for single-aisle airplanes."

Feren said that because of the Boeing incumbency, the Seattle company thought Airbus had little chance of winning the competition. "It was felt that it was going to be very difficult bridge for Airbus to get past, but Boeing was particularly shocked with the idea of airlines aggregating together and buying larger quantities of airplanes to get a deeper discount that they would have been able to sell independently," Feren recalled. "More importantly, it probably leveled the playing field dramatically, because I think if Airbus had gone head-to-head against Boeing at LAN Chile at the time, it would have been easier for Boeing to do things for them on 767s or other products to squeeze whatever competitiveness that the A320 would have had."

Both companies were aggressive. Alonso said Boeing became extremely aggressive as a decision neared. Leahy pretty much left Alonso alone in the campaign, but he was always in the background. Leahy decided pricing, terms and conditions and the number of airplanes that would be offered. The creative deal structures for the Three Amigos and were always a focus.

Boeing initially was more reserved. Feren stated, "Leahy's stock in trade as an observer was offering scaled orders to level the playing field with Boeing. I don't know if he did it instinctively or intuitively, but every time he would increase the volumes that the airlines would buy, it was a red flag for me. I thought, 'Shit, this is not going to turn out well.' He did it at America West. He did it at Air Canada. Boeing's approach is 'You need to buy. We will give you these [buying] options, and we're not going to overpopulate the skyline with risk.' The 737 had never been sold to stratospheric volumes, and there wasn't a view that the A320 was a formidable competitor. Maybe naively, but nevertheless, there wasn't."

Boeing kept saying that the three airlines only needed 58 airplanes, Feren recalled. "How are they going to take 100? What we really didn't appreciate is that I think TACA and LAN Chile realized TAM was sitting on a gold mine and that the VASP[17] guys were vastly inefficient and far more interested in expanding internationally than developing the domestic market."

The negotiations were endless and, according to Leahy, "going in circles." He became frustrated. So, he called for a meeting in a hotel with all the principals present. Finally, after a day of high emotions and dramatic back-and-forth Latin negotiations, an outline of the deal was agreed. Airbus concluded the deal in December 1997, signing an MOU for 88 firm A320s and 120 options.

---

17. VASP was a major Brazilian airline at the time.

IAE, which was struggling to gain a foothold in the single-aisle market against CFM and in Latin America, won the engine order. "This is the start of the rise of Airbus in the region," Alonso said. Leahy agrees, but points to a dramatically different strategy at Airbus. Leahy explained, "I strongly believed in local knowledge. I wanted salesmen who really knew the customer. This requires many years and spending substantial time with the customer, getting to know his needs, shortcomings and helping him see opportunities that could be achieved with Airbus aircraft. That's what Raphael and his team did."

"In my opinion, Boeing rotated their sales teams way too often. Feren's a great salesman but he clearly didn't know the Latin American airlines as well as Rafael Alonso. How could he?" Leahy posited. In fact, Boeing replaced its head of sales approximately every two years during Leahy's tenure as commercial director. "This certainly didn't help their commercial strategy," adds Leahy.

From the Three Amigos, Airbus went on to win key campaigns with VivaAerobus, Mexicana, Volaris and Interjet in Mexico. In a rare wide-body win, LAN Chile opted for the A340 over the 777. Boeing won Aeromexico and later, LATAM selected the 787. Boeing retained and grew with Panama's COPA and won Brazil's GOL.

In the 35 years Alonso was at Airbus, during which he was assigned to Latin America (plus Iberia and Spain), the company's market share went from those six A300s to 60 percent of in-service aircraft and 70 percent of the backlog by 2019. Seven hundred airplanes in the Latin American fleet start with an "A." "That's unmatched local knowledge combined with a world-class sales and marketing team," said Leahy.

ASIA

While Airbus was battling Boeing in the Americas and Europe, and they were dealing with competition from China, it was not ignoring the rest of Asia, considered the fastest-growing market in the world. Economic growth was on a sustained upward trend. Populations across the continent were moving up in classes. The region was ripe for the creation of low-cost carriers (LCC) from Japan and Vietnam to Indonesia and India.

As with the U.S., some of these campaigns were tough nuts to crack. When Leahy was promoted to head of sales in Toulouse, he was only there a few months when Airbus took an A340 out to India. "They did a demo tour around India with Pierson on board and basically nobody showed up," recalled Rao, who worked for Leahy at Airbus North America. "I was in the United [Airlines] field service office at the time. I remember it very clearly. I was in San Francisco, and I got a call from John."

"Kiran, I want you to move to India, I want to make you president of

Airbus India," Leahy said. Rao was able to contain his enthusiasm. "John, I'm not going anywhere. I'm in the U.S. now, we bought a house, we bought two cars, we've got television sets that only work in America, we've done everything. I can't move to India." Leahy said, "No, you're moving to India."

The two argued about it for about six months. "And then I ended up moving to India," Rao said. "John just put his arm around me and squeezed hard." Leahy said, "This is good for your career, and you need to listen to me when I tell you what to do." Rao went in 1996. He didn't make a sale until 2002, but he gained experience and understanding of the Indian aviation market. Rao's big breakthrough came with a new LCC called Air Deccan. It was the first LCC in India.

From there, Airbus went on to make big sales to IndiGo, which, by 2020, bought hundreds of A320 family airplanes.[18] IndiGo eventually became the biggest A320 customer. Airbus also sold to LCC Go Air, Indian Airlines, Kingfisher and AirAsia India. Although Indian Airlines would eventually merge into Air India, a big Boeing customer, and Kingfisher expanded too big and too fast, going out of business, Airbus achieved an 80 percent market share in 10 years.

AirAsia was a downtrodden, bankrupt Malaysian carrier that entrepreneur Tony Fernandes bought literally for pennies. It operated a couple of old Boeing 737s. Fernandes pumped money into it, ordered a lot of A320s, and A330s/neos and A350s through sister brand AirAsia X. He franchised both brands with JVs throughout Asia and India. Like IndiGo, AirAsia became one of Airbus's biggest customers.

Boeing just wasn't willing to take the kind of risks Airbus was. In part, it didn't have to, given its dominant position in the market. Nevertheless, Boeing would complain in the future this was because Airbus was subsidized by its home governments, enabling deals priced below where Boeing could not compete. Airbus strongly disagrees. These kinds of risk-rewards simply were not in Boeing's DNA through the late 1980s.

---

18. This is the Indian airline, not to be confused with Bill Franke's IndiGo Partners, another big A320 customer.

6

Facing Off

"The A340 was built for one airline. That's just dumb."
—**A BOEING OFFICIAL** WHO REMAINS ANONYMOUS

BY 1990, AIRBUS AND BOEING were increasingly engaged in their growing global combat. Inexplicably, Boeing still was slow to recognize the escalating threat. Granted, the wide-body A300/310 remained second fiddle to Boeing's 767, and the single-aisle A320 had only been in service two years. But Airbus already was taking its next step.

While McDonnell Douglas was spiraling down into its death throes through the 1980s and 1990s, Airbus and Boeing were moving toward another face-off. Airbus was creating the A330/A340. Boeing was designing the 777. Each would take on the MD-11, which entered service first in 1990. The A340 would enter service in 1993; the A330 followed the next year. The 777 entered service in 1995.

In the late 1980s, Airbus studied a new concept that used the A300 fuselage but with much more range. A four-engine A340 would be the long-range model, and a twin-jet A330 would cover medium-range routes, which were longer than the A300's but shorter than the A340's capability. The original concept for the A340 called for engines by IAE, of which P&W was a JV partner. It was christened the SuperFan. The forerunner of today's Geared Turbofan, the SuperFan promised dramatically lower fuel burn. The A340 concept was pushed by the Germans and Lufthansa.

IAE announced the concept in July 1986. IAE said the engine would burn 20 percent less fuel than engines of the day. It was, for the times, revolutionary. The proposed engine would use the core of IAE's existing V2500 used on the A320, adding a gearbox on the front. Had IAE proceeded, it would have made the difference in the success or the eventual failure of the A340, but it wasn't to be. IAE withdrew the engine from the market the following April.

Infighting among the IAE partners and outright opposition by P&W were the reasons, says Nick Tomassetti, president of IAE at the time. "We had an engine that was 20 percent better than anything that was flying," Tomassetti recalled. "It would have dramatically changed the way in which we proceeded with commercial airplanes." P&W had blown its market share lead years earlier by betting on the airlines moving to the 757-sized airplane, instead of focusing on re-engining the 737. GE and French aerospace manufacturer Safran, through their JV CFM International, instead won exclusivity on what became the 737 Classic with the CFM56.

The SuperFan was P&W's best bet to recapture its lead, and it blew it again. The question was why. "They didn't see IAE as the instrument to bring new technology to the industry. It was as simple as that," Tomassetti said. "We were struggling against the engineering departments at Rolls-Royce and at P&W. Fundamentally, P&W was against the idea that IAE would bring such a dominant engine to the marketplace. They were jealous, pure and simple. We had that kind of a jealous fight with the initial part of IAE for years. It wasn't something new. It was, quite frankly, the 'not invented here' syndrome. They didn't want to do it. They didn't want to take the risk, which is in any development program of an engine. So, they killed it."

Jean Pierson trekked to East Hartford, P&W's headquarters, to keep the program alive. "We didn't have a firm contract with Airbus at that time," Tomassetti said. "Pierson came to East Hartford to meet with the IAE principals or partners. He offered to let P&W put the engines on their upcoming A330, and Airbus would promote it. When he was told no by the combined IAE team, he said frankly, 'Goodbye, folks. It will be a cold day in hell before you get an engine on my airplane.'"

Yet a P&W engine did appear on the A330, due to insistence by Northwest, which at the time ordered nothing but Pratt engines for its airplanes. "That forced Pierson's hand, but it wasn't a very successful program for P&W," Tomassetti recalled. The SuperFan would have made all the difference for the A340, but IAE didn't have the "oomph" yet to force the issue. This was still in the early days of the V2500 program for the A320. "We came very close to killing the program," he continued. "If it wasn't for Pierson coming to East Hartford and threatening a three-billion-dollar penalty if they pulled the IAE engine, we wouldn't have had the IAE V2500. They really didn't care about that program."

With the SuperFan dead, Airbus now had a "glider." Airbus was forced to put the current technology CFM56 on the airplane. Hat-in-hand, Pierson went to CFM. Leahy said that knowing its strong bargaining position—driven by GE, the dominant partner in the 50-50 partnership with France's Snecma—CFM refused to grant any significant financial concessions. This made it difficult for Airbus to sell the A340 on competitive commercial terms in some campaigns where, otherwise, the plane had a good chance against the 777-200/200ER or MD-11.

The lack of thrust on the CFM56-5C would prove a weakness for the A340-300. While cruise fuel burn was acceptable for the time, field performance was a weak point. To compensate for the unavailability of the more efficient SuperFan, Airbus revised the wing to provide a bit more economy, but at best, this was a compromised solution.

Initially, the range for the A340 was 6,830nm, one of the longest for the era. The A330's initial range design was a mere 3,900nm, good for intra-Europe and intra-Asia and okay for U.S. transcontinental routes. But after allowing for winds, alternate and reserves, the early A330 was marginal for even the shortest transatlantic routes. The idea was to avoid competing with the long-range A340.

Airbus launched the program in June 1987 at the Paris Air Show. Lufthansa and Swiss were among the 10 initial customers with 130 orders. A Boeing engineer, who remains anonymous in order to speak freely even more than 20 years later, said Boeing viewed the A340 as "a mistake." "The A340 was a goof," he said. "They did the 340 for Lufthansa because at the time, Lufthansa refused to fly two engines over water. It was built for one airline, and that's just dumb. It's not a market."

Bright, a Boeing salesman who pitched the 777 against the A340 in several campaigns, was equally disdainful. "I don't think you'll find anyone at Boeing who thought that the A340 was a decent plane," Bright said. (Feren thought the A330-300 was a good airplane but agreed the A340-200, A340-500 and -600 were dogs.)

The A340 wasn't as efficient as the twin-engine 777, and it was slow. Across the Atlantic, the A340 took up to 30 minutes longer than the 777. This added to operating costs, including crew scheduling issues. "It was a great aircraft that was unfortunately plagued by bird strikes...from behind," Leahy quipped, long after production ended.

Development of the 777 involved a major change in how Boeing designed airplanes. It was the first computer-designed aircraft at the company. It was also intended to replace the 747—way back in 1990. Twins were already making inroads across the Atlantic. The 767 and A310 were plying some routes. The DC-10 and remaining Lockheed TriStars were eroding the 747 monopoly. Open Skies[19] was nibbling at the monopoly as well. The traditional hub-to-hub transoceanic model was already shifting to hub-to-secondary cities in many areas. Designing the 777 as a replacement for the 747 made sense. (It would take nearly another 30 years before the last passenger 747 rolled off the lines.)

Even then, Boeing was shifting its product strategy to a smaller-is-better model. "It was an overriding mantra for our product strategy: smaller, more capable," said a retired Boeing official who was there at the time. "We always tried to make the airplanes as efficient and as capable as they

---

19. Open Skies allows airlines from the participating countries largely unrestricted access to any city within the other's country.

could be, as small as we could make them. It goes back to why people get on the airplane in the first place. That's because they want to get someplace quickly, safely and efficiently, and anything that gets in the way of that underlying drive is contrary to why people fly. That means you want to avoid stops. You want to do point-to-point missions because all you had to do is screw up, before you're down they lose everything, miss connections. The 777 was always envisioned as a 747 replacement."

The 777 program would run 100 percent over budget, a fact that would prove relevant when Boeing executives and the board of directors considered whether to launch the next new airplane—the 787.[20] The airplane had two models. The 777-A was the "U.S." airplane: U.S. domestic service, including Hawaii. The 777-B was a transatlantic airplane. At one point, Boeing proposed putting folding wingtips on the plane. It was a concept Leahy, from his vantage point at Airbus, dismissed as marketing fantasy. In the early 1990s, composites hadn't made the impact that would be seen on later airplanes, and the wingspan was short enough that adding folding wingtips meant weight, all the while trying to figure out how to avoid encroaching on the control surfaces. Leahy proved correct. Boeing dropped the idea.

Leahy, in his own words, pooh-poohed folding wingtips. Boeing didn't do the folding wings then, but the idea resurfaced with the 777X 20 years later. The early 777-200s, including the ER model, were available with P&W, GE and Rolls-Royce engines. The A340-200/300 had only CFM56s. Entry into service for the A340 was March 1993. EIS for the 777-200(A) was June 1995.

Leahy thought that one campaign in which Airbus was close to winning with the A340 was with United. It may have been some wishful thinking. The airline was on Boeing's design committee for the 777-200. Except for the DC-10, United was an all-Boeing operator and ordered only Boeing aircraft after the DC-10. At that point, United also exclusively bought engines from P&W; the A340 offered only the CFM. (P&W thought that if United ordered the A340, it could give it a second chance to put one of its engines on the airplane following IAE's withdrawal.)

Airbus lost to the 777. United placed the first order for the 777 in October 1990. But the campaign likely helped Leahy win an order later for the A320 because by then, United was familiar with Airbus, its sales and support team—and the analysis by both sides that laid the foundation for the A320 campaign.

Nico Buchholz was an engineer at Airbus when the A340 and 777 were

---

20. Boeing didn't reveal the cost of the 777. However, one official on the program acknowledged it was more than $10 billion, and there is a published report that it was $11.5 billion. The numbers fit with the stated goal that Boeing wanted to commit to about half the 777 amount for the 787, or $5 billion.

launched. One of his jobs was comparing costs between aircraft. Boeing did the same thing, taking the Airbuses apart. Analysis went right down to the nitty-gritty items, such as brakes. It then would come to how deep is the knowledge of the buyer and the knowledge of the buyer, which in general, wasn't that deep, Buchholz said. The 777-A, according to Buchholz, "wasn't a really good aircraft, but we all know that it lay the foundation for brilliant aircraft."

The A340 had its shortcomings. The first A340, the -200, was a "nonstarter," in Buchholz's words. The -300 was a good airplane with reliable engines. The -500/-600 (there was no -400) had expensive engines tied to an expensive MRO (Maintenance, Repair and Overhaul) contract demanded by Rolls-Royce.

An early campaign was with South African Airways, or SAA. Rao, who was still fairly new to sales at the time, said SAA wanted Airbus and Boeing to bring the A340 and 777-200ER to Johannesburg for a fly-off. Airbus flew in an A340 flight test aircraft. Boeing brought a 777-200ER built for Delta. The A340 interior was filled with testing equipment and a limited number of seats but nothing in the way of a finished passenger interior. The Delta model was fully fitted out.

"John came in on the flight test airplane," Rao recalled. "He was totally mad that we brought this. He knew we were winning the campaign, but he said this could cause us to lose because we were showing a lousy airplane interior to their board, and Boeing was showing a brand new 777.

Leahy's foul mood began in Toulouse, Rao recalled. "Apparently, he slipped on the stairs going up to the aircraft. He tore his suit. He arrived in Johannesburg, and he complained because there was no one there to take him and the flight test crew through customs and immigration. He finally came through, and we went to the airline office. We saw Rolls-Royce coming out of the airline office, and he complained to the Rolls guy." At the time, Leahy was unhappy with Rolls-Royce for the lack of support for the A340 in preference to the 777.

"Then the aircraft demo flight was about to happen. The battery failed, and we couldn't start the airplane," Rao said. "After a delay for a power cart, we went off and did our demo flight. The chairman and the board and everybody in top management were all on the aircraft. Then we landed, and that was fine. Boeing then took all the same passengers."

Boeing started its take-off roll with all the SAA people on board. The chairman was in the cockpit. The plane blew up an engine. At this point, Leahy said he saw the Airbus team laughing and, he admits, he lost it. Laughing at a competitor's blown engine—which could have ended worse—was the last straw in a long line of mistakes and poor judgment.

Airbus's campaign was centered around the need for four engines in South Africa because of the hot-and-high airport and distances across the

South Indian Ocean or the Atlantic or Africa. Elementary things, like not proofing presentations after revisions, were being missed—let alone the big things like having a fitted-out demonstrator airplane in lieu of a test aircraft for sales presentations. Leahy felt the Toulouse team fell short of the standards he was trying to instill. The team's performance on the SAA demo trip did nothing to improve his disposition.

Leahy's irritation with Rolls-Royce was rooted in the fact that it supplied engines for the A340-500/-600 and the 777-200/-200ER. Boeing had all three engine makers on this model. His pique with Rolls-Royce even made it into a profile in a U.S. newspaper, *The Wall Street Journal*, which reported that Leahy didn't speak to Rolls-Royce for about a year.

"In a lot of campaigns in those days, Rolls was not supporting Airbus on the A340-600, and we would lose," Rao said. Comparing the A340-600 against the 777-300ER, with four engines vs. two, the A340's costs were much higher. To compensate, Airbus and Rolls-Royce, which supplied the engines, lowered the thrust. Lower thrust reduces the strain or wear and tear on the parts. Theoretically, this also lowered the A340's engine maintenance costs to match the two engine 777's costs. But if you did the maintenance cost per engine, we were double and that was one of the things that killed the A340-600."

Rao said Rolls-Royce was desperately trying to stay on the 777-300ER. "Rolls was sucking up to Boeing, trying to make sure that they were on the -300ER. I don't know what their politics were, but they were trying to be nice to Boeing, and we lost a lot of campaigns where Rolls basically didn't support the A340-600."

Whatever the divergent views of the 777-200/ER, Boeing created the 777-300, a stretch that added capacity with a little more range than the -200A but much less range than the -200ER (B Model). Like the 747-300 before it, the 777-300 saw only 60 sales. But when Boeing put the GE90 engine and more fuel tanks on the -300 to create the -300ER, it was a home run. EIS was in 2004. More than 800 were sold through 2019. The total 777 "Classic" sales exceeded 1,600 (including 181 freighters) through February 2020.

BOEING COUP

Airbus and Leahy suffered a huge embarrassment in the rivalry between the A340 and 777. Singapore Airlines ordered the A340-300, but Boeing swooped in and won an order for the 777-200ER. Part of the deal involved taking all 17 A340s, in their fleet as well as undelivered, in trade. Airbus wound up delivering A340-300s to Boeing. Bright was given the assignment of selling these airplanes.

"We had a big campaign to sell 777s to Singapore Airlines, and they had already committed to the A340s," Bright recalled. "Boeing had never really taken airplanes in trade. We felt like we could effectively take airplanes on trade and go do something with them. This was a blow to Leahy. It was one of the few times, I think, that we surprised him and were able to pull this off."

Boeing trying to sell a brand new, undelivered A340 rejected by the buyer presented some special challenges. The optics were terrible for the Airbus airplane. "The first thing I did was get on a plane and made a round-the-world trip," Bright said. "We went to airlines that already ordered A340s. We had these awkward conversations where I'd say, 'I am from Boeing. I'm here to talk to you about some A340s that we have.'"

As a salesman, Leahy touted the attributes of the A340 throughout his tenure at Airbus. Still, all the rhetoric and fancy brochures couldn't hide the fact that the 340 was eclipsed by twin engines, and the -500/-600 models had very expensive engines. In November 2017, shortly before his retirement and well after the 340 went out of production, Leahy candidly assessed the A340 in an interview with *Leeham News*.

"The A340 was a damn good airplane for a four-engine airplane, but we got it wrong. To a large degree, we got it wrong by listening to some very important customers about whether long-range, intercontinental, transoceanic flying would go to twins, or would it stay with four-engine airplanes," Leahy said. "When I got over to Toulouse in 1994, I was appalled by the fact that people didn't even want to look at the concept of intercontinental twins. They really were focused on the four-engine airplane. They had customers who were pushing the fact that it would always be four engines. It's no secret Lufthansa was one of them."

Leahy said some Asian customers admitted there might be twins across the Atlantic, but not across the Pacific. "'It'll never happen,' they said. We listened too much to that, rather than understanding where the future was headed." Leahy continued, "I remember being at one meeting with senior management of GE and Airbus in Venice. Brian Rowe [then-CEO of GE Aviation] was desperate to do something with the GE90 because he had gotten himself into a situation where he was trapped into being one of three engines on the 777."

At that point, the 777s were "A" and "B" models. Leahy says the A330/340 combination was selling well against those early 777s. But as one of three engine options on the 777, GE was not doing well. GE, he says, would have paid for the development costs of putting the GE90 on an A330. "Our management team just rolled their eyes, saying, 'Why would we want to do that? We've got a proper strategy: a four-engine airplane for long-haul and planes for regional flying, all with the same fuselage, all with the same wing. Ours is an unbeatable strategy,'" Leahy recalled. "I was flabbergasted. I was stunned by that. It was one of the biggest strategic mistakes Airbus ever made, missing the turn to twins vs. quads. To this day, I wish I had pushed much harder for the GE90 on the A330, which would have significantly increased its range. We would have then had an excellent alternative to developing the A340-500/600. But I was at the time the new kid on the block in Toulouse, having recently become commercial director, so I had to settle for pushing Airbus to develop the A330-200 which substantially increased the range of the A330 but did so at the cost of fewer seats. It was an excellent aircraft but due to its size, it only competed with the 767-300ER not the 777."

But there were some cases where four engines were better. The 777-200ER couldn't take off from Johannesburg and get to London. Joburg is one of those hot, difficult airports that made twin-engine operations challenging and favored the four-engine A340.

The 777-300ER, with its bigger engines and some airframe improvements, solved this problem. Rao recalled a 2002 campaign with Air Mauritius, where Boeing was pushing the 300ER and Airbus offered the A340-600. "I kept pushing the A340-600 because I knew that the 777-300ER in those days didn't have the take-off performance. We started the Air Mauritius campaign, where the -300ER could not do Mauritius to London. By the time we finished the campaign, they could easily do it," Rao recalled. "GE and Boeing pushed the thrust up to 115,000 pounds. Then they could do all these missions. Then they ended up going further than the A340-600. The biggest problem was that the 777-300ER had about 30 more seats. All of these actually affected my final thought process when we ended up doing development on the A350."

Although the A340-600 has fewer seats than the -300ER, Airbus could win some deals in the early days because of its performance. "Once the performance advantage was lost, then everything became dependent on the seats. Once it became dependent on the seats, then you suddenly realize the value of seats in long-haul flying, the value of seats in any campaign," Rao said. The 777 Classic program, through 2019, saw more than 1,600 sales. Freighters from this program were still being sold in 2021 and technically, so was the -300ER but at a trickle.

Airbus sold only 355 A340s in four models, the -200/300/500 and -600. It clearly turned out to be the wrong airplane at the wrong time, superseded by ETOPS (Extended-Range Twin-Engine Operations Performance) and the move toward twins. ETOPS permits twin-engine aircraft to operate up to an astonishing 240 minutes on one engine from the nearest airport. This dramatically improves the ability of twin-engine aircraft to fly over water or even over desolate ice caps. The economic benefits through eliminating the need for four-engine aircraft are clear.

The success of the A330, and how it evolved from EIS in January 1994 through development in the mid-2010 decade, is proof of this. Through the end of 2019, nearly 1,500 A330s were sold to 100 customers—a greater base than Boeing with the 777. By June 1987, when the A330/340 program was launched, the 767 had been in service a mere five years. The 767-300ER, which became the most widely sold model, was launched in 1984 and entered service in 1988. By the end of 2019, only the 767-300ERF was in commercial aircraft production. The -300ER saw slightly more than 800 sales. Including the 767-200 and the 767-200-based KC-46A aerial refueling tanker, slightly less than 1,200 767s were sold through 2019.

By the time the A330 was launched, the 767's design technology was 10 years old. Airbus had a fly-by-wire cockpit to Boeing's analog design. The A330/340 were essentially the same airplane and the cockpits were common to the A320 family and later A300s, with a process called minor differences training was all that was required. The 757/767 cockpits were the same, but they were different from the rest of the 7-Series airplanes: the 707/727/737/747. Engines were the same, though improved with 10 years' newer tech inserts. There were systems advancements. The A330s carried more passengers than the 767s. All in all, this made a big difference to some customers.

"The technology was years apart," said Steven Vella, an engineer and later a buyer of airplanes from Airbus, Boeing and McDonnell Douglas for lessors and airlines. By the time he compared the 767 and A330 "the 767 was coming to the end of its career and the 330 was taking off." Cockpit commonality across the A Series would become a major selling point. But creating the A330-200, a shrink of the A330-300, gave the A330 more range and versatility. The A330 began matching deliveries of the 767 in 1999 and 2000. It dipped slightly the next year but overtook the 767 in 2002. Airbus never looked back after that.

In December 2003, Boeing CEO Harry Stonecipher launched the 787 program. EIS was targeted for May 2008, in time for the Summer Olympics in China. Boeing claimed the 787 would kill the A330. The 787 was designed to replace the 767 (which itself got a new lease on life with the massive delays in the 787 program), as well as the A330. Boeing claimed the 787 would be up to 25 percent more efficient than the 767 and the A330. It didn't turn out that way.

As Airbus would later crow, more A330s were sold after the launch of the 787 than before. Part of this would be due to the massive 787 program problems rooted in the decisions to outsource many critical design elements, along with the massive shift in the industrial production plan. Coupled with booming transoceanic traffic, range improvements and major growth in passenger demand in intra-Asia and China—where the A330 was used, on average, only 2,000 miles or less—the A330 became a highly sought-after airplane.

The early 787s were, in industry jargon, "lead sleds." They were heavy, not unusual in new airplane programs, but this was especially so with the

787. One airline fleet planner specifically told his CEO to refuse any 787-8s from the first production block of 50 airplanes due to weight, design and performance issues. While this airline was a launch customer, the fleet planner was adamant his carrier should not be a launch operator.

The airline's first 787-8 was delivered from the second block of 50. The 787's entry into service, planned for May 2008, would not occur until December 2011. Production issues continued to plague the airplane, and EIS was slow for many customers.

Airbus was able to deliver the A330 sooner. It was a proven airplane. By 2011, costs had largely been amortized, so Airbus had broad flexibility in pricing, which lowered capital or lease costs for the airline. This, in turn, evened out the 787's efficiency advantages. Deliveries of the 767 spiked in 2017–2019, just as deliveries of the freighters and the tanker up-ticked against declining sales and deliveries, while the 330 transitioned from the ceo to the neo beginning in 2015.

Despite any shortcomings the 777-200 (A model) and 777-200ER (B model) may have had, these were very good airplanes. The ER took the ETOPS pioneered by the 767 to a whole new level. The added flexibility allowed by ETOPs enhanced the use by the airlines and set the stage for all twin-engine airplanes to come, wide-body and, eventually, even single-aisle narrow-body aircraft. Airbus's A340 campaign, "4 Engines 4 the Long Haul," had some early applicability, since qualifying for ETOPS was a process that strained less sophisticated airlines. ETOPS, in those days, still had limitations in the time allowed from the nearest airport. The four-engine A340 had no limitations.

Boeing's path to creating better performance for the 777 and the larger models was an odd one. In a July 1998 article in *Flight International*, reporter Guy Norris (himself an aviation reporting institution) wrote that Boeing considered adding a small third engine to the tail of the 777, which could double as the Auxiliary Power Unit (APU).[21]

"Boeing is considering the use of a third, tail-mounted engine in the 777-200X/300X that would also double up as an auxiliary power unit. The virtually unprecedented use of a thrusting APU is one of a wide range of changes being studied to improve the field performance of the aircraft, as the Seattle-based airframe builder attempts to find a launch customer for the aircraft after being beaten to several key orders by the latest versions of the Airbus A340," Norris wrote. Boeing also considered several airframe and wing changes, including adding winglets, to improve lift. In the end, it was the new engine, revised landing gear and the superior economics of the expanded passenger capacity that made the -300ER a winner over the A340.

---

21. https://www.flightglobal.com/boeing-studies-triple-engined-777x/21900.article

Through March 2020, 43 lessors and airlines ordered 820 777-300ERs.[22] Emirates Airline (EK) alone ordered 114 -300ERs (14 percent), replacing earlier -200s and Airbus A330s. Over time, EK built its business plan around the -300ER and the Airbus A380. Some inside Boeing had mixed feelings about creating the -300ER. The threat to its own flagship, the 747, was recognized. The -300ER would be the first direct step in killing the 747, for it would do many—if not most—of the missions that, up until then, had been the domain of the big jet.

In fact, there were two factions within Boeing: One argued that the 747 should be discontinued with the launch of the -300ER. Another was wedded to the prestige and the iconic profile of the airplane—and the fact that its nose-loading cargo feature made it unique in the industry. The -300ER entered service in 2004. The 747 would continue in production for nearly another 20 years. The passenger model was discontinued in 2017–18, but the last freighter was scheduled for delivery in 2022.

---

22. This reflects net orders, as listed on the Boeing website. More orders were placed initially, but some were canceled or swapped to other aircraft types.

7

The Death of McDonnell Douglas

"They are not good at running the business."
—**ADAM PILARSKI,** A FORMER McDONNELL DOUGLAS OFFICIAL

THE LONG, DOWNWARD SPIRAL OF DOUGLAS AIRCRAFT really began in 1967 when it merged with the McDonnell Corp. to avoid bankruptcy. The merger gave Douglas new life, but by 1996, the legendary line of Douglas aircraft was coming to an end. Before World War II, 80 percent of the world's passengers were transported on Douglas DC-2s and DC-3s. After the war, there was spirited competition between Douglas and Lockheed with the DC-4, DC-6 and DC-7 against the various versions of the beautiful Constellation, or "Connies." The simpler designs of the DC Series made them easier to work on, and cash operating costs were superior to the Connies. Douglas built 1,124 DC-4s/6s/7s (plus another 1,163 wartime C-54s, the military DC-4). Lockheed built 856 Connies, a 57 to 43 percent market share split, excluding the C-54s. Boeing delivered a paltry 56 Stratocruisers.

The success of the DC-9 was also the undoing of Douglas Aircraft Co. Unable to keep up with demand, production fell into disarray—much like what would happen to Boeing in 1997. Deliveries ran months late. Eastern was so irate, it sued Douglas.[23] Douglas was also hampered by the start-up of the U.S. involvement in Vietnam. Initial combat operations began in early 1965. As air war operations increased, P&W production was diverted from civil to military engines. The DC-9 was powered by P&W engines, as were the DC-8 and Boeing 707/720/727s.

By 1967, Douglas was on the ropes. A marriage with McDonnell Corp. of St. Louis, a defense contractor, was hastily arranged with the U.S. government acting as minister. But the McDonnell family never understood the commercial business, says Adam Pilarski, who was an economist at Douglas and then McDonnell Douglas after the merger. Nor did they give the Douglas Aircraft division much authority, he said. "Every six months, they were showing numbers for the last six months saying, 'Yes, we lost money

---

[23]. A white paper details this: "Overwhelmed by Success: What Killed Douglas Aircraft," by Jonathan S. Leonard and Adam Pilarski, 2014.

again, but you know the [financial] hockey stick: Everything will change,'" Pilarski recounted.

Maybe that was the problem. Long Beach, where the Douglas executives were headquartered, never met their forecasts pledged to the corporate officers in St. Louis, where MDC was headquartered. After one of the first meetings, Pilarski expressed his skepticism over the presentations made by the Long Beach executives. "How could the corporate officers believe the Long Beach group who consistently missed forecasts? How would St. Louis believe all this when these guys prove to you over and over and over and over again that they are not good at running the business?" Pilarski asked. He criticized the McDonnell family for failing to invest in Commercial. He said St. Louis micro-managed Long Beach down to the smallest decisions.

With a stable of derivative airplanes and an emphasis on cutting costs, Douglas's market share was already a distant number two when Airbus was formed in 1970. Lockheed returned to commercial aviation with the L-1011, dividing the tri-jet wide-body market with the DC-10—and ensuring neither airplane made money.

Stonecipher became president and CEO of McDonnell Douglas in 1994. He was brought in to sell MDC. "Harry Stonecipher worked 27 years at GE, then six years at Sundstrand [an aerospace products manufacturer]. He had no loyalty to McDonnell Douglas. He had no loyalty to the culture. He didn't do anything for us. He sold us," said Pilarski.

Stonecipher would go on to become "Public Enemy Number One" within Boeing. He wasn't too popular within Douglas Commercial, either, according to Pilarski. "Many people disliked him. He was not super friendly, but he was not an idiot. He knew exactly what he was supposed to do.".

Stonecipher realized that MDC did not invest in commercial for a long, long time, and there's no way Douglas could come back without investing billions of dollars. On the other hand, MDC was, at that time, the number one military supplier. A merger would basically close Douglas, and that's what happened.

In 1974, when the first Airbus A300 was delivered, MDC was in reality the leading twin-aisle, twin-engine airplane provider that year. Forty-eight DC-10s were delivered compared with 41 L-1011s, 22 747s and four A300s. The market share split was 42 percent, 31 percent, 19 percent and three percent, respectively. Boeing's share of the wide-body market by 1974 was already shrinking. The 747 was proving to be too big. Introducing 767 and 777 would restore Boeing to leadership. Neither Airbus nor Lockheed played at this time in the single-aisle market.

Initially, those at Douglas didn't view Airbus as a threat. To them, like Boeing, Airbus was just another European jobs program. But that didn't blind Douglas to the underlying economics. "Airbus was getting unlimited money from the governments," Pilarski said. "They have money, they can do good products. Why wouldn't you invest money in great things? It was very obvious that they will replace us, and Boeing didn't really want to fight them that much because Boeing basically didn't care." Yet. That day would come.

Boeing had 60 percent of the market and Douglas had less than 40 percent. The share of Douglas was coming down. Boeing didn't seem too concerned by Airbus because its sales came out of the hide of Douglas. But Boeing finally woke up to the threat and began complaining about Airbus and its state subsidies in 1992. It convinced President Bill Clinton to pursue the matter, resulting in the General Agreement on Tariffs and Trade (GATT) of 1994.

Lockheed's decision to reenter the commercial market with the L-1011 was devastating to Douglas's future. Douglas figured the DC-10 could meet a demand for about 800 planes. In the end, Douglas sold 446, plus 60 more KC-10 tankers to the USAF. Lockheed sold 250 TriStars, so the forecast was pretty close.

"Lockheed had a very bad effect because our belief was there was a market for this kind of product. With 800 planes, we can make good money off it," commented Pilarski. "Well, these bastards came in and split it with us and took away our money. St. Louis then looked and said, 'We have additional problems here, so let's not spend more money on anything.' Our engineers were, 'Hey, but we have a new product.' Yes, St. Louis said, 'We don't care about the product.'"

McDonnell Douglas explored developing an airplane with Fokker, the MDF-100, but nothing came of it. It considered a deal in which Korean interests would invest in Douglas. Nothing came of this, either. MDC also considered a collaboration with Airbus. Another goose egg.

"I think that it was basically Airbus trying to make us feel good, kind of, 'We are taking you to the cleaners, but you may not realize it, so let's pretend that we'll talk.' The cooperation would be, 'Yes, why don't you guys stop producing your planes and be a subcontractor to us on some planes?'" recalled Pilarski. But it was as much about St. Louis as anything else, he continued. "Will St. Louis have the guts to actually invest money and do something with it?"

A problem Douglas faced with St. Louis was pricing. In 1990s dollars, Long Beach needed to offer MD-11s in the $70 million price range to be competitive. St. Louis demanded pricing in the $90m range. Douglas offered to sell the MD-11 to Swissair and Austrian for $75 million. St. Louis nixed it and wanted $95 million, Pilarski recalls. In the end, a sale was completed with Swissair at a price Pilarski didn't know. Douglas offered the MD-95 to SAS, which would be the launch customer. Accordingly, SAS would receive launch customer pricing. Boeing, hoping to kill the MD-95, created the 737-600, which was the NG version of the 737-500 Classic. The market already moved beyond the -500, which sold reasonably well for a shrink but not great. Only 69 -600s were sold compared with 389 -500s.

In reviewing the proposed merger between Boeing and McDonnell Douglas, *The Washington Post* wrote:

"SAS's internal evaluating committee had recommended the purchase of 50 of Douglas's proposed new 100-seat MD-95 jetliners for $20 million each. Instead... SAS would order 35 of a new version of Boeing's venerable 737 at about $19 million per plane, a steep discount from Boeing's list price. It was clear that Boeing's strategy was to prevent Douglas from ever launching the MD-95, recalled one salesman involved in the competition."[24]

Nick Tomassetti by this time had left IAE, where he had been president, because of his disillusionment with P&W and Rolls-Royce. He joined McDonnell Douglas as head of the single-aisle programs. But after a short time, Tomassetti concluded that McDonnell Douglas "had no use for the program. The only reason that we did the MD-95 and the reason I left within a year was simply we were trying to increase the value of the company with something. We were trying to sell McDonnell Douglas. We had it on the market."

"Ultimately, Boeing bought it," Tomassetti recollected. "We had the MD-95 as the only active program at the time, and Boeing took it on." The MD-11 was already in its downward spiral. Boeing immediately killed the MD-11 after the merger. Boeing eventually killed the MD-95/Boeing 717 as well.

BOEING ADOPTS THE MD-95 PRODUCTION METHOD

"What Boeing really took on was the way in which we conceived the MD-95 program," said Tomassetti. "We made the suppliers for all of the various components do the work and also pay for the certification of what they were supplying. We had the wing guys do it, we had the nose guys do it, we had the tail guys do it. We had everybody doing their own thing. For some reason, and I'm not sure I understand this exactly, Boeing liked that concept. They weren't doing that at the time. They took that on, and it caused them one hell of a lot of problems with some of their programs," notably the 787.

Stonecipher believed spreading the risk to the supply chain was the way to make the MD-95, Tomassetti said. "Quite frankly, I don't know if Harry even knew what the hell he was doing with that. But it was a way to convince our board and the rest of the people that had to put money into the company that it was a much lower cost development of an airplane. Boeing, on the other hand, would draw the parts. The suppliers would draw whatever parts they were making up, send it to Boeing. Boeing would redraw

---

24. *The Washington Post*, April 5, 1997.

the part with their part number on it and send it back. Well, all that went away. They were able to show a reduction in the cost of development program, but at the same time they ended up with a hell of a lot of problems with the 787."

Stonecipher, of course, migrated to Boeing with the 1997 merger and became CEO in 2003 when Phil Condit resigned amidst the tanker scandal. Stonecipher launched the 787 in December 2003 after the Boeing board, which included Stonecipher and John McDonnell, debated for much of the year over costs and the production method that followed the McDonnell Douglas production model.

Stonecipher demanded Boeing get a handle on just how much it cost to produce airplanes. Until his arrival, few actually knew. As much as anyone, it was Stonecipher who drove the production method for the 787. "I knew Boeing was going to fall on its face," Tomassetti noted. "I said, 'Oh, shit, this is terrible, too bad.'" ValuJet eventually became the launch customer for the MD-95 for $18 million to $20 million.

Robert Priddy, the former CEO of the airline, remains to this day a big fan of Stonecipher, unlike most at Douglas and Boeing who paint him as a villain. Stonecipher turned McDonnell Douglas around and into a profitable company, Priddy recalls. He also characterized Stonecipher as an "everyman." While most CEOs seem to be Harvard Business School types, Stonecipher graduated from a Tennessee technical institute.

"Harry was a phenomenal guy," Priddy said in 2020. "I am a big supporter. He was sort of a Herb Kelleher," the famously gregarious people-person/CEO of Southwest. Priddy's relationship was cemented with the MD-95 deal. He issued the request for proposals to Airbus, Boeing and MDC. In preliminary negotiations, Priddy said he wanted performance guarantees written into the contact. Each agreed, and Priddy initially awarded the order to Boeing for 737NGs. But when it came time to solidify the contract, Priddy said Boeing reneged on including the guarantees in the document.

Salesmen, and an officer who later flew to Atlanta where ValuJet was headquartered, said Boeing didn't put performance guarantees in writing. "We're Boeing, we stand by our word," Priddy quoted them as saying. It wasn't enough. Priddy called Airbus, which previously said it would include the guarantees in writing. When it came time to paper the A319 deal, Priddy said Airbus also reneged. Leahy adamantly denies this. "Many Airbus contracts have performance guarantees. Priddy just wanted the MD-95 for reasons I never understood," says Leahy. Priddy, for his part, is no fan of Leahy.

Priddy called Stonecipher. Not only did Stonecipher put the guarantees into the contract, MDC also guaranteed financing. As a new airplane, and with ValuJet being a relatively new airline, MDC backstop financing was critical. After ValuJet Flight 592 crashed in the Everglades in 1996, the airline was grounded for months over safety concerns, even though the accident itself was caused by improperly labeled and loaded oxygen canisters. The ground handler, SabreTech, was principally found at fault. MDC wound up financing all of ValuJet's airplanes through its McDonnell Douglas Finance Corp. (MDFC), which became Boeing Capital Corp. after the 1997 merger.[25]

Before Boeing and MDC merged, there was an effort by MDC to hire Leahy away from Airbus. Feren, then the finance director for Douglas, received a call from John Wolf, vice president of programs for the commercial aircraft division, in the mid-1990s. Wolf said they were going to New York to interview Leahy. "What are we going to interview him for?" Feren asked. Wolf said Leahy was going to be interviewed for head of sales. "'Why would we do that?'" Feren didn't know Leahy very well at the time. They hadn't bumped into each other on sales campaigns, and Airbus wasn't very relevant in America then. Feren knew of Leahy, but that was about it.

The three met at the Tavern on the Green, the famous restaurant in Central Park. "Leahy comes in there, and he starts interviewing us more than we're interviewing him, which kind of impressed me," Feren recalls. "Even more insightful was just how much preparation he'd done. He was really drilling these questions about how serious was John McDonnell about staying in the business. How much investment are you prepared to make? He started doing a forensic examination of what he thought the viability of the MD-11 was or the MD-80. I think at the time we'd just announced the plans to go forward with MD-90, but really hadn't brought it to market yet."

The conversation got around to why would Leahy leave Airbus. "We discussed that an American would never be allowed to run Airbus global sales. He was kind of stuck," Feren said. "There wasn't really a CEO job in Airbus North America that was anything much more than ceremonial. The action was in the job he had, and he couldn't really move up to senior management in Toulouse, or so it seemed at the time. Senior executive positions were carefully guarded by European nationality. The commercial director was reserved for the British."

---

25. SabreTech was criminally charged, the only time long-time observers can think of that the U.S pursued a criminal prosecution in an airline accident investigation. SabreTech's parent closed the business. ValuJet's brand was irreversibly tainted. It later acquired a smaller airline, AirTran of Orlando, and adopted the latter's name. Rebranded under AirTran, the airline successfully grew. Southwest acquired the airline in 2010. The 88 MD-95s (by now rebranded the Boeing 717) were leased by Southwest to Delta. Southwest gradually drew down AirTran's Atlanta hub to about half the size. Boeing Capital Corp. retained ownership as the head lessor to Southwest.

Of course, this later turned out to be wrong; Leahy would become global head of sales but was never considered for CEO of Airbus because he "had the wrong passport," as he once put it. Leahy later met with McDonnell, the CEO of McDonnell Douglas, for a private breakfast in Crystal City, Virginia, across the river from Washington, D.C. McDonnell used many of the same arguments but emphasized that he believed they needed "new blood" at Douglas, especially in sales. Leahy decided to stay at Airbus at least for a few more years. He wasn't convinced McDonnell would approve the investments necessary to revitalize Douglas.

Pierson heard of the discussions, apparently from GE. Needless to say, he was not pleased, although he never directly addressed the issue with Leahy. One day Pierson casually remarked to Leahy over drinks that he should be aware that anyone who left Airbus would be considered a traitor. The message was ostensibly about Leahy's subordinates in the U.S.—but the implication was clear.

Still, Feren said, Leahy exposed the problem that Douglas had, which was there wasn't an advocate in St. Louis. Mostly, the financial forces controlled the company, and it was a very conservative company. Investing money into commercial was a very difficult and hand-wringing decision. With just a little bit of his own independent fact finding, Leahy immediately got to the nub of the issue.

Feren was impressed with how well-prepared Leahy was. "I don't mean this disrespectfully, but it was kind of cold-blooded. He didn't waste a lot of time to say 'I'm not going to do this, I'm not wasting my time on that.' Yet his candor about the potential dead-end career path he was on with his current employer was impressive. It's a very memorable experience for me," Feren said.

One can only speculate how different the fortunes of Airbus, Douglas and Boeing might have been had McDonnell successfully wooed Leahy away. Leahy was probably right that McDonnell still would not have invested the billions of dollars needed to make Douglas a viable competitor again. But would Leahy have joined Boeing following the 1997 merger with McDonnell Douglas? And if so, would he have headed sales? Would he have eventually been named CEO of BCA and, perhaps, one day become CEO of The Boeing Co.? After all, he had the right passport. This may be an interesting mental exercise, but the reality is, Leahy stayed with Airbus, Douglas Aircraft dwindled to a single-digit market share, McDonnell Douglas disappeared into Boeing and Leahy remained a thorn in Boeing's side until he retired in January 2018.

Years later, in an interview for this book, former BCA CEO Albaugh joked that Boeing should have hired Leahy and paid him $10 million a year just to go sit in the corner. "We would have come out ahead," Albaugh said.

The merger with McDonnell prolonged the life of Douglas. But with the

CHAPTER 7   **THE DEATH OF MCDONNELL DOUGLAS**

reluctance, or in the view of some, the refusal of MDC to invest in Douglas, the die was cast. Saddled with derivatives of aging technologies and a new rivalry from Airbus, there was no place to go but down. When Crandall, the American CEO, announced the exclusive deal with Boeing in 1996, he was asked why McDonnell Douglas wasn't given the chance to sell the updated MD-90 to the airline. It had, after all, the latest engines from IAE, the JV between P&W, Rolls-Royce and others. Crandall's response was biting. "[The MD-90] is old technology." Tomassetti, in 2020, agreed.

By 1996, Boeing wanted to dramatically expand its military business, in part to balance defense and commercial revenues. Boeing had no interest in MDC's commercial airplanes. The MD-11 competed with the 777. The MD-80 and MD-90 competed with the 737. The MD-95 competed only with the 737-600. While the MD-95 was a better airplane than the -600, it was an orphan. ValuJet wanted a version with more range and capacity, but that would compete with the 737-700. This was a non-starter with Boeing. Boeing wasted little time in killing the entire commercial airplane division of MDC. But before the merger could go forward, those exclusivity deals became a roadblock to approval by the European Union (EU).

At the time, the U.S. airline industry had many more players than it does today. United hadn't merged with Continental, nor had Northwest combined with Delta. TWA was still independent. Southwest had never bought anything but Boeing. Winning exclusive deals at American, Continental and Delta closed a good chunk of the U.S. market to Airbus.

The Boeing-MDC merger required regulatory approvals by the U.S. government and other countries and jurisdictions. The EU, unsurprisingly, objected to Airbus being precluded by the exclusivity deals from bidding on future orders. As a condition for approval, Boeing and the three airlines had to agree to void the deals.

American's Crandall didn't care. The deal with the airlines was negotiated in 1994, but the contract was signed in 1996 shortly before the McDonnell Douglas merger was announced. Boeing agreed to cancel the exclusivity deals, and the merger was completed in 1997. As far as Crandall was concerned, a deal was a deal. "They may have required that the exclusivity deals go away, but they didn't have anything to do with me," he said. "As far as I was concerned, the terms of the Boeing deal remained in effect. Boeing may have not been legally required to honor the deal, but I required them to honor it."

The scope of the American deal was summarized in the EU's decision approving the Boeing-MDC merger:

> American and Boeing agreed on a long-term partnership that will make Boeing the exclusive supplier of jet aircraft to American until the year 2018. American placed firm orders for 103 aircraft, including 75 orders for the next-generation 737 family of

jetliners, twelve orders for the 777-200, twelve 757s and four 767-300ERs. Based on Boeing's list prices, the order is valued at about USD 6.6 billion. American also obtained price-protected purchase rights for 527 additional jets during the more than 20-year exclusivity period. These purchase rights enable American to determine when it wants to exercise its options to buy aircraft, with as little as 15 months' advance notice before delivery for narrow-body aircraft and 18 months before delivery for wide-body aircraft, compared to the traditional 18- to 36-month delivery period. It has been reported that American did not have to pay for these purchase rights but received them in exchange for the commitment to buy only Boeing jets. At the same time, it appears that Boeing offered retroactive price reductions on aircraft purchased by American in previous campaigns.[26]

The dominance of the Big Three deals was notable. The exclusive deals accounted for 13 percent of the 20-year global market forecast of 14,400 aircraft and 30 percent of the U.S.-sector forecast, the EU concluded. The combined companies would enable Boeing to increase its market share in the overall market for large commercial aircraft from 64 percent to 70 percent and increase its customer base from 60 percent to 84 percent of the current fleet in service, the EU wrote.

In its decision approving the merger, the EU and Boeing agreed to a 10-year standstill:

> Boeing will not enter into any additional exclusive agreements until 1 August 2007, except for those campaigns in which another manufacturer has offered to enter into an exclusive agreement.
>
> Boeing will not enforce its exclusivity rights under the agreements with American, Delta and Continental announced on 21 November 1996, 20 March 1997 and 10 June 1997, respectively.

Continental merged with United in 2010. Continental management took over. Except for one expanded order from a legacy United deal for A350s, the new United remained a loyal Boeing customer. No single-aisle airplanes were ordered from Airbus until December 2019, when it became clear Boeing wouldn't, or couldn't, make up its mind about launching the New Midmarket Aircraft, or NMA. At that point, United placed an order for the A321XLR to finally replace 757s. Delta acquired Northwest, a large Airbus operator, in 2008. The Northwest management evolved into running Delta and would split its orders between the two OEMs.

---

26. European Union Decision, *Boeing-McDonnell Douglas Merger*, Case No. IV/M.877, July 30, 1977, Page 33, Paragraph 107.

8

Wake-Up Call

"We left the door cracked open just enough."
—BOEING SALESMAN TOBY BRIGHT,
ON AIRBUS'S WIN AT UNITED AIRLINES

LEAHY'S EARLY SUCCESSES selling into the U.S. market didn't shake Boeing. Nor did an order in July 1988 from Air Canada for 34 A320s to replace the fleet of Boeing 727-200s. Many of the sales were to distressed airlines, like Pan Am, TWA, Continental, Braniff II and America West. Boeing and much of the market saw these as desperation deals.

The A320 entered service in 1988, challenging the 737 family. Boeing didn't take the A320 seriously, and even Airbus's own business plan forecast a mere 400 sales over the life of the program. The single-aisle sector is where more airplanes are sold by Airbus and Boeing than any other type. Boeing called the A320 and 737-800 the "heart of the market."

The A320 was conceived in the early 1980s as a 150-seat airplane, slightly larger than the popular 126-seat 737-300 and about the same size as the 737-400, a straightforward stretch of the -300. As a simple stretch, the -400 was heavier, had worse airport field performance and shorter range. The A320 was clearly a better airplane.

United thought so. By 1992, United was an exclusive Boeing customer in practice if not yet by contract. It still had some McDonnell Douglas DC-10s in its fleet, but it hadn't ordered the successor MD-11, instead switching to become an all-Boeing purchaser. United needed a larger plane than the 126-seat 737-300. Airbus offered the 150-seat A320. United wanted Boeing to reopen its 737-300 contract to consider and renegotiate the price for the 737-400. Boeing refused. A deal is a deal, Boeing executives said, despite pleas from its United salesman, Bright, to be flexible.

Leahy exploited this opening. He and his team put together a sales package that was so compelling that by the time BCA CEO Dean Thornton understood the threat was real, it was too late. It was, Boeing's Bright recalled 27 years later, the wake-up call to Boeing that it could no longer ignore Airbus as a just another European jobs program.

"Up until that time, I feel like maybe Boeing hadn't really worried too much about Airbus or wasn't taking them too seriously," Bright recalled in

2019. "It was the United win that really started the ball rolling, and Boeing recognized that Leahy was a force to be reckoned with." Bright was on the Boeing side of the single-aisle campaign at United. At the time, United was Boeing's largest customer, taking six airplanes a month.

"Boeing internally thought United wouldn't switch to this new product," Bright said. "We left the door cracked open just enough over a small issue that let Leahy get his toe in the door, and then turn the whole thing around. When Boeing did the 737-300 deal, United didn't think they needed the 737-400. They didn't really negotiate the price that much. They just ratioed it up. They came back to us in the early '90s and said, 'We'd like to order 400s, but the price is about $400,000 an airplane too high.'"

Boeing wouldn't budge. "Well, we've got a deal, guys. We don't reopen deals. No way. Forget it. You signed." Bright said Boeing just played total hardball on this difference. That was all Leahy needed. The original 737 deal was for more than 100 airplanes. United wanted to amend the contract to swap for 737-400s at a different price than the contract allowed. When it became clear United was tilting toward Airbus, Boeing finally yielded.

"In the end, we threw in a lot more than $400,000 per aircraft to try to save the deal." Bright said. "It was probably about four times that. It all started over a disagreement of about $400,000. In the end, it was too little, too late." Bright said Thornton later acknowledged he should have listened to Bright.

"When Dean retired, I was surprised that I, as a young sales guy at Boeing, got an invitation to his retirement party," Bright said. "He took me aside and put his arm around my shoulder, and said, 'I just want to let you know that one of the biggest mistakes I made in my career was letting Airbus win this United deal.'" Bright said Thornton told him that the reason he was still employed is that Bright said the right thing all the time. "You were telling us, and we weren't listening," Thornton said.

The United A320 deal put the nail in the coffin on the 737 Classic. "Boeing clearly decided it had to do an NG," Leahy said. Boeing launched the 737NG airplane in 1993. Boeing designed a new, larger wing, which gave the NG better range than the A320 family. It stretched the -400 into what became known as the 737-800. The -800 became the optimal design in the NG family. It had 12 more seats than the A320 in what's called "Layout of Passenger Accommodations," or LOPA. This produced lower seat-mile costs than the A320, all other things being equal. The 126-seat dual class 737-700 NG entered service in the last month of 1997 with Southwest Airlines, which put 135 seats into the airplane in single-class configuration. The 737-800 became the backbone of the NG family. The economics were superb, and its reliability, honed over decades of the preceding family members, couldn't be beat.

Boeing also created the 737-900. Frankly, it was a dog. A straightforward stretch of the -800, it traded range for seats. It had only about 18 more than the -800, which in the scheme of things wasn't much of a step up. (In two classes, the 737-700 seated 126 passengers and the 737-800 had 162, a jump of 36 seats.) While the -800 could comfortably fly coast-to-coast in the U.S., the -900 was basically a two-thirds transcontinental airplane. And the airport field performance was significantly poorer than the -800—or, crucially, the A321, which had its own coast-to-coast issues. Only 54 of the -900s were built.

Boeing solved the range problem with the ER extended range variant, the 737-900ER, of which 505 were produced. Coupled with the standard -900, the 557 airplanes compared with 4,991 -800s and 1,128 -700s. There were also 69 737-600s. The 737-900ER accounted for eight percent of NG sales by the time production ended in 2019.

Airbus delivered the first A321 in 1994, the year Leahy became head of commercial in Toulouse. Through 2019, a total of 1,791 A321ceos were delivered, a 3:1 ratio vs. the -900/900ER. Comparing only 2001-2019 deliveries with the 737-900ER, Airbus delivered 1,616 A321ceos. Despite the sales advantage over the -900/900ER, the A321's shortcomings were glaring. Leahy constantly pushed engineering to increase the Maximum Take-Off Weight (MTOW) and fuel capacity to add range. The addition of Sharklets helped but didn't solve the problem. However, creating and adding the A321neo, beginning in 2017, did. From EIS through 2019, Airbus delivered 290 of the new engine option airplanes, for a total of 1,906 A321s compared with the 557 -900ERs, or a 3.4:1 ratio.

These numbers clearly showed the weakness in the upper end of the 737NG line. Leahy still wasn't happy. He constantly pushed engineering for even more range and payload. This eventually resulted in the A321XLR, or "John's airplane," as some in engineering and programs called it.

EXCLUSIVE DEALS

Shortly after Boeing lost United—and apparently tired of buying deals at the last minute—Phil Condit, the CEO of The Boeing Co., met with American's Crandall to craft the exclusive procurement deal. According to Richard Cherney at American, Condit and Crandall sketched out the outline of a formal, exclusive supplier contract in which Boeing would become the sole airplane provider to American.

Airplane deals typically are complex contracts, with credits, performance guarantees, maintenance cost guarantees, etc., negotiated and often later disputed. Not this time. "This basically got done on a cocktail napkin because it was Crandall's desire to forgo the other goodies, the spare parts and price guarantee, and maybe inflation cap and all those kinds of things. They are of value, but they are a little bit harder to quantify. Crandall said, 'I want it all up [on] the nose of the airplane.' That makes it very easy, because then you can ask, How many airplanes are we talking about? Roughly, when are we talking about? What's the net concession rate?" Cherney explained.

"Someone has to write a whole bunch in there about access to spares or various guarantees or top caps or any of that stuff, which would take a lot more than just the back of a cocktail napkin," Cherney said. "It was, 'Here's what it is, here's what the concessions are and, in exchange for going exclusive, we want an MFN.'" MFN stood for Most Favored Nation status, also known as MFC, or Most Favored Customer. The concept meant that no other customer would get a price better than American paid for its aircraft, or American would receive a check for the difference.

Leahy was totally in the dark. One of Crandall's officers, Arpey, called to tell Leahy a deal was in the works, but it was too late for a counteroffer. "I was pissed off by the exclusive deal," Leahy later recalled. "I was in a state of shock. 'You must be joking,' Leahy told Arpey. 'Why would any company eliminate competition going forward?'" Arpey didn't have an answer.

"We tried to come in, but at this point, basically I think Boeing came to the conclusion that no matter how painful it was, it was better to give the current management anything they wanted to get an agreement for 20 [Boeing] years. Because although it might be painful now, over 20 years Boeing will find a way to get it back. And sure enough, they did," Leahy said. He believed Boeing knew it could claw back revenue over time on issues like escalation, support costs, etc. "That is one good reason why we had a chance to get back in with the neo at American in 2011."

Pilot preference was also a factor, Crandall recalled in 2019. "The pilots always preferred Boeing airplanes," he recalled. "And Boeing, of course, was willing to go a long way to keep Airbus out of America, which they did for a long time. The consequences were a combination of the fact that the pilots preferred Boeing airplanes anyway, and Boeing was able to offer a deal, which we thought was as good or better than anybody else was going to do on any sort of a continuing basis. It looked like a sound business deal and that's why we did it. I think it's definitely premised on the fact that pilots preferred Boeing airplanes."

Meantime, Boeing ran into problems of its own making. Ron Woodard, the BCA president, had vowed to crush Airbus through increasing production to outstrip Airbus's capacity to build airplanes. The problem was that Boeing's production ambitions for the 737 and 747 outran its ability to keep up. Suppliers missed delivery schedules, disrupting production. Traveled work—essentially missing pieces on the airplanes as they rolled off the production line—ballooned. Delivery schedules to customers were missed. Boeing was forced to shut down the 737 and 747 production lines for a month to catch up. Ultimately, it took two years to fully catch up, said Gary Scott, a Boeing manager at the Renton factory during the debacle who later became president of Bombardier Commercial Airplanes.

CHAPTER 8   WAKE-UP CALL

For the first time since World War II, Boeing reported an annual loss. Woodard was fired. A shareholders' lawsuit, relating to the Boeing-MDC merger, alleged Boeing had known of the production problems at the time of the deal and consummation of the merger but hadn't disclosed them. Boeing settled for tens of millions of dollars. Despite key losses at Northwest and United and the near miss with Piedmont, Boeing's arrogance continued unabated, said critics. Two campaigns that should have been Boeing's turned into victories for Airbus.

The second iteration of Frontier Airlines began operations in 1994, not long after the United fiasco. A number of former executives from the first Frontier were founders. The first Frontier was almost exclusively a Boeing 737 operator. The second Frontier relied on used, leased 737-200s. It later added the 737-300. With this incumbency and executive history, Frontier was considered a solid Boeing customer. As a small airline, flipping fleet types was also a "big deal," further adding to Boeing's confidence that Frontier would be a 737 operator for the foreseeable future. Thus, it was a shock when Frontier, in 1999, signed agreements to acquire A318s and A319s. The first delivery was in 2001. By mid-2005, all the Boeings were gone.

JetBlue was founded in 1998 by David Neeleman, who had been a co-founder of Salt Lake City-based Morris Air. Deliberately, Morris was patterned after Southwest, using 737-300s and simplified reservations/ticketing systems. Southwest acquired Morris. Neeleman made the transition but didn't get on well with Southwest CEO Herb Kelleher. They parted ways, with Neeleman constrained by a non-compete clause. So, he went to Canada and founded WestJet. This low-cost carrier also relied on 737s.

When the non-compete expired, Neeleman returned to the U.S. and founded jetBlue. Initially, the plan had been to hook up with Richard Branson and license the Virgin brand, but terms couldn't be reached. With Neeleman's long history with 737s, Boeing assumed he would choose the 737 for the new airline. In fact, his business plan featured the 737. Thus, he surprised Boeing and the industry by placing a large order for A320s.[27] Through 2020, neither JetBlue, Frontier nor Neeleman ever bought another Boeing airplane.

---

27. Neeleman later founded Azul Airlines in his native Brazil, using the locally produced Embraer E195 for his fleet. When Azul expanded and required mainline jets, Airbus got these orders, too. Later still, he invested in Portugal's flag carrier, TAP Air (TAP.) Still later, in 2017, he announced plans for another U.S. carrier, codenamed "Moxy." An order for 60 A220-300s was placed in 2018.

9

Launching the A380

"It was very conceptual and futuristic."
ROBERT LANGE, DESCRIBING THE A380 CABIN PLANS

AIRBUS BEGAN EXPLORING THE CONCEPT of a double-decker, super-jumbo jet in the 1990s. At the time, the Boeing 747-400 was the largest commercial passenger airliner. The -400 nominally seated 416 passengers in a two-class configuration. The Airbus concept, dubbed the A3XX, nominally would seat 550 passengers, about a third more. In high density, single-class seating, the airplane could seat almost 900 people.

Throughout the early conceptual stage, Airbus collaborated with Boeing to explore joint development of the airplane. Discussions began in 1992. Studies continued until 1995, and the project formally ended the following year. Bob Lange, who was in sales and marketing at the time, managed the first A3XX cabin mockup for Airbus.

"It was very conceptual and futuristic," Lange said in an interview for this book. "Its single aim was to demonstrate that with so much real estate, you had the possibility to do things that were completely different. John [Leahy] and I used to do a double act with the VIP mockup visits and the airline CEOs who were visiting those mockups at the time."

The campaign to launch the program at Singapore Airlines pitted the A380 against the Boeing 747-500/600. This was a stretch concept with added range and other improvements. The -500 would seat 462 passengers. The -600 would seat 548 passengers. It was Leahy against Conner, at the time Boeing's vice president of sales for Asia/Pacific.

"Singapore was the kingpin of the widebodies at that point," Conner recalled. "Whatever Singapore did, everybody would follow. I'm down there with my team bringing in the 747-500, -600. We were just working the heck out of this thing. I've got a letter from Phil Condit that says, 'If you guys buy the airplane, we'll launch the airplane,' because we hadn't launched it yet. Then we start getting down [to] the short strokes, and it's down to best and final. I'm sitting in the hotel, having lunch and there is Leahy over there with his team getting ready to go in to go to Singapore.".

With Leahy was Airbus CEO Noel Forgeard. "He was bringing in all the big guns," Conner said. "It's just me and my team, and I'm down there go-

CHAPTER 9 LAUNCHING THE A380

ing, 'Hey, it would be good if we could get Phil here, if we could get Alan or Seddik here.'" But Conner couldn't get them. "I just can't seem to get anybody to come down there."[28]

Conner said Leahy and his team put an amazing offer on the table for the A380, which included walkaway rights. Conner remembered that Leahy told the airline that if, for some reason, the airplane didn't do what Airbus said it could do or didn't do various things, that they could walk away from the deal. "Our guys just were not going to launch the airplane that somebody can walk away from the deal for a variety of reasons," Conner said. "I kept saying no. Leahy put that on the table and that was what I had to go up against. I couldn't get our people back home to match that."

The A380 was so much larger than the 747, airlines would also have to invest millions in airport infrastructure. Conner said Airbus offered to help on this, too. "Leahy said to them that they would invest and help with the reconstruction because they had to do the new jet bridges and all these different things," Conner recalled. "At least this is what I was told from Singapore. Any time they have to do a bus gate, then they would get compensation for that. There were just a lot of different things." Boeing was willing to match many of the offers made by Airbus, but Conner said it drew the line at the walkaway.

As part of any campaign, Boeing and Airbus would evaluate the performance of the competing aircraft and commercial terms to the extent they knew them through the customer. The two OEMs would denigrate and dismiss the opposing airplane and offer. "We were telling Singapore how the A380 was going to be heavy. We were taking the typical Boeing engineering approach to all these different things, putting all these risks of this big beast on the table," Conner said. "Singapore used that to throw these risks back at John, and John just said, 'Well, fine. If that happens, this is what we'll do.' John basically took all the risks away that they kept bringing up to him."

In a sense, Boeing helped sell the A380 to Singapore through this approach. "In typical John fashion, he used our sales pitch against us and took all those things that would be of concern away. He gave Singapore a deal that they couldn't refuse, or that we were unwilling to match at that point," said Conner.

Leahy scoffs at the "walkaway" element of the deal. He said Singapore may have told Conner this, but denies a walkaway feature after delivery was part of the offer to Singapore. Leahy admits that he gave Singapore the right to cancel the order if, several years before delivery of the first aircraft, Airbus was forced to admit that the performance of the A380 was

---

28. Phil Condit, CEO of the company, Alan Mulally, CEO of BCA, Seddik Belyaman, head of BCA's sales.

significantly worse than promised and couldn't be rectified. It all depends on how walkaway is defined.

Walkaways typically are associated with leases and with a manufacturer providing the leases. Leahy said Singapore was purchasing the airplanes. Singapore arranged lease financing on some of them but with a third party—not with Airbus. Leahy said Airbus couldn't launch an airplane program with a walkaway after delivery. "That would make no sense, but we were willing to stand by the performance of our aircraft."

However, he said the Singapore contract included provisions that if the airplane failed to meet guarantees or was substantially delayed, the order could be canceled. Performance guarantees include negotiated margins before any penalties can be paid, as well as the extent of delivery delays. If the aircraft is delayed too long, the order can be canceled. This is widely known within the industry—and by those who closely watch it—but less well-known to outsiders. Boeing's experience with cancelations for the 737 MAX daylighted this concept for all to see.[29]

Leahy said that virtually all operators kept their orders for the A380, despite all having the right to cancel after two-plus years of production delays. Leahy viewed the 747-500/600 as a threat to pricing. But the bigger issue, he said, was meeting London's new noise regulation called QC2. Initially, the A380 engines didn't meet the quieter noise standard. (Nor, for that matter, would have the 747-500/600, which relied on the 747-400's older-generation engines.)

QC2 was an essential requirement for Singapore. On a Friday visit with the CEO, Leahy was told that the A380 must guarantee QC2 at London. He said "best efforts" were meaningless. Leahy returned to his hotel and called Jürgen Thomas, head of A380 program. Thomas was in the U.S. but immediately flew into action. He worked around the clock through the weekend with the engine manufacturers to hammer out a guarantee that satisfied Singapore. Rolls-Royce was able to agree by Tuesday of the following week.

Conner didn't come away empty-handed, however. He sold Singapore more 747-400s to bridge the airline to the A380s. But had Boeing been willing to offer the airline a walkaway on the -500s and -600s, Conner believes he would have won and launched these new models. Leahy disagreed. "Singapore wanted the A380. They wanted QC2. They wanted the all-new aircraft. We just had to find a way to make it work commercially."

Conner thinks Boeing executives really didn't want to launch the -500/600 anyway. There wasn't a new engine for the -500/600, which was needed for

---

29. The MAX contracts generally allowed cancelation after a 12-month delay. During the gestation of the 787, some customers canceled some orders as delays mounted.

CHAPTER 9 LAUNCHING THE A380

the larger airplane and for better economics. The wing would be tweaked but not new. And the concept for what later became known as the 787 was already floating around within Boeing.

To this day, the belief in some quarters persists—mainly with Boeing fans and Airbus critics—that Boeing sagely plotted a course to entice Airbus into committing to the A380 while planning its own new airplane program. Key Boeing officials involved at the time today deny they maneuvered Airbus into developing the A380. There was no grand Machiavellian scheme to entice Airbus into committing billions of dollars, manpower and industrial resources into a program that they thought was doomed from the beginning.

"I don't believe we sucked Airbus into doing this airplane. I think we saw that they were going to go down that path, and I think our guys looked at the market for a -500, -600 and the size of the market," Conner said. "Then they looked at the market for an airplane that was point-to-point, a smaller 787, and they thought that was the better path to go. I don't believe they thought that there was a market big enough for two in that size of airplane."

There was also the theory that the A380 was simply a Leahy ego airplane. "None of us believed in the A380," recalled Bright. "We just thought that was all about John's ego at the time, that he wanted a big airplane. I don't know how he would justify what's happened to the A380. Maybe he could argue that it really showed Airbus is a leader in the industry."

Albaugh, who at the time was at Boeing's defense unit but moved to become CEO of BCA in 2009, thought the A380 was a "politically driven" airplane. "They wanted to have the biggest airplane. We wanted to have the airplane that the market wanted [in the 787]."

Not surprisingly, Airbus players insist neither ego nor politics played a role. Instead, there was a conviction that Boeing was subsidizing sales of other airplanes with profits from the 747. Some were convinced that Boeing would sell the 747 to an airline and then later swap the order to the 777, cutting Airbus out of sales for the A340. Or that Boeing had large margins on the 747 that could be used to cross-subsidize other models. Boeing salespeople said there were some cases where this occurred, but it was not all that prevalent nor a strategy.

The 747 was launched in 1966, entering service in 1969. For the first five or 10 years, the 747 was unique among airplanes. It was truly the only reasonably efficient long-range airplane in the 1970s—if you could fill all the seats, a caveat Airbus's Enders later said about the A380. But it also was before deregulation and Open Skies. "That was back when the airplane was flying from New York to Johannesburg three times a week because it was too big," recalled a Boeing salesman of the era. "It couldn't support daily flights. They had to wait and gather people up to fill it. It was kind of hard to decide what sort of pricing structure actually made sense because it just was what it was."

As other airplanes were developed, the market for the 747 began to erode, undermining the subsidy theory advanced by Airbus. By the 1990s, when the A380 was conceived, McDonnell Douglas produced the DC-10-30 and MD-11, Airbus had the A340 (the A330 was then still a medium-range airplane) and Boeing had the 777-200ER.

The writing was already on the wall, but Airbus wasn't reading it. A controversial study, *A Shadow Critical Project Appraisal: The A380 Program*, issued in March 2002, forecast that Airbus would never make money on the airplane and only about 400 aircraft would be sold over the life of the program. The study was conducted by Aaron Gellman, an academic; Hans Weber and Richard Aboulafia, both consultants; and George Hamlin, a former Airbus employee in the U.S. office who got crosswise with Leahy and became a vociferous Airbus-Leahy critic after he left. The study was funded by Boeing. Hence, Airbus and others dismissed the objectivity of those writing it. There was no question Boeing's funding cast a shadow over the report. Aboulafia insists Boeing had no input into the study. However, Leahy was doubtful.

As it would turn out, the group was correct in that the program never made money for Airbus, but they were optimistic, even with the dismal sales forecast. Airbus only sold 251 A380s against the 400 predicted by the study. The larger number, however, included freighters, which Airbus dropped in 2006. Freighters would be about 100 of the 400 aircraft.

Boeing's lukewarm feelings toward the 747-500/600—and new direction for what would become the 787—didn't prevent Condit from vowing to make trouble for Airbus and the A380. Condit, according to one account, threatened to file a trade complaint if Airbus launched the A380 program. Boeing didn't file a complaint then but running for cover under trade complaints would be a recurring theme in the coming years.

Apparently, Boeing wasn't above pursuing other pressures. In its 1997 decision approving the Boeing-McDonnell Douglas merger—three years before Airbus launched the A380—the EU wrote:

> There are indications that Boeing's existing buying power may have had some influence on the access of Airbus to suppliers as risk-sharing partners. For example, it has been widely reported that at the beginning of the year, Northrop Grumman decided not to participate as a risk-sharing partner in the development of the A3XX. Following its refusal, Northrop Grumman announced that it had been awarded a USD 262 million contract to upgrade AWACS radar by prime contractor Boeing. Boeing also recently awarded to Northrop Grumman a USD 400 million contract to produce passenger and cargo doors for its 737, 757 and 767 aircraft. In this context it should also be noted that supplies to

Boeing represent by far the largest part of Northrop Grumman's commercial aircraft business. After the proposed merger, these supplies would be combined with Northrop Grumman's supplies to MDC's defence business which are in terms of absolute figures even higher than the existing commercial supplies to Boeing.[30]

FORECASTS

The forecast for the Very Large Aircraft (VLA) market was as controversial as the A380 itself. The sector was defined by Airbus and Boeing as beginning at 400 seats on up. Both companies used their biggest airplanes in marketing materials to represent this sector: Airbus pictured the A380, and Boeing used the 747. The other twin-aisle airplanes—from the A300/767 to the A330/340, MD-11 and 777—fell into the medium wide-body category, as would the 787 when it finally emerged in 2003.

Airbus's VLA 20-year forecast from 2000 through 2019 always contained a projection that 1,300 to 1,700 VLAs (including freighters) would be needed. The variance depended on the year. In contrast, Boeing's forecast mostly went down, down, down during the same period until 2018—the last year Boeing segmented the sector—when its forecast was fewer than 500, mostly freighters. Critics of Boeing's forecast noted that its figures went up and down, depending on how much emphasis was being placed on the 747 in any given year. One former Boeing employee, who worked on the Current Market Outlook, said Boeing had two versions—one for internal use and another, usually more aggressive version, for public consumption.

Critics of the Airbus forecast wondered just what in the world it was sniffing. In fact, as Airbus officials would years later defensively point out, the forecast was the "addressable market," not the actual "demand." (Boeing would slip into this for its NMA forecast, masking the realities of its difficult business case.) Airbus, therefore, hid from public view just how many A380s it truly expected to sell.

But a revelation from another source unmasked this figure. In a patent infringement lawsuit filed by Rolls-Royce against P&W over technology used in the A380 engines, Rolls-Royce revealed in a footnote that Airbus expected to sell 650 A380s over the life of the program.[31] Former Airbus

---

30. European Union Decision Case #IV/M.877, July 30, 1997, (c),(ii), Page 33, Paragraph 107.

31. Rolls-Royce provided the Trent 900 engine for the A380. P&W was part of the Engine Alliance JV with GE Aviation, which provided the competing GP7200 engine. At the time, P&W and Rolls-Royce were partners in IAE, maker of the V2500 engine used on the A320ceo and the McDonnell Douglas MD-90. The V2500 is also used on

executives now say the number was closer to 500, and this included over 100 freighters.

Years later, Airbus explained that the VLA sector, which always had been represented by the 747 and A380 in promotional materials and presentations, really represented all airplanes over 400 seats. Since nominally this was only the 747 and A380, it's how the sector was viewed. But there were a few carriers that configured the 777-300ER (Air Canada at 465) and A330-300 (Cebu Pacific at 440) with more than 400 seats. Therefore, these counted as falling within the plus-400 seat, VLA sector, in Airbus calculations.

Well, yes, maybe. But these configurations were few and far between and minuscule in the scheme of the VLA sector. Furthermore, when Boeing launched the 777X program, the 777-8 fell squarely in the medium-sized wide-body category (at 350 seats). The 777-9, however, fell squarely in the plus-400 seat VLA category (at 425 seats). Boeing, however, engaged in a dismemberment of the VLA sector definition in its Current Market Outlook forecast, classified the 777-9 as a medium-sized wide-body—a preposterous move considering the definition (plus-400 seats) used for decades. As with Airbus hiding its true, internal demand for the A380, Boeing's decision to classify the 777-9 as a medium wide-body hides the true demand of the -9

FOCUS OF TRADE COMPLAINT

The A380 became a millstone around Airbus's neck and not only because of the lack of sales and financial drain on the company. Condit didn't follow through on his threat to file a trade complaint. But in 2004, Stonecipher authorized action, and the A380 became one of the areas of dispute in the international trade complaint between Boeing and Airbus before the World Trade Organization (WTO).[32] Elements of the A380's financial support from member states was one of those ruled to be a prohibited subsidy.

After Enders announced the termination of the A380 program, Airbus claimed that this released the company from any obligation to cure the illegal subsidies under previous WTO rulings. The company pointed to launch aid provided for the A300, A310 and A340 that were also subjects of the

---

the Embraer KC-390. The lawsuit was eventually settled with P&W buying out the Rolls-Royce share of IAE, a decision Rolls-Royce regrets to this day because Rolls-Royce effectively exited the far more lucrative single-aisle airplane engine market. Airbus was keen that IAE be the vehicle to sell and service the P&W Geared Turbofan, because it had doubts about P&W being able to execute the program smoothly, which proved painfully to be the case.

32. WTO cases are government-to-government, in this case the U.S. Trade Representative vs. the European Union. In reality, this is Boeing vs. Airbus.

CHAPTER 9 LAUNCHING THE A380

Boeing complaints. Because these programs ended, Airbus said, the WTO found no further applicability under WTO rules, which are about forward harm, not retroactive harm.

With the A380 termination, Airbus argued that this same principle applied. By this time, of course, the A300, A310 and A340 had been out of production for years. The last A380 delivery was scheduled for 2021, so it wasn't quite an apples-to-apples comparison.

10

Moonshot

"What we really need is lower costs."
—AIRLINES AFTER 9/11

CONNER CAME HOME FROM SINGAPORE DEVASTATED. He failed to launch the 747-500/600. Leahy succeeded in launching the A380. When he sat down with Condit, however, the CEO didn't chastise him. Rather, Condit said don't worry about it; we have something better. Boeing had two concepts percolating. One was the speedy Sonic Cruiser. The other was a traditional tube-and-wing design, but much more efficient than any airliner flying then.

The Sonic Cruiser was a futuristic-looking airplane. It had similarities to a Super Sonic Transport, which was natural since it was a Mach 0.98 concept. Its economics were pegged as equal to the Boeing 767. The chief attribute was speed, nearly 150 mph faster than the long-haul airliners in use.[33] The tube-and-wing airplane was the concept that became the 787. At this stage, it was labeled the 7E7.

SONIC CRUISER

In 2000–2001, Boeing floated the concept of a high-speed, subsonic aircraft that cruised at Mach 0.95–0.98 (vs. Mach 0.72–0.84 for the airliners then in service) with transoceanic capability. The futuristic-looking airplane was basically a NASA (National Aeronautics and Space Administration) design. It captured the imagination of airlines and public alike. Airbus dismissed it as just another "Boeing paper airplane." Aside from this being a predictable dissing from Boeing's rival, the concept came on the heels of the defunct 747-500/-600, so viewing the Sonic Cruiser as hype wasn't altogether unreasonable.

---

[33]. The last airliner designed to fly at Mach 0.97, or around 700 mph, was the Convair 990 at the start of the 1960s jet age. Convair had all sorts of aerodynamic issues with the "speed bumps" on the wings and engine pylons. Fuel consumption was high compared with the 707 and DC-8. Only 37 990s were sold. At the time, the 880/990 program generated the largest corporate loss in American history.

CHAPTER 10 **MOONSHOT**

Airbus pointed out the technical challenges of an airplane flying just below the speed of sound. This wasn't just sour-grapes rhetoric. A salesman for P&W pointed out that the Sonic Cruiser had to be able to fly supersonically in case of cruise upset. The plane would be in a flight envelope where a "bow wave" of air builds up, causing resistance that affects efficiency.

The 767's economics were still considered efficient by standards of the day, but by 2000, the 767 was a 20-year-old design. The Sonic Cruiser needed new systems and advanced technologies, as well as better passenger experience. Boeing noted that the Sonic Cruiser's speed would save an hour for every 3,000 miles. This saves time across the U.S. to Hawaii and on north-south routes where time zones have minimal effect. But there were limitations for practical usefulness across the oceans and on key intercontinental routes.

Conner presented the Sonic Cruiser concept to Singapore Airlines, which wasn't interested despite its remote geography. The Cruiser would get to London two hours sooner, but not enough time was shaved off to eliminate the need for relief crews. Other transoceanic airlines, whether across the Atlantic or Pacific, faced the same challenges. The plane, Conner remarked, was a "tweener." It wasn't a supersonic airplane, but it wasn't fast enough to fit into airline schedules efficiently.

REAL OR DISTRACTION?

Airbus officials at the time didn't think the airplane was a sincere effort, but merely a distraction cooked up by Boeing because the 747-500/600 failed. There are those to this day who believe this to be the case. Boeing people in sales and product development insist the Sonic Cruiser was real. Bright, the top salesman at the time the Sonic Cruiser concept was unveiled by BCA CEO Alan Mulally, believes it was.

"Yes, we all believed it was real. Mulally, I think, really wanted to take the company in that direction and take the big step," Bright said in 2019. "Unless it was being pulled over on me at that time, I was a believer that that was the direction the company was headed." Others at Boeing, in sales and engineering during this era, agreed.

"Yes, it actually was real," said one who, even years later, requested anonymity in order to speak freely. "There are a lot of people that think that was some sort of a game that we were playing with Airbus or something," this former employee recalled. "The genesis of the Sonic Cruiser was one guy who thought, instead of trying to make an airplane go fast, what happens if we take a fast configuration and slow it down? Slowing it down meant from being the supersonic airplane to just under Mach 1. We started working with it and, lo and behold, that damn thing looked like it was going to work."

Boeing, however, never focused on one concept when developing new airplanes, then or now. As always, the product development department was looking at multiple concepts. "We actually started a parallel development," this same employee recalled. "The primary focus was on the Sonic Cruiser. There was always a more conventional layout but utilizing the same technology suite so we could make the trades back and forth to see what we were giving up with speed."

There were 25 or 30 airlines participating in the project, trying to decide what the right answer was. "There were airlines that were enthusiastic over the Sonic Cruiser," said the engineer. "I remember a meeting with American Airlines CEO Don Carty and his lieutenants. We started going over the possibility with him. Then he stopped the meeting and said, 'I want the first two years of production,' and his team turned ashen. There wasn't any negotiating room."

"This was the business traveler war," the Boeing official said. "They all realized that the guy that had a big Sonic Cruiser fleet got all the business travel because you chopped 20 percent or 30 percent off the trip time with basically 767 fuel economy. It was a no-brainer to them." Over time, American would have figured out, at some point, that other carriers would eventually have the Sonic Cruiser and the advantage went away. "But they were tripping all over themselves for it," said the Boeing employee.

Scott Carson, who was in BCA finance at the time and later CEO, concurred that the Cruiser was real, but agreed it served a secondary purpose. "We presented it to the marketplace as a choice they can make. Did they want more performance for about the same price as the 767? More performance and speed? Or did they want more airplane, which the 787 ended up being for about the same dollar? Which was more important to them, and the industry chose [the 787]," he said. "The Sonic Cruiser was also an awfully good distraction, by the way." But the concept was presented to the industry in sincerity.

"I think it was real," Conner said. "I know that we had two options: the Sonic Cruiser and the 787, as it came to be. I was there in Singapore when we pitched the Sonic Cruiser. I remember the response from Singapore [Airlines] was, let's see, we arrive two hours earlier or we leave two hours later. That really doesn't work for us to fly into London, or to fly into these other places. It means we don't leave until 2 a.m. and we arrive in London at 4 a.m. That doesn't really work. People want to arrive at six and be able to put a full day in. They don't want to stay up till 2 a.m. and leave." The value of that extra speed started to become a scheduling nightmare for Boeing's customers. What they wanted was to have the fuel efficiency and be able to plug into their existing schedules and the smaller airplane, Conner said.

CHAPTER 10 **MOONSHOT**

IF NOT THE SONIC CRUISER, THEN WHAT?

While Boeing wrestled with these issues, the terror attacks of 9/11 upended all the thinking and settled the matter. Speed was no longer enticing. A highly efficient airplane with dramatically lower costs than the 767 was now demanded by the carriers. The U.S. airline industry teetered on bankruptcy.

Boeing scrubbed the Sonic Cruiser and focused on the concept that became the 787. "You listen to your customers. They said, 'Well, what we really need is lower costs.' Boeing did an about-face and went the other direction," Bright recalled. But there was another problem facing Boeing: Questions, entirely serious, arose in the marketplace wondering whether Boeing would invest in a new airplane at all. The dithering over the 747 derivatives, development of the poor-selling derivatives in the 757-300 and 767-400, and the McDonnell Douglas influence on shareholder value caused airlines, lessors, analysts and others to question Boeing's future commitment to commercial aviation.

When Condit resigned in 2003 over the USAF tanker scandal (Chapter 25) and Stonecipher returned as CEO, the questions multiplied. Stonecipher's reputation from the decline of McDonnell Douglas commercial products and disdain for engineering vs. profits was well known. Cost cutting was high on the list. So was outsourcing with industrial partners, a tactic Stonecipher pursued at McDonnell Douglas for the MD-95 (later known as the Boeing 717) and potential new airplanes.

Development of the 777 under Condit ran twice over plan, $10 billion to $11.5 billion, in the early 1990s. Mulally, the CEO of BCA, was told to keep the cost to Boeing for the 7E7 at around $5 billion, according to press reports at the time. Mulally proposed an industrial partnership that looked remarkably like those explored by MDC in its waning days.

An April 2003 article in *The Wall Street Journal* by veteran aerospace reporter Lynn Lunsford cited unidentified sources on Boeing's board over the deliberations of the 7E7. At this point, the board hadn't yet authorized the program. The emphasis on cost cutting raised a concern with one board member, Lunsford reported. The director warned that too much cost cutting could prove detrimental and give Airbus an opportunity to make inroads in Boeing's market share.

This board member was Jim McNerney, who ironically would succeed Stonecipher and become the face of cost cutting and the war on the unions to trim costs. McNerney would also have to deal with the pain and agony to come with the 787. Stonecipher went on a cost-cutting drive that many said later would put Boeing on its decline as an engineering-driven company. The McDonnells and Stonecipher appeared to be taking Boeing down the same, failed path they followed at MDC.

From 1997 through early 2003, the focus was on derivatives, reduction of R&D investment and emphasis on shareholder value. Yet, Boeing's engineers were homing in on the 7E7 design. The new airplane wasn't necessarily going to be composite, the feature that really made the 787 so attractive. Just as Boeing had teams working on the Sonic Cruiser and the 7E7, there were two teams working on two 7E7 concepts. One concept was a traditional aluminum fuselage, and the other was composite.

Getting to the point of launching the program had its own turbulence. "There were definitely two camps: the people that wanted aluminum and the people that wanted composites," recalled a key player. "I think it drove a healthy tension to try to ferret out what the right answer should be."

In the end, the composite design won. Much to the surprise of many, Stonecipher launched the program in December 2003. A planned entry-into-service of May 2008 was targeted, barely four-and-a-half years later. The industrial partnership and snap-together final assembly were keys to the plan. Even so, suppliers were skeptical.

One supplier, attending the annual conference of the Pacific Northwest Aerospace Alliance, told a reporter on the sidelines it didn't believe for a minute, even when Boeing awarded it the contract, that the 787 could be produced in less than seven years. (Entry into service was December 2011, eight years after program launch.)

What drove the May 2008 target? China wanted the airplane, now called the 787, in service before the Summer 2008 Olympics, the first time the country hosted the global games. "That drove the schedule," says a former Boeing employee who was involved at the time. "We created a schedule. It wasn't insane, but it had no contingency in it."

"I think part of the rationale was that, because of the way the work was divvied up, there was a lot of stuff that on a normal program would have been more sequential. In theory, these were going to be done in parallel. We spent a lot of time putting the schedule together. We knew it was going to be tight, there's no question about that. But there were a lot of things that we certainly didn't anticipate that really blew it up," the employee said.

As the 7E7 was finally unveiled, it was a medium-sized, twin-aisle, all-composite airplane with new generation engines. It was an all-electric airplane, meaning systems previously powered by conventional methods would instead be powered by batteries or generators. One of these was eliminating bleed air for heating and pressurizing the cabin and de-icing. Larger windows that dimmed electronically were chosen over traditional window shades. A new production method akin to prefabrication was planned, with suppliers "stuffing" the fuselage sections with all the systems previously installed by Boeing. Boeing created a global industrial partnership, and outsourced design and production to unprecedented levels. Final assembly was to be a snap-together process using the prefabricated fuselages, sharply reducing costs. The new approach to design, production

CHAPTER 10 **MOONSHOT**

and assembly called for a timeline of a little over four years from program launch (December 2003) to entry into service (May 2008).

It was a breathtaking airplane. It was a breathtaking departure from previous designs. It was a breathtaking approach to production and assembly. It was, as a successor to Condit would famously label it, a "moonshot." It also would become breathtaking as one of the costliest industrial screw-ups in global program management and implementation. But this was yet to come.

SLOW SALES

Publicly, Leahy and the Airbus team dismissed the 7E7 as another of Boeing's line of paper airplanes, including the 747-500, 747-600, 747-X and the Sonic Cruiser. Privately, Leahy was seething.

When the A380 was launched in 2000, Rolls-Royce, GE and P&W assured Airbus the engines (RR Trent 900 and the GE-Pratt Engine Alliance GP7000) were the latest technology. Yet three years later, Rolls-Royce and GE had newer engines at least a half-generation ahead of the A380's. The engines were 10 percent more efficient, quieter and had lower emissions. Given how long it takes to develop engines, these had to be on the drawing boards when Airbus planned the A380. Years later, as Leahy was ready to retire, he pointed to the 787's engines as one of the reasons the A380 struggled. Had these been offered for the A380, Leahy said, the economics would have been significantly better.

Despite the promise and innovation of the 787, sales initially were awful. "I got a call from Harry," Feren recalled in 2019. "Harry said, 'Hey, I want you to go over to the 787.'" That was a stupid idea, Feren thought. "You want me to be the program manager? I don't think I'm qualified to be a program manager." Feren said Stonecipher replied, "Of course you're not, you idiot, you'll be the marketing guy."

Feren responded, "I've got this really cool job selling airplanes in North America. I really enjoy it. I've done a pretty good job at it, so, is this a negotiation?" It wasn't, and off he went traveling around the world. "We were coming out of 9/11 and the world was really set for a rebound," he elaborated. The 767 was 20 years old. The 777 was already 10 years old. A new airplane was needed.

Boeing's position in the market was threatened by Airbus, and the 787 was its way back. "There was a very high likelihood that our competitive posture in the middle market was going to be eroded," Feren said. "Airbus had stumbled around with an A300 and A310, but they started to get things figured out with the A330. My perception was the A330 was a more viable threat to our long-term business model if we didn't do something."

Yet by the end of 2004, the first year the airplane was offered, there were only two orders for 54 aircraft. One, for 50, was from All Nippon Airways (ANA). The second, for a mere four, was from a start-up airline, Blue Panorama of Italy. "You have to put in perspective just how horrific 9/11 was and just how wounded the balance sheets were for our customers and just how raw they were about nearly having lost their business," said Feren. "You didn't have a lot of people placing big orders for anything. We scrambled around to cobble together a collection of people that was not the robust or the most dynamic launch group you've ever seen."

"That was my problem when I was head of sales," said Bright. "I have to remind people that we had trouble giving those airplanes away." The airlines were still recovering from 9/11 and, Bright says, Boeing's pricing was "off." None of that mattered to Stonecipher.

By the end of 2004, Feren was reassigned. Bright was gone. Carson got the call to replace him from Stonecipher. He was, in some respects, an odd choice. "Harry called me and said you're going over to run sales," Carson recounted in 2019. "I told Harry I have no sales experience. None. He said, 'Yes, but you kept Connexion sold to the board for four years.' Connexion was the program I'd been running at the time." Connexion was Boeing's foresighted attempt to link airplanes with Wi-Fi internet connections. However, it was a failure. Airlines and the traveling public weren't ready to connect to airborne Wi-Fi yet.

When Carson moved to BCA, the sales force was demoralized. Boeing shrunk following 9/11, but Airbus continued building airplanes at established rates. Some at Boeing claimed the subsidies provided by the Airbus states allowed this. Others pointed out that Airbus, due to European labor laws, couldn't economically furlough employees, so it may as well continue to crank out airplanes at pre-9/11 production rates. As for Leahy, he saw opportunities to gain market share while Boeing was down due to U.S. airlines still in recovery mode and facing the continuing scandal over the KC-767 tanker deal.

BCA typically held annual sales meetings in January. "That first sales meeting we had was an all-hands gathering of the team, and we talked about goals for the next year," Carson said. "The tone that came through was, what chance do we have? We don't have John Leahy. I remember turning to the guy that had European sales at the time, and I said, 'What you do have, though, is me, and I have you. I'm not worried about whether or not we can do this. I'm worried about us getting off our dead butts and getting out there and getting it done.'"

Boeing ended 2005, Carson's first full year as head of BCA sales, with 939 net firm orders for 7-Series. Commitments, including contracts not firmed up, exceeded 1,000 for the first time in Boeing's history. And 179 of these firm orders, or 19 percent, were for the 787. Boeing went from two customers to 19 for the new airplane. Carson said the difference was that he got his team talking more to customers to find out what they wanted in a deal. He had more pricing flexibility than Bright had in 2004. (Bright said that Stonecipher's departure in March 2005 removed one obstacle to pricing flexibility.)

Carson also put a damper on the "Leahy Tracking" that the sales team had been doing. BCA's team was chasing him rather than selling airplanes. "It was mystifying to come into an organization where what you need to do is cultivate your customers, and they would have a weekly meeting where they reviewed, 'Where's John this week? Who's John talking to this week?'" Carson said. "I don't care where John is. I care about what our customers need. That was kind of an 'aha' moment for me, but I think for the team as well. I told them, 'I don't really care.'"

"Where's John?" apparently emanated from Stonecipher's anger over poor sales. It didn't help that his wrath hit *The Wall Street Journal* (another Lynn Lunsford story) on December 20, 2004. Not only did Stonecipher complain about the poor sales performance of BCA, he took BCA CEO Mulally publicly to task.

"Where's John?" was one of the focuses in Chicago, Carson said. "'How come you guys aren't doing any better? We see Leahy all over the world. Why aren't you out there where he is?' The guys decided that's what we have to do. We have to know where John is so that we can be there too."

Carson was not buying. "It's like, wait a minute," he recalled. "If John's talking to a customer and if it's a customer he already has locked up, why don't we go spend our energy somewhere where someone needs us?"

Leahy, unaware of Carson's comments in 2019, had the same philosophy: The business was all about relationships. In a separate interview, he said that he told his sales team they always had to be in contact with the airlines and lessors. It was their job to know of potential campaigns. By the time a formal request for proposals was issued, Leahy's team had better know beforehand it was coming. If they didn't, they had probably already lost the deal.

Relationships mattered at Airbus and at Boeing. Conner succeeded Carson as CEO of BCA in 2009. The 787 was grounded for three months in January 2013 after a ramp battery fire on a Japan Air Lines (JAL) 787 in Boston and following a near-fire with a battery on an ANA 787 during take-off in Japan.

BCA was holding one of its annual sales meetings. Sales officials, customers, guests and others numbered about 1,000. Willie Walsh, the CEO of British Airways, was a speaker. The airline placed an order for the 787, even though the airplane was grounded. Walsh told the crowd he did so not because "Boeing said the airplane would be fixed" but rather "Ray Conner said the airplane would be fixed." This kind of personal relationship was more important than a corporate one.[34]

---

34. Walsh would repeat this move in 2019 when the MAX was grounded. He signed an MOU for 200 MAXes at the Paris Air Show.

Conner has a different take on sales in 2004 than Carson. He said a lot of deals were in the works by the time Carson arrived; they just hadn't come to fruition in time to save Bright. "Toby had been fired, and Scott came in," Conner recalled. "We had a lot of deals. We were in the midst of a lot of deals, and this was a brand-new program. Harry had gone out and said that we were going to sell 200 of these things before such and such a time. It was taking some time to get those things done, and we just didn't have them done."

Conner, assigned to the Americas, had deals at Northwest and Air Canada in the works. "Both of these were huge," he said. "They were the two largest Airbus wide-body customers in North America. One of them was the largest wide-body customer that they had, period, in Northwest. We had deals that we were working, they were close to being done, and I think that we're all in that same position at that point." Conner landed orders from each. He "caught us napping," Leahy recalled. "We were complacent with both Northwest and Air Canada. The results speak for themselves."

"We just were not quick enough to close the deals to save Toby's job," Conner said. Regardless of the reasons, with Carson heading sales and Stonecipher gone, coupled with more pricing flexibility, orders for the 787 took off. "Toby was treated very badly by Boeing. If Boeing management had just given him a little more time, he would have delivered," said Leahy.

From 2005 to 2007, Boeing sold 514 787s. And then sales tanked as the industrial, design and production problems began to emerge. Boeing's entire business plan for the 787, from the materials to the design to the industrial plan, was the "moonshot" characterized by CEO McNerney.

11

Trouble in Toulouse

"Airbus doesn't yet have a simple and clear organization."
—**CHRISTIAN STREIFF,** AIRBUS CEO

THE A380 WAS IN PRODUCTION when Boeing launched the 787 in December 2003. The A380's target date for entry into service was 2006, six years after launch. The 787's EIS was supposed to be two years later. At the time, EADS was still very much a two-headed company. One was in Paris; the other was in Munich. Airbus's headquarters were in Toulouse, but the two EADS halves conflicted with each other on a regular basis. Each wanted to be dominant. British and Spanish cultures further complicated development. While the multi-national, bicephalic approach had worked since Airbus was formed, it also had inherent flaws.

Tom Williams, who was executive vice president of programs and customer support at the time, observed that the old GIE model had worked fine on the development of some planes like the A320, A330 and A340. But Airbus was still effectively five companies: four GIE members and the central entity. The five different organizations were not pulling in the same direction, because the previous logic was that each one should maximize its own earnings.

"They were never entirely sure aircraft would make us money and that was always a bit opaque," Williams said. "They relied on a very complex, bartering process and, I think, clearly making the single corporate entity back in 2000 was the right thing to do, but it didn't materialize overnight." In fact, it would be years before there was a recognition that the best people for a job didn't depend on which passport they carried, nor where the work was to be done. It took a disaster with the A380 program to bring all this to light. Even then, many more painful years would pass before Airbus transitioned to a commercial company.

The passport mentality was slow to go. That kind of thinking was rife throughout the system, Williams said in 2019, shortly after he retired. "It wasn't so much the physical issues that were the problem because guys knew how to build all the bits. It was more of overcoming the mindset issues and the huge differences in standards. For example, you could find that you go and visit a subcontractor doing welding, and he was working to a German standard and specification. But the Brits then would say, yes, but that's not compliant with our specification, and they've got to be re-certified again if they want to make bits for the British part of the airplane."

Williams said there were "really crazy legacy issues to overcome, and it put a lot of inertia in the system that we had to work really hard to overcome. There was the combination of bureaucracy. There was more a mindset of that your standard is the best standard, and theirs is weak because it can't do this or can't do that, and I wouldn't say we really overcame that fully until we came to the A350."

Through the A380, Airbus was still stuck with a legacy of the different approaches. What brought the whole system crashing down? The A380 was launched in 2000 with a 2006 EIS target. In May 2006, Airbus officials were still confident—at least publicly—that the first delivery would occur by the end of the year

Charles Champion, who headed the program, and Gustav Humbert, president of Airbus, reiterated all was fine in interviews immediately before and during the Berlin ILA air show in May. Although a few delays already had been experienced before then, both assured a reporter that the program was on track.

After the Champion interview was published but before Humbert's, Airbus announced a major problem of such proportions that EIS would be put off until 2008. The cost would run into the billions of euros. Heads rolled. Champion was reassigned. Humbert accepted responsibility as president of Airbus and resigned. Noel Forgeard, co-CEO of parent EADS and non-executive president of Airbus, wasn't so noble. He claimed complete ignorance of the massive screwup. Nevertheless, he was forced out as well.[35]

French authorities would later investigate several EADS/Airbus executives for insider trading for selling stock shortly before the wiring issue and resulting financial charges were revealed. The executives' defense was that they sold their stock in a pre-determined window, and the sales conformed with company procedures. The executives were eventually exonerated.

Thus began several years of rotating leaders at EADS and Airbus as the A380 fiasco was resolved. Louis Gallois was named to replace Forgeard as co-CEO of EADS. Enders, the other co-CEO on the defense side, remained. An outsider, Christian Streiff, was named president of Airbus in July.[36] Streiff had no allegiances to the internal political factions, yet he lasted only a few months.

---

35. https://www.flightglobal.com/former-eads-co-ceo-noel-forgeard-reiterates-defence-after-resignation/68264.article

36. https://www.airbus.com/newsroom/press-releases/en/2006/07/christian-streiff-confirmed-as-airbus-president-and-chief-executive-officer.html

CHAPTER 11   **TROUBLE IN TOULOUSE**

In a speech to employees October 3, just four days before Streiff resigned, he said Airbus had to develop an A380 production and delivery schedule customers could count on. The industrial snafu meant Airbus would deliver far fewer A380s over the next few years than had been planned, beginning with the first to Singapore in October 2007. Thirteen A380s were planned for delivery in 2008, 25 in 2009 and full production ramp-up in 2010, when 45 were projected for delivery. This represented an average delay of one year, Streiff said.

Reality would fall far short of these projections. The electrical harnesses problems were the root cause. There were, Streiff explained, 530km of cables, 100,000 wires and 40,300 connectors. "It is twice as complex as for our next largest aircraft, the A340-600," he said. "The depth of the problem was not fully understood in June. The full analysis over these past weeks has revealed it is much worse than expected."

The industrial problems added costs to the A380 and delays meant revenue shortfalls as compensation had to be paid. "This drain on our cash is compounded by the threat from the persistently weak dollar that penalizes the competitiveness of our Euro-zone manufacturing," Streiff said in explaining the need for Power 8, his recovery plan for Airbus. "We also have to face the difficult pricing, and we must generate cash to afford the A350 XWB and continue investing in our future."

The Power 8 name was derived from Streiff's vision that Airbus would generate "power" through changes in eight "modules" of the transformation plan. By the time of the October 3 speech, planning of Power 8 had been underway for two months. Streiff said another two months was needed to implement it. He also pointed out that Airbus was not an "integrated" company.

"Airbus doesn't yet have a simple and clear organization," Streiff said. "There are shadow hierarchies, leftovers from the never-finished integration. And the change we bring about must also include the management culture. Until recently, it has been more a 'green light culture' where truth was not brought to light." (The latter is often a common complaint across many corporations. It would be one of those at Boeing, especially when it came to the 787.)

Yet, three days later, news reports emerged that Streiff tendered his resignation to Gallois and Enders. Company spokespersons denied it, but it was confirmed the next day. Streiff had been on the job only three months. In an interview after his October 7, 2006, resignation with the French newspaper *Le Figaro*, Streiff was blunt.[37]

---

37. *Flight Global* published the English translation: https://www.flightglobal.com/christian-streiff-delivers-tough-warning-as-he-leaves-airbus-ceo-job/70022.article

"I have gradually come to the conclusion that the management style of Airbus did not allow for the success of my plan," he told *Le Figaro*. "The organization and management of EADS have as their main objective the delicate balancing of people, of power and of positions. This formula could be efficient during a normal time, but it is no longer appropriate for a company that is going through a serious crisis."

Streiff wanted to streamline the top organizational structure, eliminating the duplications between the French and German factions. He wanted a simpler decision-making process. And he wanted "to have the necessary operational powers. As the days went by, when discussions proved to be difficult, I formed the conclusion that unless I left, I would not be able to advance the situation," Streiff told the French paper. He said there was an inability to talk about the changes he thought necessary.

Streiff said he was not fully aware of the depth of the crisis at Airbus when he took the job the preceding July. In 2019, Enders was dismissive. "I wouldn't assign any role to him in looking back. The guy was on board only about three months." Enders said anybody would have needed to create a Power 8-type program.

"He was a strange guy," Enders said. "He was a nice guy. But he had this funny idea that even though he was brand new in the industry, and we were in a big crisis, he should be left all alone, and there should be no oversight by Louis or me. How can that work? We were under such pressure and then, all of a sudden, he resigned."

With Forgeard and Humbert out, Champion reassigned following the A380 crisis and Streiff jumping ship barely three months into the job, Airbus needed to move quickly. Enders stepped up. "I threw my hat in the ring then and said, 'Look, I'll do the job,'" he recalled in 2019. "There was some opinion that I wouldn't survive in Toulouse. They would eat me alive in a couple of months. So, Louis, as a Frenchman, would be better connected."

Gallois became the next CEO of Airbus but retained his co-CEO slot at EADS. "Louie did a good job," Enders said. "It was a double job. He was still co-CEO. It was a kind of a transition time. It was strange but fortunately, we sorted out the government shift in summer 2007, where in retrospect it looks, 'How could we ever survive seven years with two chairmen and two CEOs?'"

Gallois' leadership at Airbus was instrumental in keeping Leahy there. Having flirted once with McDonnell Douglas, Leahy—upset with all the turmoil and the unending European politics—again considered the idea of leaving. Gallois persuaded Leahy to stay.

CHAPTER 11 **TROUBLE IN TOULOUSE**

BECOMING ONE AIRBUS

The A380 crisis and executive turmoil was the catalyst to begin transforming Airbus into one company. While the cultural differences between France and Germany could never be eradicated, production differences were reduced. "The crisis allowed us to be far more brutal with the integration than we otherwise would have been," Enders said. "If you look back and say, 'What is the origin of the production problem of the 380?' it was that the management had not been fruitful enough with the integration."

The era also influenced the direction of Airbus, Enders said. There was a time in the early 2000s when everything seemed to run well, the dollar/euro exchange rate was very much in favor, and Boeing had its problems. "Why do any tough moves?" Enders recalled. "The kingdoms or the fiefdoms in Hamburg and in Toulouse were largely untouched. It was called the single corporate entity, but it wasn't. It wasn't really until the crisis that allowed us, really, to move much faster and more brutally than we would otherwise have done."

Williams agreed. Like Enders and others, Williams said the A350 would ultimately be the beneficiary. Williams, Enders, Fabrice Bregier and Guillaume Faury credit the crisis with transforming Airbus. Williams said Enders and his team "pushed really hard then to make sure that the 350 was probably the first integrated aircraft in terms of not just design standards, PLM [Product Life Cycle Management], configuration management and also the full cascade of requirements right through the system. It was the first time that we'd had common approaches to things like carbon-fiber components. The same machine tools were specified for the plants in Spain as in Germany on carbon fiber and before that, this was a totally anathema. There's a divorce. If one side said this was the best the other side would have worked hard to prove that it wasn't."

Nevertheless, Williams continued, "We sensed we can't keep doing this. It really was the catalyst to force people to say, no, we need to change, and I think then we did. We didn't just to finish that. We didn't fully manage the transition. If you think of the bridge 380 and A400M, the A400M was still kind of the halfway house. It was almost there, but not quite, but it was only really on 350 that the job was done properly."

The success of the A350 Program goes largely to Bregier and Didier Evrard. They learned from the failures of the A380 and made the A350 the most successful design and industrial program Airbus had ever developed. The A380 was in many ways a transition airplane, with a mix of then-current technologies and emerging ones in the areas of advanced materials. Sixty-one percent of the A380's structure was aluminum; 22 percent was composite; and three percent was a new material called GLARE, or glass laminate aluminum reinforced epoxy, which is a form of composite.

GLARE is considerably more expensive than aluminum but also a lot lighter, an important factor for an airplane the size of the A380.[38]

While the A380 crisis was going on, Airbus was immersed in two other airplane programs that weren't going well. The military A400M transport/cargo plane would become a financial black hole that would dog Gallois, and later Enders, throughout their tenures as CEOs and beyond. Launching the A350 involved false starts and miscalculations.

---

38. Airbus once said building one A380 is the equivalent of eight A320s.

12

Try, Try Again

"The company had been unprepared for 787 and had been panicking."
—**TOM ENDERS,** AIRBUS CEO

WHEN BOEING LAUNCHED THE 787 IN DECEMBER 2003, Leahy was taken by surprise. The last thing Airbus needed was a third major airplane development. It was well underway with the A380—this was 2003–04—and in the early stages of the A400M program. The A400M is sized between the Boeing C-17 and the Lockheed Martin C-130. A high-speed turboprop, the A400M is Europe's attempt at providing a competitive alternative to the cargo/transport missions dominated by the U.S. since World War II. Remarkably, the C-130 first flew in 1954, as did the 707. Unlike the 707, modernized versions of the C-130 are still in production in 2020.

The C-17 was developed by McDonnell Douglas. Production continued after the 1997 merger with Boeing. The final C-17 rolled off the assembly line in 2015. The A330 Multi-Role Tanker Transport was Airbus's entry into new-build military cargo/transport/tanker airplanes. It's proven highly capable, but it lost the USAF competition in Round Three.

The A400M's marketing pitch is new technology compared with the C-130. Unfortunately, as with some airplanes, success often rises and falls with engines. And engines, in this case, proved to be the A400M's Achilles heel. When the project was conceived all the way back in 1982, the Future International Military Airlifter (FIMA) group was a JV between Aerospatiale, British Aerospace, Lockheed (there was no Lockheed Martin at the time) and Messerschmitt-Bölkow-Blohm. Lockheed dropped out in 1989 to pursue the C-130J Super Hercules. Italy's Alenia and Spain's CASA joined the JV. The group was renamed Euroflag. Development of the A400M paralleled the A380. The A380 EIS was targeted for 2006, and the A400M was targeted for 2009.

Specifications required a new, powerful turboprop engine. The SNECMA engine initially selected proved unable to meet the requirements. In 2002, Airbus issued a new request for proposals. P&W Canada, probably the premier turboprop engine maker in the world, offered the PW180. Europrop International, a new consortium, also submitted a proposal. The engine was 20 percent more expensive than the PW180. Nevertheless, Airbus selected Europrop in what was widely described as a politically driven decision. Thus, when it came time to respond to the Boeing 787, Airbus tried to minimize its investment and workload. Its cash and engineering resources were already stretched.

Airbus needed a response to the 787. But, immersed in the costly A380 and A400M programs, aggravated by the industrial wiring fiasco with the A380 and the technical challenges of the A400M, there was little appetite for yet another new airplane. "I was initially skeptical of the A350," Enders recalled in 2019. "I thought we had too much on our plate. We hadn't solved the 380 crisis. We knew there was A400M coming behind. Then there was the cost problem that led to dollar-to-euro exchange rate that led to the Power 8 program. The company had been unprepared for 787 and had been panicking. All that led me to the conclusion that we should be careful launching a 350 program at the time."

Lange recalled that Airbus's engineer community said then that they could not understand how Boeing could deliver the performance of the aircraft that they were promising. (The engineers were proved right, as it turned out, but this was yet to come.) "It wasn't just a question of the program timing and the program missions," Lange said. "There were so many things that were part of the mission concepts. They were promoting it with a single pylon which was usable for either of the choice of engines. People were captivated by that. It never came to pass. There were a few other things about the aircraft that never came to pass. It was really sexed-up, but the problem was they couldn't meet those claims."

Airbus had a known quantity in the A330. "I think for a period of time, John's external position was that we didn't need to react to the 787 because it wasn't what it was being promoted to be," Lange recalled. "That wasn't sticking. Then it became clear that we needed to react, and we were reacting with two drivers. One was performance, which mainly came through the re-engineering. The other was the time to market, where John would always emphasize that being early to market was key. We were already behind."

By 2006, Airbus was probably looking at an EIS in 2011 against the 787 EIS in 2008. In the end, the 787 EIS was in December 2011. And due to Airbus's own missteps, the A350 EIS slipped to 2015. Airbus launched the A350-800/900 in 2005. But it was little more than a warmed-over A330, with GEnx engines and a composite wing. Boeing predictably sniffed its disdain at the effort.

So did the industry. In pure economics, it might have been a good airplane, but it was never going to win the image battle against an all-new aircraft. The A330, a 1980s design, was a very good airplane. But compared with the 787, the effort was clearly a make-do, even with the changes and upgrades. In comparison to the A380 structure, the A350 was a major step

CHAPTER 12 **TRY, TRY AGAIN**

better: 40 percent was composite, and 31 percent was aluminum. The wing accounted for most of the composite materials; the fuselage and other components were metal, in contrast to the composite 787.

Airbus won orders from lessors International Lease Finance Corp (from Leahy's good friend Hazy) and GECAS (whose sister company, GE Aviation, made the engines) as well as several airlines, including Singapore, US Airways and others. Even so, the reception was lukewarm. The A350 development was another illustration of how Airbus couldn't get its wide-body program correct the first time. Or even the second, third or fourth times.

The A350 program would go through five versions before Airbus settled on the winning design. The first A350, the re-winged, re-engined A330, became known informally as A350 V1.0. The initial lukewarm reception was evident from the ILFC order. Hazy had, up to then, purchased more airplanes from Airbus and Boeing than any other customer. Hazy was also an early customer for the Boeing 787, ordering 74 of them. He ordered just 20 A350 V1.0s. Small orders were placed by other loyal Airbus customers.

In March 2006, a huge trade group held its annual U.S. conference in Orlando, Florida. Leahy and Hazy were among the day-one speakers. Leahy, with his usual Airbus marketing presentation, was followed by Hazy as part of a top-tier panel of lessor CEOs. The event kicked off on Monday.

The preceding Friday, Hazy was in Seattle taking delivery of the first 777-300ER for ILFC customer AeroMexico. Present at the ceremony was aviation reporter Bryan Corliss of the local paper, *The Everett Herald*. Over the weekend, Corliss wrote a short news item about the delivery in which he quoted Hazy as saying he wasn't satisfied with the A350 proposed by Airbus. Corliss didn't elaborate.

Another journalist was in Orlando for the meeting and read Corliss' item on-line. When the Q&A session opened on the lessors' panel, the journalist asked Hazy about the comment in *The Herald*. Hazy called out, "Is John Leahy still in the room?" Leahy, standing in the rear, shouted back, "Yes." Hazy then proceeded to criticize the A350 V1.0 as a makeover of the A330, with a metal fuselage and similar systems vs. the ground-breaking 787. As soon as Hazy finished speaking, the journalist rushed back to Leahy and asked for his reaction. Leahy pointed out that Hazy was a customer—but for only 20, Leahy was reminded. Otherwise, he didn't have much to say.

Within days, the CEO of Singapore publicly criticized the proposed A350. A short time after this, Airbus announced it was going back to the drawing board. The result was a year's delay and a few billion dollars more in development costs.[39]

---

39. Leahy didn't speak to the journalist for a year after this. The author is that journalist.

There are those to this day who believe the Q&A with Hazy was a set-up. It wasn't. The journalist's question was in reaction to Corliss' short news item. It was a natural question. But the ramifications were profound. Although the public criticism by Hazy and Singapore elevated the challenges Airbus had with its initial A350 design, in fact, behind the scenes, industry reaction was already harsh. The sales team already encountered resistance, and Emirates, a key customer, abruptly terminated a presentation mid-stream.

In 2019, Rao recalled some of the sales efforts. "We did a lot of campaigns, and at this point, there was no product strategy at Airbus," he said, itself a surprising revelation. "It was hidden somewhere in engineering. John was out there, fighting a lot of 787s against the original 350 version. We lost at Northwest, we lost at Air Canada. Then, in the Christmas of 2005, we lost at Qantas.[40] When we lost at Qantas, at that point, John decided that the original 350 wasn't going to be in the aircraft to do the job."

Rao was reassigned from sales to a team for further development of the A350 in early 2006. Presentations were made to Hazy, Singapore and Qatar Airways, all in a last-ditch effort to sell V1.0. Then came Emirates and its president, Tim Clark. "I went with John to do these presentations. I don't know if they ever coordinated amongst themselves, but each one of the presentations ended with the airline telling us it's not going to work. Clark was the final one, and that was done in Toulouse. I was again tasked to do the presentation. I started the presentation, and half an hour into it, in front of all the top management of Emirates and all the top management of Airbus, Clark said, 'Kiran, stop.' Then he just ripped the airplane apart, and we ended up being told to design a new aircraft."

Rao and the team were basically put in a room for six months and told to come up with a concept for a new A350. Improved versions with a composite fuselage were conceived, but Airbus still didn't get the A350 right, even after this revamp. The initial redesign version included a composite fuselage overlaid on a metal skeletal structure. This, too, came under criticism. Geoffrey Thomas, then of *Air Transport World* (*ATW*), reported that Airbus was going to change this to a composite structure. He said Airbus vehemently denied it and forced *ATW* to retract the story. Not long after, Airbus did, in fact, change to a composite skeletal structure, just as Thomas reported. Thomas laments that he missed winning "News Story of the Year" because *ATW* pulled it from its website.

It took until late 2006 to come up with what would be called the A350 XWB. XWB stood for Xtra Wide-Body. The fuselage was wider than the 787 but smaller than the 777. This time, Airbus offered a three-member family,

---

40. Qantas would firm the 787 order in March 2006.

straddling the 777 and 787. The A350-800 competed with the 787-9, the -900 was across from the 777-200ER and the new -1000 competed with the 777-300ER. The -900 was the baseline design, with the -800 being a straightforward shrink and the -1000 a straightforward stretch. Even then, the "final" version wasn't up to snuff.

Deprived of cash by huge cost overruns on the A380 and A400M programs—and faced with already ballooning costs on the R&D for the A350—Airbus took a "Hail Mary" pass by trying to cover two Boeing programs with one aircraft family. When Airbus launched the A350, one of its marketing messages was that the 787 was too small. The larger A350-800/900, Airbus claimed, fitted into this trend for larger aircraft. However, this thesis ran headlong into the contradiction that the A350-1000 was actually smaller than the competing 777-300ER: 350 passengers vs. 365. Some felt (and said so at the time) that Airbus was trying to do too much by covering the 787 and the 777 sectors with one family of airplanes, and that, in any case, the -1000 should really have been about 380 or 385 passengers. It wasn't long before the folly of this approach reared its head.

The revised A350 was, like the 787, all composite. But whereas the 787's fuselage was a single-barrel construction, Airbus elected to design the A350 fuselage as giant panels attached to a composite skeleton. Airbus claimed this was less costly and less technically complex.

Boeing, predictably, criticized the A350 in every respect. The A350-800 was less efficient than the 787-9. As a shrink, it had poor economics. The A350-1000 wasn't up to the advertised mission. The panel design was bad. The skeletal structure was bad. And so on.[41] The trouble was that Boeing never had anything good to say about Airbus airplanes and data was often exaggerated, either in favor of Boeing or against Airbus. It's like the boy crying wolf: Boeing's negativity wasn't always credible. The company began showing presentations with question marks through the -800 and -1000, suggesting Airbus wouldn't proceed with one or both.

Given Boeing's penchant for hyperbole, one had to be skeptical. But the only people who mattered, the customers, began to express doubts over time, including those who ordered the A350-800. For the -800, it was simple: The operating costs were about the same as the larger -900, always a prob-

---

41. Years later, one supplier to Airbus and Boeing said the panel approach was the better one. Still later, in 2021, Airbus began showing the cargo airlines and lessors a freighter concept for the A350. It turned out that the panel design lends itself better to a freighter model than Boeing's barrel approach does. It's unclear if either company gave a lot of thought to this when the 787 and A350 were initially designed.

lem with a shrink. As for the -1000, it was falling short of the advertised performance.

Eventually, *Leeham News* broke the story, on June 5, 2011, that Airbus and Rolls-Royce were going to modify the design of the -1000's engine and wing to provide more thrust and longer range. At the Paris Air Show a week later, Airbus confirmed this. The changes to the engine, to provide a 97,000-lb. thrust, were (in engine terms) minor but enough to require some different parts and spares. This reduced engine commonality between the three family members and in the process, deeply angered Clark, a launch customer of the -900/1000.

In the process of upgrading the -1000, Airbus failed to consult or even inform the airlines, Clark and others claimed, further increasing their anger. Still, the -1000 remained nominally at 350 passengers vs. the 777-300ER's 365. This put the -1000 at a revenue disadvantage to the -300ER, something Rao pointed out in the competition between the A340-600 and the 777-300ER. But on trip costs, the -1000 beat the 300ER by a wide margin: 25 percent by Airbus calculations, 20 percent by Boeing analysis and about 22 percent by *Leeham*'s analysis.

The A350-900 whipped the 777-200ER and -200LR as well. About the same seating capacity, the trip and per-seat costs instantly obsoleted the -200ER. As an ultra-long-range (ULR) airplane, the -200LR served a different purpose, a niche. But when not doing a ULR mission, the -900 was the better choice. (Airbus created an A350-900ULR in 2019.)

While the -800 recorded a respectable 180 orders at this early stage in the program, the sub-type became less attractive as the economics became better understood. Perhaps, more to the point, development of the A350 began to come under resource pressure. The -900 and -1000 were the more important of the three family members. With some customers—and even some within Airbus—cooling to the -800, the model was sacrificed as more engineers were devoted to the larger siblings. Once it became clear the -800 was a goner, A350 customers cited the -800's mediocre economics compared with the -900—along with "de-risking" the development and production—as reasons to swap to the larger -900. Airbus said it would make more profit on the larger aircraft.

"If we had to go and do it all again, I would have gone for a four-aircraft family with two engines," Rao recalled in 2019. "We needed a smaller engine for the -800 and -900 and a bigger engine for the -1000 and the -2000 because, in the end, the engine was too big for the -800 and too small for the -1000. When you put the -800 up against the 787-9, it was a smaller airplane. The 787-8 didn't sell too much either, but the 787-9 was better."

The -2000 Rao referred to as a 425-passenger A350 that would have competed directly against the 777-9. Airbus considered launching this model after Boeing moved forward with the 777X program. But by then, Boeing had locked up more than 200 orders from Emirates, Etihad and Qatar for the 777-8 (350 passengers, more than 9,000nm range) and the 777-9 (425 passengers, 7,600nm). With these customers off the table, Airbus couldn't build a business case for the remaining, limited market.[42]

This left the question of how Airbus would compete with the 787-8 and 787-9. The A330—the airplane the A350 was supposed to replace—caught its second wind when the 787 had 3.5 years of delays. The -8 proved to be overweight, and Airbus dramatically improved the A330 through Performance Improvement Packages (PIPs). Sales surpassed 1,500, the majority coming after the launch of the 787. It was a marvelous showing, but as the 787 finally got past its problems and entered service, sales began to taper off. Even low prices couldn't head off the looming gap between the backlog and production rate of 10 per month.

By December 2013, it was clear Airbus had to proceed with a re-engined A330 if it wanted to continue production and have something to compete against the 787. The next month, it was also apparent the A380 needed new engines to compete with the twin-engine 777-9. Airbus would have some tough decisions ahead, including whether to re-engine the A320 family and gamble on how Boeing would respond.

---

42. Airbus was also afraid the A350-2000 would cannibalize demand for the struggling A380. In the end, Airbus probably is thankful it took a pass on the 425-seat sector. Subsequent events proved Boeing may have backed a sales loser in the 777X. Market fragmentation, the very premise for the 787 over the A380, proved to be damaging to the 777-9 as well.

13

Falling Apart

"That was a decision that caused a lot of angst throughout the whole system."

—RAY CONNER, ON THE COMPRESSED TIMELINE FOR THE 787

WITH THE DRAMAS OF THE TANKER COMPETITION LOSSES AND WINS— and the WTO complaint going on—Boeing got to work producing the 787 Dreamliner, a name chosen by an informal public contest. Airbus couldn't decide how to respond to the 787 and when it did, its own false starts hampered its efforts.

With analysts, customers and aviation geeks wondering for months whether Boeing would ever launch a new airplane, the 787 signaled Boeing was "back." Then, in 2005, Boeing launched the 747-8, the next and final iteration of the legendary airplane. Equipped with the new GEnx engines designed for the 787, aerodynamic improvements and an extended upper deck for a few more passengers—taking the 747-8's capacity to 465—Boeing seemed back to its aggressive, competitive roots.

The company launched the 787 amid sky-high hopes and industry-wide excitement. The dramatic operating cost savings, composite design and industrial approach to production were all game changers. Boeing held regular media conference calls with progress updates, something unprecedented in the industry. The industrial partnership and snap-together approach to the final assembly was designed to lower costs and dramatically shorten launch-to-entry into service.

Although historically the industry, across companies and oceans, had taken around four years to develop airplanes and put them into service in the past, launch-to-EIS time was increasing by 2000. Airplanes were becoming more sophisticated, automated and filled with advanced technology. Writing software was an immense effort.

Technological transformations were leaps ahead of the 707, 727, 757, 767 and even the 777. Technology for the 787 and A350 was well advanced over the once ground-breaking, fly-by-wire Airbus product line. There were sophisticated health monitoring systems to identify problems quickly or even proactively. This makes it easier for mechanics to have parts ready when a plane arrives at the gate. In turn, it reduces delays. Auto-throttles, one of the earliest advances, makes piloting the aircraft easier—though some auto-throttle failures led to crashes. Flight envelope protection and fly-by-wire, both Airbus innovations, were major advances.

The 787 was the first "all-electric" airplane. In this context, the engines did not provide "bleed air" for pressurization of the cabin, heating, deicing wings and air conditioning. Electrical power did these things. (Airbus, in the A350, stayed with bleed air, forgoing the relatively small benefit in relation to the cost of going electric.) The 787 also required a prodigious amount of software. The increased reliance on electrical power required use of a lithium-ion battery of great power. An electronic board coordinated all the inputs and outputs to all the other advanced systems.

The industrial design, production and final assembly partnership exceeded even that practiced by McDonnell Douglas. And all this had to be done from the December 2003 program launch to the May 2008 EIS. It was a recipe for one of the greatest industrial disasters of all time.

SETTING THE MAY 2008 EIS

The timeline, just four years and five months from launch to EIS, was aggressive. In the past, Boeing's delays had been measured in months, except for the 747-100 program, which suffered from engine, not airplane, delays. Problems with the 787 emerged internally fairly early on in the program, but Boeing's periodic media progress calls gave few hints. Nor was information shared with aerospace analysts on Wall Street. There was little hint outside the company of how serious the problems were as Boeing counted down to the planned rollout on July 8, 2007 (7-8-7). Boeing had done a good job of containment.

One of those outsiders earliest to tumble was Joe Nadol, the aerospace analyst for JP Morgan. Nadol covered Boeing and many of the publicly listed suppliers that fed parts and components to BCA, including on the 787. One of the better analysts on Wall Street, he worked his supplier source at the 2007 Paris Air Show in June. It was here that Nadol was informed by suppliers that the 787 was in serious trouble. He raised the red flag in a research note issued after he returned to New York.

Nadol later told a reporter that Boeing's investor relations department in Chicago went "tilt." Without providing details, he said IR attempted to discredit him and his research note, plus it froze him out of earnings calls and meetings. After Nadol's report, other analysts began sniffing out the problems. Separately, reporters and bloggers also began learning of the growing issues.[43]

---

43. Nadol died in February 2015 when a commuter train from New York hit an

It became a race against time to meet the rollout date. Boeing planned a global event. There would be live satellite feeds and a webcast for anyone interested in watching. Every 787 customer was invited for front-row seats before a stage of events, hosted by NBC News anchor Tom Brokaw. Brokaw, a solid, lifetime newsman, wasn't happy in this role, but he explained that NBC was owned by General Electric and a GE engine was one of those powering the 787. When GE called, Brokaw felt he had little choice but to emcee Boeing's extravaganza. And it certainly was an extravaganza. Few companies do parties better than Boeing.

For those who couldn't fit (or weren't even invited) into Boeing's 787 assembly bay in Everett, the stadium for the Mariners baseball team south of downtown Seattle was rented. There, big screens televised the events. For aviation geeks, the coolest event was the entire 7-Series line of airplanes swooping into Boeing Field minutes apart, starting with the 707. There were no commercially operated 707s, but a company called Omega flew the 707 on for-lease aerial tanker missions. The former MD-95, renamed the 717, came next. A FedEx 727-200A followed, then a 737, 747, 757, 767 and 777. It was a fabulous piece of theatre.

Back at Everett, the massive doors of the hangar opened to reveal 787 Number 1. Reaction to the plane was everything Boeing had hoped—globally, across the U.S. and locally. The 787 gleamed in the sunlight. Nobody outside Boeing knows how much the extravaganza cost, but the return on investment had to be measured in multiples.

Yet within weeks, stories began to emerge that airplane Number 1 wasn't all that it seemed. Reports indicated some of the doors weren't real; suggestions were that some were cardboard. Components were missing. Some began calling the first 787 a Potemkin airplane.[44]

At the rollout and before, McNerney and others at Boeing cited the plan for the first flight in September 2007, two months away. It soon became clear this was a pipe dream. Number 1 was, indeed, incomplete at rollout. Reporting emerged that Number 1 had missing parts, components that didn't fit properly, and temporary fasteners connecting airplane sections. Reports later surfaced that the temporary fasteners were from the home improvement store Home Depot, but this was never confirmed. Some believe it to be hyperbole. Nevertheless, this became one of the symbols of the 787's problems, which grew and grew.[45]

SUV on the tracks during the evening rush hour. He and five others in the lead car died in the ensuing fire.

44. This refers to purported fake settlements erected at the direction of Russian minister Grigori Alexsandrovich *Potemkin* to fool Empress Catherine II.

45. One of the leaders of the 787 program told this author the temporary fasteners weren't from Home Depot.

CHAPTER 13 FALLING APART

Some composite fuselage sections were mismatched. The wing-to-body join failed to mate properly. Design and production issues with Italy's Alenia, Mitsubishi's wing, Vought and the Vought-Alenia JV in the new 787 production plant in North Charleston, South Carolina, caused major delays and cost overruns. As the most advanced airplane being designed for commercial aviation at that time, software development was vexing.

In April 2008, less than a year after rollout and a month from the targeted EIS, Boeing announced a third delay. Officials now projected 25 deliveries in 2009. Boeing said on a program update call on April 9 that the new delay wouldn't impact earnings, but Wall Street analysts were already forecasting compensation costs.

As the airlines lined up for compensation, forecasts of customer penalties payable by Boeing were all over the map:

- Morningstar: $800 million to $1 billion
- Cowen & Company: $4 billion
- Goldman Sachs: $3 billion
- Lehman Brothers: $3 billion to $5 billion
- JP Morgan: $3.5 billion to $4.5 billion
- Wachovia: $2 billion to $3 billion

These weren't the only costs. Boeing had previously announced it added $1.5 billion to engineering and production costs, but this was an old figure. During the program update, officials said there would be more added, although they deferred any discussion of details to the earnings release at the end of the month. It was obvious that Boeing wasn't going to book any meaningful 787 revenue in 2008 due to the delays. Costs continued to mount.

By comparison, the two-year delay in the A380 program was forecast to cost Airbus approximately €6 billion (about $8 billion) through 2010, when the delivery schedule was expected to be back on track. This included penalties, production costs and lost or deferred profits. Airbus had fewer than 200 orders for the A380 when the problems arose.

The financial impact for the 787 would not show up as a "hit" to the bottom line in one massive write-off, however. Boeing uses "program accounting" to amortize costs across the entire production run. This means that while the break-even sales point had ballooned to a figure that Boeing didn't announce, the charges were buried in the cost of each airplane.

At this stage, the depth of the problems still wasn't apparent. After the April 9 program update call, Nadol wrote in a research note, the "new schedule seems reasonable but [there are] still lots of unknowns. Substantial risks remain. We are focused on issues such as the sanctity of the design of critical structures and certification concerns, such as lightning strike and electromagnetic interference." Paul Nesbit of JSA Research, generally viewed as pro-Boeing in his remarks, was quoted by *The Everett Herald* as writing that "there is 'no compelling reason' to believe Boeing will meet its new schedule."

Carson, by now CEO of BCA, ducked a question from an analyst on the earnings call about when, over the course of the 900 orders outstanding, would Boeing catch up on the delivery schedule. He said this was still being assessed. Nadol wrote that he didn't think the program would catch up until there were 900 cumulative deliveries, something he forecast for 2017.[46]

The first flight finally occurred December 15, 2009—more than a year and a half after the planned May 2008 EIS. It was a typical, miserable Puget Sound rainy winter day at Everett. By the time the 787 landed at Boeing Field, heavy rain and high winds moved into downtown Seattle. Boeing spokesman Bernard Choi, himself a former newsman for Seattle TV station KING, bravely anchored the event from under an umbrella as a driving rain pummeled him.

Despite the gloomy weather, the flight test crew and everyone else were all smiles after the 787 parked in front of the Museum of Flight. Still, a writer given to clichés might have said the weather cast a pall over the entire event. The 787's troubles were far from over.[47]

More design, industrial and assembly problems emerged over the course of the next two years. On November 9, 2010, a test flight was on approach to land at Laredo, Texas, when a fire erupted in the electronics bay. According to reports, the crew was lucky to land safely.[48] "The fire affected the cockpit controls, and the jet lost its primary flight displays and its auto-throttle, according to a person familiar with the incident. The pilot lost some use of the flight and engine controls, which on the Dreamliner are electrically activated," *The Seattle Times* reported. There were 30 to 40 people on board; they evacuated by emergency slides. Nobody was hurt. The program was delayed again while the source and cause of the fire was determined. It ultimately was traced to an electrical box. Metal shavings which shouldn't have been present caused a short that started the fire.

The 787-8 didn't enter service until December 2011. The short-range 787-3 was canceled, and the largest member of the family, the 787-10, was postponed. The latter was finally launched in May 2013 with an order from

---

46. Through 2017, Boeing delivered 636 787s, with the EIS coming in December 2011, not 2009. Boeing didn't deliver the 900th 787 until 2019.

47. Eleven years later, the first flight of the 777X, delayed a year, was finally scheduled for January 24, 2020. The first attempt was a rain-out. The flight took place the next day, also a cloudy, rainy day. True to form, a pall seemed cast over the 777X as well.

48. https://www.seattletimes.com/business/electrical-fire-forces-emergency-landing-of-787-test-plane/

Singapore.[49] Historically, break-even was achieved after about 400 deliveries. The airplane didn't turn cash-flow positive until late 2015, when a total of 363 airplanes were delivered—nearly four years after EIS. Cash-flow positive, however, is not the same as program break-even. Over the course of the program, Boeing racked up $32 billion in deferred costs and deferred tooling costs. By year-end 2020, Boeing had whittled this down to $20 billion.

The number would have been higher were it not for reclassification of the first three test airplanes as R&D expenses. These three airplanes had been modified so much to fix design and production problems that they were unable to be sold. Two became museum static displays in Japan and Seattle. The third was scrapped. The other three test airplanes were sold as VIP aircraft.

A group of the airplanes became known as the "Terrible Teens." These were heavy and had a lot of reworking. It took salesmen years to sell these aircraft.

What went wrong? Boeing executives interviewed for this book pointed to several factors. The only hope that Boeing had for 787 launch customers were ANA, Japan and the handful of Chinese carriers. There wasn't a U.S. airline that was in a position to do anything because these were still struggling after 9/11, a former Boeing executive recalled. The Chinese carriers said, "We'll launch, but we want the airplane for the Olympics."

"That drove the schedule," the executive said. "There were a lot of things that we certainly didn't anticipate that really blew it up. A lot of people think the fastener story was absurd. It was not really the issue, but it was a huge, huge problem." Conner agreed. Although he wasn't part of the program planning—his role came later—Conner said just the fact that the plane was composite, not aluminum, had an impact on the supply chain.

"Based on my discussions with people, initially it wasn't an all-composite airplane, it was an aluminum airplane. A lot of the suppliers that we'd chosen, the methodologies and those kinds of things that we were building everything around, were for a more traditional type of airplane," Conner said, looking back. "Then we made a decision that we wanted to go down this composite route for efficiencies, for airplane performance's sake. Of course, nobody was really set up to do that. We had to do new airplanes in a less expensive way. Everybody always tries to figure out how to do new airplanes in a less expensive way."

Walt Gillette, the lead engineer on the 787 program, was tasked with implementing all these things, which were non-traditional for Boeing. What

---

49. The program's official launch was at the Paris Air Show the following month. EIS was March 2018.

was non-traditional? It was the McDonnell Douglas MD-95 approach described by Gary Scott in Chapter 8.

Boeing gave limited specifications to suppliers and then it was up to them to design to meet those specs. Previously, Boeing did all the detail design for systems and structures, providing very detailed specifications, "almost to the point of designing it ourselves," Conner said. By moving to a non-traditional method, "I think we were a little naive in our approach to that."

When the suppliers came back with their designs, "our engineering teams would say, 'No, that's not what we want,'" Conner said. "There was a lot of confusion around design, and I think there was a view from Walt that we always designed way too much margin into our airplanes so we could have a lot of growth and those kinds of things. I think it then became more of a point design, as opposed to a design that had the ability to grow and do all these things."

There had been debate within Boeing's engineers over the respective merits of a composite vs. metallic airplane, but this is not unusual at Boeing or any other aerospace manufacturer. Studying alternatives and assessing trade-offs between them were normal. "We looked at all the final trades and made the decision to use composites," the former Boeing executive said. "Then we had to convince Chicago that that was the right thing to do."

As things fell apart, Boeing's unions were quick to say, "We told you so." They demanded that Boeing bring the 787 work back in-house from outsourcing. The IAM 751 members, who assemble the airplanes, and SPEEA, the engineering union, blamed outsourcing for the problems. To some degree, so did Boeing. But it wasn't this simple.

With all the focus on the industrial partner snafus at Vought in South Carolina, Alenia in Italy and multiple Japanese providers, it's easy to forget that suppliers, not the industrial partners, were tagged with the initial delays. At first, a critical shortage of fasteners was identified as the prime culprit. The fasteners were supplied by Alcoa; this is a normal part of the supply chain, not an outsourcing issue. Likewise, flight control software from Honeywell was an early problem. This, too, was a supply chain issue. Software systems integration had problems as well—another supplier, not an industrial partner.

In its own defense, Honeywell said Boeing was eight months late delivering engineering specifications required to write the flight control software code. Design changes by Boeing also required Labinal, a wiring supplier, to undertake redesigns. And so it went. The ripple effect of all the various issues, large and small, contributed to the delays and complications.

SPEEA blamed outsourcing engineering work, specifically the use of Russian and later, Indian engineers. Russians were imported under so-called H1B work visas to work on the program. Work was also outsourced into Russia itself. It later emerged that tasks sent to India, mostly on the 747-8, required rework by SPEEA, but one of the key Boeing execs on the 787 program denied the Russian work was inferior.

"I don't think that was a big deal," the former Boeing officer said. "The Russians did an absolutely magnificent job and if you think about it, at the time we had the cream of the crop of Russian aerospace engineers because they had nothing else to work on. While they did pretty much all the engineering on the large cargo freighter [the Dreamlifter, an extreme modification of the 747-400F], we had the best stress engineers working on that thing. I don't think that outsourcing was an issue. There certainly were some issues with the way the engineering was done on some of the major suppliers. I think that was our fault for the most part. We probably should have had more oversight on them but those major suppliers were, and some are OEMs. Mitsubishi designs and builds their own airplanes. Finmeccanica, the same thing. It wasn't like these guys were folks that [had] never done Tier-1 engineering work."

Still, Boeing had to check the work coming into Seattle for assembly. In the end, Boeing says it didn't find a lot that was wrong, but it didn't know. "You can't not know," said the former officer. Meanwhile, the Charleston operation became an industrial nightmare for Boeing. There were two operations there. One was owned and operated solely by Vought; another was a JV between Vought and Alenia called Global Aeronautica. Large sections of the fuselage were produced in these plants.

Quality control, design and production issues plagued the plant. By March 2008, Boeing had had enough. It bought out Vought's interests. Boeing became a 50-50 partner with Alenia in the Global Aeronautica JV. The aft end was produced by the JV. The former officer said the program started out well but halfway through the program, Vought, which was owned by hedge fund Carlyle Group, was put up for sale. "They stripped a lot of resources out to improve the numbers to put it up for sale and those were resources that were absolutely necessary for their part of the work statement," a Boeing executive said. "In the end, that's why we ended up buying that."

New airplanes almost always gain weight as design moves to production. The 787 was no exception. It became unusually heavy, as new airplane programs go.[50] Range, performance and economics were reduced as a result. "We came out heavy, and we were just totally honked up. It was a mess," Conner said. He agreed that Boeing turned too much responsibility over to suppliers. "We went to stuffing the airplane[51] with our suppliers. We turned

---

50. The Lockheed L-1011 was a notorious example of an overweight airplane. The L-1011-1, the first model, became known as the "lead sled."

51. "Stuffing the airplane" means installing systems before shipping the fuselage sections. Previously, fuselages would be "stuffed" on the final assembly line.

over a lot of the design to the suppliers, but we didn't give them the appropriate level of specs that would guide them in the appropriate way with respect to their design. Then we ended up with a mess in some of those cases."

Conner also said Boeing didn't execute its supplier management in the detailed way that it did in the past. "We let them go on their own. We didn't have a consistent tooling methodology. Every supplier had a different tooling methodology in terms of how to build this composite structure. It was brand new structure, composite, and we were just learning and relearning, like we almost were starting when we were with the aluminum airplanes."

Conner added that Boeing tried to do too much at once with the 787. "I guess the fundamental thing is typically you only limit yourself to maybe three to five major changes from one airplane to another airplane. We did step changes from the 777 to 787. It would have been just enough to go with just structure on its own, going from aluminum to composite. But we went aluminum to composite, and we went to a more electrical structure. We went to a non-bleed structure. We did all these different things that were major changes that put us over the top."

Committing to a May 2008 EIS for the Summer Olympics in China was a mistake, Conner said. "I think they took a year or so out of the program to support the Chinese for the Beijing Olympics. That was a decision that caused a lot of angst throughout the whole system. You don't take a year out of the program to do that."

The departure of Mulally, CEO of BCA, to become CEO of Ford Motor Co. was also a blow. Conner, who worked with Mulally at BCA, believes he could have made a difference. For all of Carson's attributes, engineering wasn't one of them, and his management style was very different. "Alan was very equipped to deal with all that stuff," Conner said. "Had we realized how far behind we were, I know Alan would've really been in attack mode on that for sure. That was not Scott's strength at all."

The 787 program was launched by Stonecipher in December 2003. He was ousted two years later and succeeded by McNerney. The timeline shows the 787 crisis happened on McNerney's watch, and he gets the lion's share of the blame for the debacle, including letting Mulally leave in 2006 just as it was becoming clear internally that all was not well.

But Conner says McNerney gets a bad rap; he inherited decisions made by Stonecipher. "Harry put tough limitations on our team about how many people we could have working on the program in Seattle. That drove a lot of decision-making down the road with respect to what we could do. We could only do final assembling, and it needed to be just so many people. There were a lot of things that were driven on the '87 that were part of edicts that came down from Stonecipher. That forced the team then to structure their '87 in a different way and ended up hurting us."

CHAPTER 13 **FALLING APART**

This was a business model that was essentially followed by McDonnell Douglas, where Stonecipher had been CEO. Yet Boeing had been warned against this approach by a Boeing engineer, Dr. L.J. Hart-Smith, in February 2001—almost three years before the 7E7 was launched and two years before Boeing board member McNerney warned of an over-emphasis on cost control.

In a 15-page white paper,[52] Hart-Smith—a former McDonnell Douglas employee at the Douglas Aircraft Co. Long Beach facility—made the point that outsourcing didn't necessarily result in better profits or efficiencies. "The subcontractors on the DC-10 made all of the profits; the prime manufacturer absorbed all of the overruns," was a blunt statement in the "Abstract." "A strong warning is included about the perils of sub-optimum solutions in which individual costs are minimized in isolation. Indeed, the importance of *thorough* planning, accounting for all interdepartmental interactions, cannot be over-emphasized."

In the Introduction, Hart-Smith wrote, "Outsourcing is commonly looked upon by management as a tool for reducing costs. But the unresolved question is '*which costs?*' In addition, there is the matter of 'what is the effect on *overall* costs?' The most important issue of all is whether a company can *continue* to operate if it relies primarily on outsourcing the majority of the work that it once did in-house."

Hart-Smith continued, "The experiences of the former Douglas Aircraft Company would suggest that, in the context of the aerospace industry at least, it cannot. In the more general context, it should be obvious that a company cannot control its own destiny if it creates less than 10 percent of the products it sells."

The paper discussed benefits of outsourcing when it is done well, but the warnings were clear. And for the most part, the latter were ignored as the 787 program was launched. "The inescapable problem with outsourcing work that *could* be done in-house is that it *necessarily* increases the tasks and man hours to carry out the work way above those needed to perform *all* assembly, including most subassemblies, at *one* site," Hart-Smith wrote, a point that proved to be prescient.

After reading Hart-Smith's paper, one must wonder whether Stonecipher ever did. Since the paper is critical of the McDonnell Douglas way of doing things at Douglas Aircraft, and it was Stonecipher who launched the 7E7, one conclusion is that he didn't.

Leahy and his sales team took full advantage of the 787's woes. With repeated delays and increasingly angry customers, Airbus sold more A330s

---

52. "Outsourced Profits—The Cornerstone of Successful Subcontracting."

after the 787 program was launched than it did before. It was a statistic the promotion-minded Leahy cited at every opportunity.

Because McNerney warned the Boeing board in April 2003 about excessive cost cutting, when the debate over the 7E7 was going on, Conner may well be right about McNerney's getting a bad rap over how the 787 crisis unfolded. But one thing can be laid squarely at McNerney's feet that didn't help matters as the program unraveled. It was his war on the unions, which threatened to rip BCA apart.

14

Labor Wars

"Labor disputes are affecting our customer relationships."
—**BOEING CEO JIM McNERNEY,** IN A LETTER TO IAM 751 MEMBERS,
OCTOBER 2008

AMID THE 787 PROBLEMS, Boeing got into a nasty fight with its tough labor union, the International Association of Machinists and Aerospace Workers District 751. This mouthful is more colloquially known as IAM 751. District 751 members were the ones assembling the airplanes. A smaller, almost sideshow fight went on concurrently with its engineers and professional technicians' union, the Society of Professional Engineering Employees in Aerospace, or SPEEA. Of these two major unions, the IAM 751 was, by far, the most aggressive. It was also prone to strikes.

The Machinists signed their first contract with Boeing in 1936. The Great Depression still gripped the nation. Following World War II, the IAM called its first strike against Boeing in 1948. It lasted 146 days. Boeing didn't have another strike by the IAM until 1965. This one lasted 19 days. Then, in 1977, there was another that lasted for 44 days, and another, in 1989, for 48 days. Then again in 1999, for 69 days, and in 2005, as the 787 was in production, for 28 days. All strikes had economic elements to it: pay, benefits, pensions, etc. But by 2005, outsourcing on the 787 became a top issue.

Boeing increasingly outsourced work on its 7-Series airplanes. Part of this was tied to supplier offsets in exchange for orders. Some of it was a need to offload smaller components to more efficient suppliers. Some of it was done, theoretically, for cost-cutting purposes.

The 2005 strike was mainly about recovering economic givebacks from the 2002 contract, agreed in the wake of 9/11 and at a time the U.S. airline industry was decimated by the terrorist attacks. Then, Boeing was much more dependent upon the U.S. industry than what evolved over the next decade when market demand shifted to Europe and emerging markets in Asia, China and India. The strike, as with all of them, halted deliveries. In 2005, the cost to Boeing was estimated at $70 million a day.

In the run-up to 2008 contract negotiations, outsourcing became the key rallying point. The IAM 751 produced a colored chart showing the amount of work IAM members did dating back to the 737. At the time, what is now

Spirit Aerosystems in Wichita, Kansas, was Boeing Wichita. IAM members did then what Spirit does today—build the fuselage. IAM also produced most of the 757. But when it came to the 747, 767 and 777, IAM-produced components fell dramatically. With the 787, it fell even more. The 787's final assembly, with only one FAL, in Everett, was minimal.

When Boeing selected Everett for the FAL after a national site selection competition (nearly won by North Carolina), Boeing said the FAL would need only several hundred employees—a sharp drop from other wide-body lines in Everett and only a fraction of IAM members at the far more widely produced single-aisle 737 lines in Renton.

In 2008, a strike was pretty much a foregone conclusion. Strike sentiment was high at the union. By this time, the problems with the 787 program were very public for all to see. And the union's "I told you so" to Chicago was at a fever pitch. The IAM contract expired in September. It turned out to be an unfortunate timing. The union struck September 7. The same week, the stock of investment bank Lehman Brothers collapsed, losing 77 percent of its value. Lehman declared bankruptcy the following week. "The Great Financial Crisis" was underway.

Predictably, Boeing managers criticized the IAM for going on strike at a time when the global economy was suddenly going south. They weren't alone. The criticism was a bit unfair, however. Nobody foresaw a global financial meltdown when the strike vote was taken, nor when the strike deadline was set. But having walked out, and despite the cost to Boeing, neither side was willing to retreat.

On October 6, a month after the walkout, McNerney sent a tough memo to employees. He wrote that IAM concessions were necessary to cut Boeing's health care and pension costs. Labor unions had hurt the auto industry over the decades with costly contracts, McNerney wrote. He warned that lower costs in the U.S. South could mean reduced airplane production in the expensive Pacific Northwest. He warned of emerging competitors in Russia, China and Canada.[53] He warned that Airbus was becoming more competitive. McNerney wrote, in part:

> Labor disputes are affecting our customer relationships.
>
> While we've disappointed customers for other reasons in recent years, too, we believe this track record of repeated union

---

53. China was designing the COMAC C919 and Russia the Irkut MC-21, both direct competitors to the Airbus A320 and Boeing 737. McNerney's warning was hardly short of irony. Boeing increasingly, though selectively, outsourced to China and Boeing used Russian engineers, both inside and outside of Russia. The previous summer, Canada's Bombardier launched the C Series, a competitor to the smallest A320 and 737 family members.

CHAPTER 14 LABOR WARS

work stoppages is earning us a reputation as an unreliable supplier to our customers—who ultimately provide job security by buying our airplanes.

Boeing and the IAM quietly returned to the bargaining table in early October. A month later, a settlement was reached, and union members returned to work. Little was changed in the contract, however, including no change in outsourcing. "The union didn't win a damn thing," gloated Kostya Zolotusky, an always quotable if sometimes too-candid officer at Boeing Capital Corp. But neither had Boeing won the key concessions it wanted.

The contract of the other principal union, SPEEA, also expired in September. A white-collar union, SPEEA's membership didn't like strikes. And compared with the IAM, which could draw on strike funds from tens of thousands of local workers or hundreds of thousands nationally, SPEEA was small and weak. It's first contract with Boeing was in 1948, the same year the IAM struck Boeing for the first time. It didn't call its first strike until 1993—and then it was for only one day.

In October 1999, members voted to authorize a strike, its second. After some back and forth, including federal mediation, the union struck on February 9, 2000. They stayed out for 40 days, a remarkable show of solidarity, especially through Seattle's miserable, cold and rainy winter months. For the next 20 years, SPEEA would fight labor battles regularly, sometimes in court, but it never struck again.

Having battled to a draw at best in 2008, the IAM 751 was about to get its ears pounded in by McNerney and his management team the following year. While the IAM was still on strike, another drama was unfolding simultaneously, one that would have ramifications for Washington State's Gov. Christine Gregoire, who was running for re-election for a second term. Democrat Gregoire was elected in 2004, defeating Republican State Sen. Dino Rossi by a mere 133 votes after three recounts and a court review. Rossi and the Republicans nevertheless believed they were robbed. This set the stage for a rematch in 2008 when Gregoire's first term was up.

In October, when Boeing and IAM negotiators met at a hotel across from Sea-Tac Airport, union members held a rally outside. Gregoire, mindful of the 2004 election and her razor-thin margin, showed up at the rally in support of the union. She needed labor solidarity to win re-election. While awaiting her turn to speak, one of the IAM leaders boasted that Washington was the fourth most-unionized state in the country.

Gregoire defeated Rossi in the 2008 election with 53 percent of the vote. She achieved her objective, winning union support. But in Chicago at Boeing's corporate headquarters, as well as BCA's headquarters at Longacres in Renton, executives sourly took note of her appearance and support of labor during the strike—and of her snubbing the state's largest employer.

It was also not lost upon Boeing's leaders that Gregoire and the state government seemed to take Boeing's presence for granted. During her first term, the governor didn't even attend two of the international air shows in London and Paris to promote Boeing and Washington-based aerospace companies. The state's presence at these shows and others was minimal.

The strike came back to haunt IAM 751 and Gregoire the next year. Although Boeing was a long way from resolving the problems with the 787 program and delivering the first airplane to ANA, sales were good enough to see that a second assembly line eventually would be needed. The unions, state and local elected officials, and Gregoire naturally wanted the second line in Everett. South Carolina officials urged Boeing to locate the second FAL at the North Charleston facility.

Boeing launched a bake-off between Washington and South Carolina for Line 2. Boeing repeatedly said the decision would come down to whether the IAM 751 would renegotiate the 2008 contract and grant significant givebacks on health care and pension benefits. Internally, the study weighing the pros and cons of locating Line 2 in Everett or Charleston was called "Project Gemini." It was no whitewash. The study clearly outlined the risks of locating Line 2 in Charleston, which, in 2009, was still sorting out problems (and would be for the next decade). In fact, in some places in the PowerPoint presentation to the board of directors, obtained by the union in response to its filing a complaint with the National Labor Relations Board (NLRB) over the Charleston decision, the cons outnumbered the pros.

Boeing created two teams to evaluate its options. The "Red Team" was assigned to the Charleston option. The "Blue Team" considered the Everett option. Financial figures were blacked out in copies obtained by the media, but other information in the August 24, 2009, document was revealing.

Boeing listed as Next Steps on August 26—two days after the PowerPoint presentation—initial permit filing in South Carolina, retention of legal and engineering firms, and incentive negotiations with the state. Washington elected officials and union leadership were to be informed of these actions the same day. A meeting with 751 leadership was planned the next day with negotiations to begin in September.

Management clearly outlined cons: skill dilution from management and engineering to manufacturing support; short-term adverse impact on productivity due to the creation of a "greenfield" facility; significantly greater startup costs and risks to schedule and customers; negative impact on program profits; and political backlash from Washington state.

In October, Boeing announced the obvious: The second FAL would be in Charleston. IAM 751 blasted the decision. In press statements and its house publication, *Aero Mechanic* (November 2009), the union decried the move as simply a bad decision, given the state of the 787 program. IAM members were working overtime to sort out the design, production and industrial

CHAPTER 14   LABOR WARS

problems brought on by the outsourcing (as were SPEEA members). IAM members enabled Boeing to boost production on the other 7-Series lines, notably the 737 and 777, to provide badly needed cash flow to the company.

The Everett Herald reported on October 30 that U.S. Sen. Patty Murray of Washington, a strong Boeing partisan, went to bat for Everett. The *Herald* reported, "Boeing executives only half-heartedly penciled in Everett for the coveted production line, discouraged Murray from rallying on the city's behalf, held bad memories of the strike and Gov. Chris Gregoire walking the line, smarted from battles with state legislators and purchased a South Carolina aerospace company. On February 9, Murray heard firsthand about South Carolina's favored status from Boeing executives Tim Keating and Phil Ruter. Charleston topped the list of choices with Everett scrawled along the margin, its chances slim if not none. They suggested Murray not waste her immense political capital trying to alter the course of events set in motion by Boeing's big boss, Jim McNerney."

The paper continued, "Everett's chances already seemed next to nil given the bitterness stirred by the Machinists strike in 2008. McNerney had reached wit's end with the union. He had shareholders pressing for profits, customers demanding deliveries and little patience for a work force eager to strike." For its part, Boeing spokesman Tim Healy told *Leeham News*, "We were utterly serious about reaching an agreement. And we told the IAM quite precisely what we needed from them and when."

Conner, at the time vice president of supply chain management and operations, and Doug Kight, vice president of human resources for BCA, went into detail in a message to BCA managers and human resources's employees entitled, "Why Our Discussions with the IAM Were Unsuccessful."[54]

> We'd like to emphasize that Boeing considered many complex factors in this decision. Working with the union to achieve our objectives of production stability and long-term cost competitiveness was one of those factors.
>
> Unfortunately, that offer fell short of what would have been needed for Boeing management to recommend to the board that the second 787 line be put in Everett.
>
> We stated that we needed an extension of at least 10 years to the current contract. We offered annual wage increases of two percent, a bit higher than the average increase that our IAM-represented employees have gained over the last 30 years. We offered annual pension increases at the same rate. We offered to

---

54. https://blog.seattlepi.com/aerospace/2009/10/29/boeing-to-workers-talks-were-in-good-faith-unions-offer-fell-short/

introduce an annual incentive plan that could have boosted income annually for our employee.

In the end, we told the IAM clearly and repeatedly that their offer did not meet the objectives we had set out for a proposal to the Board of Directors. We asked them if they were sure that this was the best they could do on a range of issues, and they said it was.

In one area, Boeing officials simply misled Gov. Gregoire. She had asked what kind of incentives Washington could offer in its campaign to win the second FAL. Officials said none; incentives weren't an issue. The only thing that mattered was the union. Gregoire took Boeing at its word. In a slick 32-page pamphlet touting the attributes of Washington—things Boeing already knew well—incentives were mentioned only once in a single paragraph. Even then, the mention concerned past, not future, action. When the South Carolina incentives were revealed, Boeing effusively praised state and local officials for their generosity.

South Carolina jurisdictions offered incentives from the state to the local level with a value that never was publicly confirmed but widely reported to be nearly $1 billion. When this was revealed, Gregoire, other elected officials and observers felt flimflammed. So did the union.

Although the union allied with management in the fight to win the KC-X USAF aerial refueling tanker contract over their common enemy, Airbus, there was little in the way of harmony. On March 26, 2010, five months after Boeing chose Charleston over Everett for the second 787 FAL, the IAM 751 filed an unfair labor practice complaint with the NLRB. Boeing, the union charged, selected Charleston in retaliation for the 2008 strike.

"Boeing officials have repeatedly stated that the decision to move manufacturing to South Carolina was based on our union members exercising their legal right to strike for better wages and working conditions," said Tom Wroblewski, president of 751. "Retaliation and threatening statements like those are illegal because they send a message to workers that they should not stand up for their rights at the bargaining table. We will not allow this unlawful intimidation to stand as we prepare for the 2012 contract negotiations."

Boeing spokesman Healy dismissed the complaint as "meritless." But observers unaffiliated with Boeing or the union cited repeated statements by Boeing executives (from McNerney on down to Healy), that all pointed to the 2008 strike and the need for long-term, no-strike contracts as the driving factors in the Line 2 decision. These were impossible to explain away. The NLRB complaint would hang over labor relations for the next few years. McNerney's war on the unions would heat up twice more, even more bitterly than the debate over where to put the second 787 FAL.

CHAPTER 14 **LABOR WARS**

Development of the 747-8 became collateral damage to the 787 issues, and Boeing's overall product strategy going forward also became a casualty. Simultaneously, another threat to Boeing was emerging in 2008, one that Boeing officials initially dismissed as irrelevant. This came not from Toulouse, at least not at first. Instead, it came from north of the border, from teeny, tiny Bombardier, the inventor of the regional jet.

15

Upstart and Disruptor

"If you had any chance for success, it had to be a game changer."
—**GARY SCOTT,** TO THE BOMBARDIER BOARD OF DIRECTORS, UPON BEING HIRED AS CEO OF BOMBARDIER COMMERCIAL AVIATION

WHILE AIRBUS AND BOEING WERE DUKING IT OUT FOR SALES, whose airplanes were best and in the interminable dispute before the WTO, a threat to both companies was forming from an unexpected source. Bombardier made trains, corporate aircraft and regional airliners. It was now planning a new-design airplane for the 100- to 150-seat sector occupied by the A318, A319, 737-600 and 737-700.

In 2004, plans were floated for the 110-seat C110 and 130-seat C130 (two-class configurations). These were five-abreast, single-aisle designs. The C110/130 was an unremarkable airplane. The fuselage was standard aluminum, common for the day, and the wings were also metal. The engines were off-the-shelf technology.

The idea went nowhere. The cool reception in the industry caused Gary Scott, the new president of Bombardier, to recommend shelving the airplane for the time being. Five hundred and fifty of the 600 employees assigned to the program were reassigned. The remaining 50 continued R&D. But the C110 and C130 concepts were the forerunner of what eventually was launched as the CS100 and CS300. The 2005 program was called C Series, the name adopted in 2008.

Although the concepts projected a cash-operating cost reduction of 10 percent, which was "okay" for some airlines, Scott believed a 15 percent improvement was truly required. He had been with BCA for 28 years, starting in 1973. Scott grew up on the finance side of the house, moving around in different divisions, including customer services, de Havilland (Boeing owned de Havilland from 1986–1992), Everett and Renton, and moved into general management in 1995 when he took over the 737/757 programs as VPGM. This experience was crucial to his thinking at Bombardier.

In 2002, Scott was named president of the Civil Simulation and Training Group of CAE, a company that among other businesses provided simulators to the airline industry. Scott's group was based in Montreal. Two years later, Bombardier recruited him to head the C Series program. Scott retired in 2011. "When I was hired by Bombardier, one of the things I told them, and we agreed to beforehand, is that we need a game-changing airplane," Scott recalled in 2019. "You need about a 15 percent better cash operating cost than what's available in the industry today." A new plane had to meet all the price and other criteria, while also meeting significantly improved environmental standards.

The original C Series didn't meet these goals. "We had a 10 percent better airplane, but we were using essentially existing engines, and existing materials and systems," Scott said. "I told the board that we should not go forward. During that time in our discussions with the engine manufacturers, we learned that Pratt was really maturing their technology on the geared turbofan. Initially, we were targeting 2010 for the C Series, but if we waited until 2013, they could have an engine for us."

Waiting until 2008 to re-launch the C Series also allowed more use of new technologies for the fuselage and expanded use of composites compared with the 2005 iteration. The design was revamped to use aluminum-lithium alloy for the fuselage forward of the tail. The tail section and empennage were composite, as were the wings. Most importantly, Bombardier selected the P&W Geared Turbofan engine.

Bombardier's original budget was about $3 billion, one-third underwritten by launch aid and other subsidies from the U.K. government for the Belfast, Northern Ireland, plant, the Quebec Provincial and Canadian federal governments, and tax breaks from Montreal at Mirabel Airport. This was similar to the structure that Boeing and the U.S. Trade Representative targeted against Airbus and the EU.

The GTF promised conservatively a 15 percent cash operating costs savings, sharply lower noise footprint and significantly lower emissions than the GE CF34 that was used by Bombardier's own CRJ and Embraer's new E-Jet. The E-Jet family entered service in 2004.

"We were able to upgrade all the systems in the aircraft," Scott said. "By 2008, we had an airplane that was actually going to have at least 20 percent better fuel burn, 15 percent better cash-operating cost, plus all the other improvements from passenger appeal, environmental impact that we were targeting as well. We went back to the board, got approval to offer and started to get serious with the airlines in 2008."

LAUNCH CUSTOMER—AND DISAPPOINTMENT

The next year, Bombardier received a big endorsement for the revised C Series. Lufthansa launched the C Series at the 2009 Farnborough Air Show. Nico Buchholz, Lufthansa Group's fleet planner, wanted to send a message to Airbus that there now was an alternative to the duopoly in mainline aircraft.

Airbus and Boeing largely ignored Buchholz. The order was for the CS100, intended to replace the aging Avro 100 and CRJs at Lufthansa Group's affiliated carriers—not the mainline Lufthansa. The CS100 didn't compete with Airbus or Boeing—just Embraer. Then a U.S. company, Republic Airways Holdings, announced a firm order in February 2010 for 40 CS300s and an equal number of options.

Airbus dismissed the C Series. Officials, led by Leahy and supported by Executive Vice President Williams, ramped up the rhetoric, trashing Bombardier and the C Series. But by the end of 2010, Airbus announced the launch of the A320neo. The timing made it appear that Airbus was prompted by the Republic order. Contrary to widespread belief, it was not, Leahy insists.

One of Republic's carriers was Frontier Airlines, which operated A319s and A320s exclusively. The CS300 was an ideal replacement for and a direct competitor to the A319. It was also common industry gossip that Bombardier had a CS500 design—a direct competitor to the A320.

Airbus was already testing a GTF engine on its A340 test bed, which many in the industry viewed as a dry run for the prospect of re-engining the A320 family. Throughout the rest of 2009, Leahy publicly dismissed the idea of putting the GTF on the A320. The A320, with the CFM56 and IAE V2500 engines, was selling well—so, Leahy said, why mess with success? He was intrigued by the progress being made internally but given that he had large quantities of existing A320s to sell, he did not want customers postponing orders while waiting for a possible new aircraft.

Yet by May 2010, Airbus clearly was gearing up to proceed with the re-engined A320. At the pre-Farnborough Air Show press briefing, Leahy and Williams fired warning shots across Bombardier's bow. Airbus, Leahy declared, was not going to let Bombardier do to it what Airbus did to Boeing: quietly sneak up and become a real competitive threat. Airbus, Leahy said, would compete on price and, it was becoming clear, with a new, re-engined A320 family.

Williams, a Scotsman with a wickedly candid way about him and an elbow-sharp sense of humor, was less obtuse. "We're going to carpet bomb them out of existence," Williams declared at the same press briefing.[55]

Airbus was true to its word. It dropped the price on the A320 in head-to-head competitions, offering airlines a larger airplane for close to the price of the CS300. This was not as difficult as some observers believed because the newly designed C Series costs were much higher than an amortized A320. One firm calculated that the C Series cost about $33 million to pro-

---

55. Whether intended or not as a clever play on words, carpet bombing required bombardiers.

duce, including overhead. This meant Bombardier had to sell the airplane for at least $36.3 million to make a 10 percent margin. Airbus could, if it really wanted to, sell its amortized airplane around this figure in 2010 dollars.

So could Boeing if it wanted to, and Leahy successfully emphasized that Bombardier lacked a true world-wide support organization. Although Bombardier had one in place for the CRJ regional jet and Q400 turboprop, neither came close to matching those operated by Airbus and Boeing. Airbus blocked Bombardier from several deals. "They are not even remotely comparable to Airbus or Boeing," Leahy would tell prospects. It was true.

But there was an element of smokescreen to the Airbus rhetoric as well. "The Republic order did not prompt the launch of the neo," Leahy said in 2019, denying widespread conclusions at the time. "We did not take Republic seriously. We were building our business case. We had finally finished negotiations with the engine guys, which were not easy. We had launch customers ready to go, including IndiGo [of India], and we had serious interest from the major lessors."

"It wasn't so much about Republic but more a general issue that we could see with competitiveness of the C Series. It was an argument strongly made by Kiran [Rao]. The C Series definitely prompted the neo but not necessarily due to Republic," Williams said.

Airbus launched the A320neo family in December 2010. Boeing would follow with a re-engined 737 in July 2011. Boeing initially took a laid-back approach toward the C Series. Albaugh, the CEO of BCA until 2012, said he'd compete against the CS300 with the 737-700. The -700 was fully amortized and Boeing could slash the price to offset the economic disadvantage of the small and technologically aging sub-model.

Boeing ignored Bombardier until the latter nearly landed a big order from United in early 2016. Boeing sold the 737-700 to United for a reported price of less than $24 million.[56] Then, Bombardier won a deal with Delta the following April. This prompted Boeing to file a trade complaint against Bombardier a year later.

Albaugh, who headed BCA at the time, explained Boeing's thinking in 2019. "Having an installed base is a huge deal," he recalled. "We had installed bases at all the major airlines of the 737. Are airlines really going to want to bring on a new airplane type that doesn't have the logistics tail the 737 has? By the way, we incrementally were making the 737 better. Our view was that the NG, with a lot of the tweaks that we had made over the years, was still going to be very competitive with the neo. We thought the -700 would be very competitive with the C Series. The other thing you got to remember is, we didn't really have much of a market for the 737-7, except

---

56. There was more to the United deal than just price, as will be described later.

for Southwest. Did we really think that Southwest was going to want to go to a mixed fleet? I think it was more of a threat to the 319 than it was to the 700."

This view would come back to bite Boeing in 2016. Despite Albaugh's vow to fight the C Series by low-balling the 737-700, Boeing generally left Bombardier alone. Faced with Airbus's sledgehammer, the smaller company's sales force had its hands full, but this wasn't Bombardier's only problem.

After winning the Lufthansa Group and Republic orders, there were few other sales of note. Korean Air Lines, a good brand name, placed an order for 10 CS300s, but that seemed to be part of an industrial offset. Other orders were from names that hardly instilled a sense of industry buy-in.

Odyssey Airlines placed a small order for 10 CS100s. Odyssey was a London start-up that planned to run the airplane in business-class configuration between London City Airport and New York. But it had little funding and looked to raise money through crowd funding on the Internet. That didn't work, and the crowd funding scheme was ridiculed by observers and pundits.

PrivatAir, a tour company, placed an order for five CS300s. The company eventually went out of business. Iraq Air placed a small order. The country risk spoke for itself. Ilyushin Aircraft Finance, a Russian lessor, placed a big order for 30. But as international sanctions were placed, following annexation of Crimea and interference in the 2016 U.S. presidential election, IFC couldn't raise the financing it needed. The order was cut back sharply.

Bombardier forecast it would have 300 orders by the time the C Series entered service, intended for 2013. But like the new airplane programs at Airbus and Boeing—and despite claiming lessons learned as a supplier on the 787—the development schedule soon fell behind. Problems emerged with the cockpit software. The Chinese, assigned the fuselage production, fell way behind. Other challenges came up and so did the costs. The $3 billion budget soon ballooned to $5 billion.

With concurrent development of two corporate jets and neglect of the sales of the CRJ and Q400 programs, Bombardier desperately needed cash flow. It couldn't cover all the commitments. The balance sheet picture was available for all to see, and it wasn't pretty. The company's stock traded between C$1.50 (about $1.19 in the U.S.) and C$2.50, or approximately US$1.99, and credit rating agencies rated the company as CCC—a high-risk bond investment and one which some banks can't buy.

The poor balance sheet and doubts about Bombardier's longevity hung over the C Series like the sword of Damocles. "Customers wanted to know that Bombardier is going to be there 10, 20, 30 years from now in the commercial aircraft space, just like Boeing or Airbus," Scott said. The general global economy also became an obstacle.

The C Series was launched at the 2008 Farnborough Air Show, which was held in July. In September-October, the financial crisis began, precipitated by the collapse of Lehman Brothers in New York. It soon spread across the globe. Financial institutions were collapsing at a rate not seen since the Great Depression.

"The whole world went into a financial crisis and Bombardier with them," Scott said in 2019. "Before that, Bombardier looked great, the balance sheet looked great, the business aircraft was doing well, the CRJs were still doing well, the trains were doing well, but all that started to turn south."

And there was another reason, too. "If you look at when Delta ultimately bought the aircraft [2016]," Scott said, "a lot of the airlines still had time. They could still wait and see how the airplane developed as it moves through design and in the flight test. They could wait and see whether that real airplane was going to deliver on all the objectives that we had set out."

This, as it turned out, is partly why Airbus passed on acquiring the C Series program when approached in 2015. Enders wanted to see the airplane certificated and in service to be sure it wasn't a dud. Leahy was intrigued with the airplane and a potential deal but didn't think it was worth the asking price. Nevertheless, he told Enders, "We could make this aircraft a commercial success."

Burdened by development costs of the Learjet, Global and C Series that were bringing down Bombardier, the Learjet 85 program was canceled in 2015. The lack of sales on the CRJ and Q400 also hurt, depriving Bombardier of desperately needed cash flow. The corporation was in an inexorable decline.

16

Creating Neo

"The engine technology was basically it."
—**KIRAN RAO,** ON A RE-ENGINED A320 VS. A NEW DESIGN

AIRBUS HAD BEEN TESTING THE P&W GEARED TURBOFAN on its A340 test plane but professed little interest in re-engining the strong-selling A320. Few believed this disclaimer. By 2008, Airbus was beginning to wrestle with this decision.

Deciding what to do to improve the A320 family was no easy feat. The C Series posed a threat to the A319, even if Airbus dismissed the plane publicly. Airbus had to decide whether to launch a new airplane program or simply re-engine the A320. The A320 design and technology dated to the 1980s, so in absolute terms, the basic concept still had a lot of life left in it.

During the first decade of the 21st century, Airbus was also swimming in development problems. The A380 was two years late due to the infamous miscues over connecting wiring. The A400M financial and technical disaster was still unfolding. The A350 had had several false starts. The A330 and the A320 were keeping Airbus afloat. The last thing the bean counters wanted was another $10 billion airplane program.

Still, engineers were more interested in a new airplane. Leahy was skeptical. "Somewhere in strategy, people were pushing a new single-aisle," said Leahy. And engineers always want a new aircraft. "What can you get? If you had your 10 or 12 billion, in our case euros, what would you get? The engine is going to be new. What are you going to get out of the airframe? They couldn't get more than about five percent. They would come up with everything, an all-electric airplane,[57] electric brakes, everything under the sun, laminar flow composite wings, and they'd only get about five percent. How do you take 12 billion dollars, you've only got five percent for the airframe, and you're going to try to sell that when your competitor just hangs new engines on?"

Barry Eccleston, an ex-engine guy with Rolls-Royce, made the same argument. It would be the same set of questions over at Boeing, which is why,

---

[57]. This means systems were powered by batteries and generators, not that the power plants were electric.

unbeknownst to Airbus, Boeing was looking at something entirely different. Re-engining was hardly a new idea. Throughout commercial aviation, airplanes had been re-engined dating to the piston engine days. In the jet age, the Douglas DC-8-60 Series became the Series 70 using the CFM56, the first application of this engine on an airliner. Boeing, of course, re-engined the 737 with the CFM56.

"If we moved with the neo, we would be competitive against the C Series, and Boeing would have a tough time to do a neo version of the 737. We all know why that is today.[58] There wasn't technology available to build an all-new airplane. A composite fuselage, composite wing and everything else transferred down to a little airplane, like a 320 or a 737, don't bring you that great an advantage. The engine technology was basically it," Rao said.

"It was a calculated risk that if we allowed Boeing to respond with a new airplane, and we went to the neo, they would come so late and so expensive and the advantages that they would get would not be that great," Rao elaborated. "The decision of the neo was based on that. That Boeing could not launch an all-new airplane."

"You've got to bring something to the market that provides a significant step forward," said Scherer, then head of strategy for Airbus. "If you're going to invest 20 billion [euros] or 15 or whatever it was at the time in a new program, you better have a long technological run. With the technological proposition that you're investing [in], it better create at least a double-digit advantage for your customers."

Scherer couldn't find this leap with a new airplane. "I was a big believer in open rotor engines because at one point, we have to decarbonize to end the dependency of this industry on fossil fuels. Anything that saves fuel is good. Open rotor saves 30, 35, 40 percent if you integrate it well with the fuselage, compared to the then-current turbofan engines, and so we have to study that," he said. But technological challenges hadn't been solved in 2008-10, or even 10 years later.

Boeing and McDonnell Douglas studied open rotors as far back as the 727 and MD-80. It's still being studied today. Noise was an issue. The rotor rotation created noise that wasn't mitigated by a nacelle or shroud. Cruise speed is slower, not much of an issue on 90-minute flights. But the A320 and 737 can fly up to eight hours under the right conditions. The open rotor cruise speed would add time, crew and maintenance costs, which would offset at least some of the fuel savings.

Blade separation is a risk. Jet engine nacelles are supposed to contain fan blade failures and separations, which they usually but not always do.

---

58. Rao was referring to the technical difficulties Boeing had, exposed for all to see because of the two fatal MAX crashes. He was not referring to the accidents or the grounding.

Without a nacelle or a shroud, a blade separation risks fuselage penetration. It was for these reasons that Joe Sutter, the legendary Boeing engineer, once said Boeing would never put an open rotor on an airplane.

When the A320 entered service in 1988, it had advantages over the Classic 737-300/400/500 series. Passenger experience was better on the A320, and so were range and economics. Technology also was much more advanced. The NG airplane was slightly better than the A320 baseline aircraft. The A319 was slightly better than the 737-700; the A321 clearly outclassed the 737-900 and 737-900ER. Overall, the two families were about even, and commercial terms often were the deciding factors in a sales campaign.

"By re-engining the A320, we could regain the advantage the A320 originally had because of the curvature of its geometry, which is more suited for high bypass ratio engines," Scherer said. "That's how it started. Everybody thinks we precipitated it through a decision to equip the A320 with Pratt. That's not true. It was very important for us to make sure that if we re-engined the A320, that our main competitor would do the same thing on the 737. How do you make sure that happened?"

CFM was the exclusive engine supplier for the 737. "CFM had everything to lose if there was a whole new generation of airplanes," continued Scherer. "If CFM could make sure that Boeing was going to re-engine the 737 with a CFM engine, and CFM could secure a deal with Airbus to re-engine the A320 as well, that was the only way GE had to maintain to hold on to their 75 percent market share in this segment."

In early 2010, Enders and Leahy met privately for a small breakfast in Washington with David Joyce of GE and two of his key executives. Recall that GE owned 50% of CFM, so Joyce was also representing the joint venture's interests. It was clear GE didn't want to see an all-new 737 replacement. A re-engined 737 was their strong preference. All agreed a re-engined A320neo was the key to making this happen.

"The whole idea was to maintain a relative status quo because that was in the interest of the two arguably most powerful players in the space, namely CFM and Airbus," Scherer said. "Once I had a deal with CFM, I knew they were going to make absolutely sure they had the same on Boeing's side. That's when I realized we had a winning proposition. The first deal was actually between CFM and Airbus."

Leahy insisted that the re-engined A320 family have a dual-engine choice. "The big issue of the day was should we develop a new single-aisle or should we look at doing a re-engined A320," said Eccleston. "With my engine background, whenever I was back in Toulouse, I would make the point that most of the airplane efficiencies usually come from new engines, and we have new engines available." Airlines needed reliable airplanes that could do six to eight flights a day, day after day after day.

"The last thing you want is the potential failure and all the unreliability that might come with brand new technology," Eccleston said. "So, my argument in Toulouse was, 'Let's keep the airframe and just put the new engine on it. We'll get most of that improvement on the back of the new engine.' Other folks felt it was much more important to develop new technology, develop a new airplane, get a lead on Boeing."

The debate in Toulouse carried on in 2009. Meanwhile, Eccleston met with American, mostly keeping them apprised of where Airbus thinking was on the future single aisle. In 2010, Airbus officials had to fish or cut bait. The real threat was Boeing and their "New Small Airplane," Leahy said. "By 2009/2010, we saw a relatively inexpensive way to substantially improve our product vs. the 737 and also block their NSA by forcing them into the MAX."

"The A320 and 737NG were very similar in performance and price," Williams said. "From a competitor's point of view, you could argue a little bit. The 737-800 has a slightly longer fuselage. There wasn't a real huge competitive advantage between them. You don't have to worry about the smaller C Series. The bigger one is definitely going to be a problem. The seat-mile economics are going to be great. It's a brand-new structural design, and the weight per seat for the structures is going to be far better than the 319. Then they'll rule you out of the 319 market share and eventually, they'll do what Airbus did to Boeing on the 320 vs. 737. That was really the driver behind the whole thing."

Williams' characterization was precisely the argument Boeing used in its dumping complaint to the U.S. Commerce Department against Delta's C Series deal—except Boeing engaged in overkill by suggesting little Bombardier would eventually bring down the entire U.S. aerospace industry if left unchecked.

"The C Series was never going to be a major commercial threat," Leahy said. "If we built the whole neo business case around the C Series, you'd never get the board to go along with it. It was a small, marginal airplane competing with the A319, without a product support network. It was never going to sell well on its own. We had a better airplane when you start looking at a neo. We've got an airplane that has the product support network and which fits into a family. You have people like American and United and British Airways and others who say, 'I want commonality. I don't want several fleet types. What I want is to have an airplane that fits in.'"

Boeing knew the 737NG was reaching the end of its life. The NG was an improvement over the 737 Classic. The engines were upgraded but remained the solid CFM-56. The 737-400 was stretched six feet to become the 737-800, capable of seating 12 more passengers than the A320 in standard LOPA. These 12 seats would give the -800 modest CASM advantage over the A320. By the time the last one was delivered in 2019, around 5,000 had been sold. The 737-700 also sold well; 1,128 aircraft were delivered, 15 more than the -300 model it replaced. The 737-600, a shrink, was a sales bust. The improvement over the 737-500 saw only 69 sales compared with 389 deliveries for the Classic -500. The last four were delivered in 1999.

Boeing developed the 737-900, a stretch of the -800. It had fuselage plugs to increase the capacity, but the extra weight cut its range; the airplane could only fly two-thirds of the way across America. Only 54 of the original -900 were sold. Boeing beefed up the weight and added tanks to create the -900ER, with full U.S. transcontinental range, but field performance of both sub-types was poor. The take-off runway requirement was markedly longer than the -800. It was worse than the A321. The -900ER saw only 505 sales, a mere 7.3 percent of total 737NG passenger orders.

The entire industry knew Airbus was considering re-engining the A320. At the same time, Boeing was designing a clean-sheet replacement for the 737, but Boeing also had a team working on a re-engining design. This was a fallback in case its hand was forced by Airbus. Albaugh, and the then-head of the 737 program, Mike Bair, talked down the thought of re-engining the 737, even as it was being developed. They wanted a new, clean-sheet airplane to replace the 737.

Albaugh held a webcast employee "Excellence Hour" January 14, 2011. During the event, he spoke about the prospect of re-engining the 737. According to a transcript, it was clear he didn't think much of the idea. "I think Airbus will find re-engining the A320 more challenging than they think it will be. When they get done, they will have an airplane that *might* be as good as the Next Generation 737. We think we can continue to make incremental improvements to the 737 to make sure that it is a more capable airplane than even the re-engined A320.

"At the same time, while we haven't made a firm decision, I don't think we will re-engine the 737. It's really hard to come up with a compelling business case to do that. We think the right answer [is] to probably do a new small airplane that might come out toward the end of this decade. We'll make that decision probably sometime in the middle of this year," Albaugh continued. "Every customer I talk to has a real hard time understanding why a re-engined airplane makes sense. Airbus says it will cost them a billion euros to re-engine. My guess is it's going to cost them considerably more than that. The engines are bigger. They are going to have to redesign the wings, the gear. It's going to be a design change that will ripple through that airframe."

Albaugh said that a re-engined 737 gives about a two to three percent economic benefit to the customer. "Right now, in our view, the 737 gives our customers about a five percent or six percent better economic value than the 320. They eat up about half of that with the re-engined 320, and we continue to incrementally improve the 737." Leahy publicly wondered what they were smoking in Seattle.

Boeing nevertheless devoted considerable engineering resources to studying a 737RE, as the re-engine was informally known, as well as an entirely new design. "We were basically keeping the RE effort alive as a stalking horse for the new small airplane effort at that time," recalled an engineer on the program years later. "It was good that we did, too, as we were able to put something together really quickly for that whole American Airlines debacle and get the MAX started as quickly as we did. The new airplane, as it was defined then, was struggling to beat a re-engined 737 from a performance standpoint and–if it contained significant composites–we had no idea how to build it at any kind of 737-like production rate, never mind all the handwringing about the where."

Boeing wanted minimal changes for the re-engine concept, but gaining significant improvements remained elusive. As for the preferred solution, "at that time, they couldn't make up their mind whether it would be a single-aisle or a twin-aisle," an engineer said. At one point, "the wind was blowing toward a new airplane." The 737, he said, was structurally old technology "with a 707 nose on the same-sized body. We could never come up with anything better than a 737 and bring it to life." So, the engineer said, the 737RE was dropped.

Just two months later, in an interview with now-defunct *Aircraft Technology* magazine, Bair also spoke of the prospect and was equally dismissive. He said engineers had figured out how to re-engine the airplane with either the P&W GTF or the CFM LEAP-X. "We've done a lot of work [on the potential of putting a new engine on the 737]," he stipulated. "We understand what the assignment would be if we decide to do that." By this time, Boeing had been through the "concept feasible gate" that validated re-engining could be done. "We figured out a way to get a big enough engine under the wing that even if we had more space, we wouldn't put a bigger engine," said Bair.

He also said the nose gear would have to be lengthened about eight inches, which, in fact, is what happened in the final design. The economic improvements were projected at the low teens, according to Bair. This proved to underestimate the actual benefits, which came in around 15 to 16 percent better than the 737NG after aerodynamic clean-up was finished.

Bair also said Boeing looked at engines from P&W, CFM and Rolls-Royce. The re-engining cost budget was targeted for between $1 billion and $2 billion, Boeing insiders said.[59] Boeing Co. CFO James Bell publicly pegged the cost at about 10 percent of a new airplane, widely believed to be about $10 to $12 billion in the 737 class. Bair said that with few exceptions, when

---

59. Years later, in 2019, a retired Boeing source said the final budget was $3.5 billion. There was constant pressure to reduce the budget. He said $900 million ultimately was cut. Neither figure was confirmed independently.

Boeing showed the 737RE to customers, they asked if "there was something else we can do?"

Boeing thought a new airplane could be ready by 2019 or 2020. "I try to avoid saying 'replace the 737,' because what we're doing is something a little bit different," Bair said. "We're trying to figure out what does the world want in 2030, in 2035? That's when this airplane will be kind of at its prime. On the surface, it's hard to imagine what worked well in 2000 is going to work well in 2030."

While Boeing leaned toward a new airplane but dawdled, Airbus was closing in on its decision to launch the A320RE. "If you looked at where we were with the ceo vs. the NG, we were actually slowly losing market share," Leahy said. It wasn't a 50-50 duopoly. It was 48–52, 47–53 in Boeing's favor, leading up to the launch of the neo. "The 737-800 was a very good aircraft," he would say internally. "We need to respond."

Despite its public rhetoric, Airbus officials were quite aware of this and internally at least, admitted the 737 was probably a little bit ahead of the A320 in maintenance costs. The 737-800 was also probably a couple percent better than the A320 in fuel burn. Plus it had more seats.

"What are we going to do about this?" Leahy said. Airbus needed a 15 percent leap for the A320. Engineers saw they could get there but couldn't see how Boeing would be able to match. "Most of our engineers were assuring us that they couldn't figure out any way that Boeing was going to be able to match the performance of the neo because their engine was going to be smaller, they had the short landing gear, they couldn't figure out what to do with that, etc. Boeing would do something to improve the airplane, but it would never be as much an improvement as we were able to get going from the ceo to the neo."

It was indeed a real struggle but in the end, Boeing was able to get about the same gain over the NG with the 737RE. The successor to the 737-800 still had a small advantage over the A320RE. The A319RE and 737-700RE also were about even, as the latter was originally conceived. But the A321RE became a slam-dunk winner over the re-engined 737-900ER. (There was no larger model in 2011.)

By the fourth quarter of 2010, Airbus decided it would bet on the re-engined approach. In December, Virgin America became the first airline to commit to the new airplane, by now called the New Engine Option, or neo. The legacy family was renamed the Current Engine Option, or ceo. In December, India's IndiGo signed a contract for 100 neos.

After the launch and follow-on orders, with AirAsia's and many others' splashy announcements at the 2011 Paris Air Show, Airbus had more than 1,000 commitments for the neo. But Boeing was still indecisive. The ambiguity was driven in no small part during this era by the continued 787 debacle, which had not entered service at the time.

"What we have done is taken this option [737RE], and it is truly an option, and we've put it on the shelf," Bair said in that March *Aircraft Technology* interview. "We can change our mind and exercise it at any time if we decide if that's the right path, or something happens in the industry that makes it more compelling. It's hard to imagine what that might be."

In July, the month after the air show, that "something" happened. Airbus and American dropped a bomb on BCA headquarters in Longacres and corporate headquarters in Chicago.

17

Launching MAX

"We view this whole affair as [a] triumph for Airbus."
—ROBERT STALLARD, OF RBC CAPITAL MARKETS

WHEN AMERICAN'S ARPEY CALLED BOEING to alert sales that an Airbus deal was about to happen, a "bomb" went off at Longacres. Boeing was still undecided whether to launch a new airplane design to replace or to re-engine the 737. If Boeing wanted a new airplane, there still was no decision whether to go with a twin-aisle or a single-aisle design. Bair and Albaugh wanted a new airplane. More studies had been done in favor of the twin-aisle design than the single aisle.

It is accepted fact in the industry and media, especially at Airbus, that the American deal forced Boeing's hand to proceed with the re-engined 737 rather than build a new airplane. There were questions that hadn't been settled, such as what the starting size of the airplane would be. Boeing indeed was studying such a design, but the focus was on a twin-aisle airplane starting at 180 seats—or slightly larger than the 737-800, which then was typically configured with 162 seats in two classes.

A composite airplane with an elliptical design, with the aim of a cost basis, sales price and economics of a single-aisle aircraft, was the goal. If this sounds like the NMA Boeing considered later, it's not a coincidence. "Imagine that," said a former Boeing executive in 2019 when asked about the similarities.

The code name then was FSA or Future Small Airplane. This later morphed into NSA. Most people viewed this as New Single Aisle airplane, but it stood for New Small Airplane. The new single-aisle design never got beyond the base starting size, or slightly larger than the 737-800, says a former Boeing executive.

But the biggest issue: Boeing couldn't wrap its hands around production. Albaugh said Boeing couldn't figure out how to produce a composite NSA at the production rates necessary to match the 737's. The unidentified Boeing executive interviewed for this book expanded on Albaugh's remarks. "It wasn't a question of achieving the same production rate as the 737, which in July 2011 was 31.5 a month, a far cry from 2019's 52 per month. It was a question of how quickly Boeing could get production up to the 737's rate.

CHAPTER 17 LAUNCHING MAX

"We could be three years later to market with the better airplane," this executive said, "but it would take a long time to ramp up the production to the same level. The airlines couldn't stand for this."

Getting the NSA's cost, price and operating economics down to that of a single-aisle airplane—the same Boeing talking points for the NMA—were key considerations in 2010–11, as they were in 2018 for the NMA, Albaugh and Conner agreed. "Maybe the engineers wanted to do the new airplane and I think it would have been a very good airplane," Albaugh recalled in 2019. "When the analysis was done, the new airplane would have given us around 20 percent improvement on efficiency. We were advertising a re-engined plane with 10 percent to 12 percent improvement, but a lot of people thought we could get more.

"We went out and talked to a lot of airlines. We talked to Southwest, United and American. They all said they wanted the new airplane, but they also said, 'We're really worried about this thing not being on time, and we're worried about the risk of you guys being late, especially in light of the 787 performance,'" Albaugh said. "There was a good chance it would have cost more than we thought because the track record would indicate that everything cost more. The airlines really didn't want to wait that long, so they drove us. A lot of people say that it was the American deal that prompted the decision to re-engine the 737. It was really all three of them."

There were technical issues, too. "There were a lot of risky things," remembered Albaugh. "You think about that, and you compare to 787 where either the Technical Requirements Maturity Level for 787 wasn't real high. The TRL level of the new airplane wasn't real high either. The maturity of the technology was just low." Launching the 737RE, with a 10 percent to 12 percent improvement, to be date certain on delivery (2017), and to be pretty certain of the cost, is what really drove Boeing to make the decision, he said. There was a lot of speculation that, because of the 787 and the 747 programs, with the problems, delays and cost overruns, the board of directors never would have approved another new airplane. Albaugh couldn't confirm this.

"Obviously, I briefed the board of directors on it. I can't recall any specific conversations where they put it that way. Everybody always says, 'It's going to be different this time.' I'm not one of those people. I've had too many train wrecks on development programs to think that would ever miraculously happen as planned. To me, the deciding point really is, could we deliver that new airplane on time, on schedule, on budget? Based on our track record with the 787 and the 747, there was a good reason to think that that wasn't high probability," Albaugh said.

Conner agreed that the airlines wanted airplanes sooner than later. "The customers drove us to do the 737 re-engine. We had two solutions. We had a new airplane, and we had a MAX. The customers wanted it. Sooner was better."

Lest some think this is revisionist history on the part of management, the IAM 751's newsletter, *Aero Mechanic*, reported at the time: "While Boeing executives continued to talk up the all-new airplane option, behind the scenes, customers were telling them they had strong doubts about the company's ability to deliver. Given the problems with the 787 and its reliance on a globally outsourced supply chain and inexperienced manufacturing workers, they didn't believe Boeing could bring its proposed new plane to market on schedule."

"The customers wanted something they could count on, so they pushed Boeing to go that route," said 751 Business Representative Tommy Wilson. Ramping up production would have been a big issue. "We would've had to create a whole new production system because of how many airplanes we're building on the NG at the time," Conner said. "That would have said that you were going to have to put off an all-new airplane that would've been coming into the marketplace in terms of volume. You could have dribbled that for a while, but it would have taken a long time to give the benefit to the marketplace, and the marketplace wanted the benefit."

Conner said he had a different plan. "I presented it, and we got a little off track with the NMA after I left. The airplane evolved into something that was much more than presented. The twin-aisle airplane Bair's team worked on was a three-member family beginning at 180 seats with a more modest range.[60] Conner said his concept "was going to lead to something else. Think about Embraer. I thought about that in 2015." This concept emerged publicly in 2017, when Boeing and Embraer announced they were forming a JV.

Boeing's family would start at 180 seats and Embraer would come in below, down to 100 seats. Each family would have the same flight deck, a feature Airbus adopted with the A320 and subsequent airplanes. Albaugh confirmed the favored new design was a twin-aisle airplane, but Conner said what became the NMA went beyond what was needed.

When American announced its record-breaking order July 20, 2011, Airbus got firm commitments for 260 A319ceos/neos and A321ceos/neos. This was in addition to more than 1,000 firm commitments to the neo that Airbus booked by mid-year. Boeing won an order for 100 737-800s and 100 737-8s. The first ceo deliveries were scheduled only two years hence, in 2013.

Boeing's hometown newspaper, *The Seattle Times*, didn't mince words. The headline said it all: "Big 737 order still leaves Boeing with egg on face."[61]

---

60. Wall Street aerospace analyst Doug Harned of Bernstein Research floated the idea of a 4,000nm twin that more closely overlapped (or succeeded) the A321 and 737-900ER. This sounded very much like the concept Bair's team worked on and the airplane Conner hinted at.

61. https://www.seattletimes.com/business/big-737-order-still-leaves-boeing-with-egg-on-face/

CHAPTER 17 LAUNCHING MAX

A picture from the press conference aptly conveyed Albaugh's feelings. He looked like he had swallowed a lemon. Aerospace reporter Dominic Gates wrote, "Boeing raked in around $10 billion worth of commitments for 200 Renton-built 737s Wednesday. Usually that would be a good day. Yet Boeing Commercial Airplanes chief, Jim Albaugh, was forced to confront analysts' suggestions that the company's product strategy is in tatters."

The Times continued, "'We view this whole affair as [a] triumph for Airbus,' wrote Robert Stallard of RBC Capital Markets. Stallard, surprised that Boeing would unveil its new strategy during a customer news conference alongside Airbus, headlined his note to clients: "A strange way to launch an aircraft."

Gates wrote, "In her note, Heidi Wood of Morgan Stanley called Boeing's strategy 'reactionary.' Boeing's hasty decision to re-engine the B737 is a clear indication of the success and strong competitive positioning of the A320neo." In early 2011, Wood also predicted that Airbus would have 1,000 NEO orders by the 2011 airshow. She was ridiculed in the press and by her Wall Street peers. Actually, Wood slightly underestimated the figure.

Bright, who was a top Boeing salesman when he left in 2004, watched the events in 2011 from afar. In 2019, he recalled that he thought Airbus manipulated Boeing into producing the MAX. "Boeing went from one week saying 'We're building an all-new airplane' to the next week [saying] 'We're just going to do a refresh,'" Bright said. "I think Airbus just played it beautifully.

"I was outside and watching this. I had very close friends at Boeing I was talking to. I had friends at high levels in Boeing, and they were going, 'We're building a new airplane, we're building a new airplane.' And then literally, in about a two-week period, they went from building a new airplane to building the MAX," Bright added. Being outside, he didn't know what new design Boeing was leaning toward, though he said he thought it "looked very much like the NMA."

Aside from the embarrassing American debacle, 2011 was a year when things began to look up for Boeing. On February 24, the Pentagon awarded Boeing the KC-X aerial refueling contract for the USAF. After losing Round Two to the Northrop-Airbus bid, this was a huge victory for Boeing and a bitter defeat for Airbus. The first flight of the 747-8I was March 20. (EIS would be June 2012.) The 747-8F entered service October 12. The 787 finally entered service with launch customer ANA on October 26.

All this good news was overshadowed by another dust-up with labor. Boeing may have had egg on its face over the American deal and being forced into launching the 737RE, but it gave Chicago the chance to nail the IAM 751. It appeared the company was able to get a measure of revenge for the 2008 strike.

If putting the 787's second FAL in Charleston was the first major battle in McNerney's war on the unions, the 737RE was the second—or so many people thought—as they watched events unfold from the outside. Albaugh quickly told IAM 751 and the press that, of course, the 737RE would be assembled on the existing 737 FALs in Renton. McNerney just as quickly said, Not so fast. That decision hasn't been made. It was a stunning statement. It appeared to be a public rebuke of Albaugh and one that made no sense. With two assembly lines in Renton now, and available space for a third, where else would the airplane be completed?

Action on the complaint filed by 751 with the NLRB in 2010 was heating up in the summer months of 2011. The stakes were high for Boeing and the union. The 2008 contract was up in 2012. Talks were slated to begin early that year.

With the threat that the MAX might be assembled elsewhere, 751 put a new contract to vote in December 2011. The percentage of those voting in favor of the contract was 74. The agreement and vote came months ahead of the 2008 contract expiration. Negotiations and votes usually came down to the wire. The new contract extended to September 2016. It guaranteed the MAX production would be at Renton. Production was to go from 35 per month to 50 per month. Part of the agreement included withdrawal of the NLRB complaint.

The union won a two percent wage increase and cost-of-living adjustments, incentive-based bonuses, increases to the formula for pensions, improved insurance benefits and a ratification bonus. It agreed to higher insurance co-pays for premiums. "Boeing's leverage in the talks was its offer of the 737 MAX in Renton, which secures well-paid union jobs," *The Seattle Times* wrote. "The union, for its part, had leverage through Boeing's discomfort with the NLRB case."

How serious was the threat to put MAX into a non-union environment? And what of the public split between McNerney and Albaugh? "Well, it was a good cop, bad cop thing," Albaugh said in 2019. "I'm not sure we had it all that well orchestrated. This was really a three-cushion bank shot. We had the NLRB case we wanted to get settled. We had to make a decision on where to put the MAX, and we didn't want to have any strikes in Puget Sound. I think we got to a place that worked for everybody. The NLRB suit was dropped. We got the MAX with the NG. We got a four-year commitment from the union on no strikes. It worked out for everybody."

Albaugh wouldn't discuss whether the threat to build the MAX elsewhere was real, but a Boeing executive later conceded it made no economic sense to move it. "I was down in North Carolina looking at the GE facility down there. I get this call from my general counsel," Conner recalled. "He said, 'Shit is going to hit the fan,' referring to the conflicting assembly line messages. There hadn't been a decision. Jim McNerney just didn't want to be that quick with that draw.

"I think Albaugh was of the assumption that that's where we do it. It didn't take long for the union to figure out, 'We could have another South Carolina situation on our hands,'" continued Conner. "All McNerney said was, 'Look, we haven't made that decision.' That's all he said. Jim [Albaugh] made an assumption that we would do it. It came out like this big controversy, but it wasn't that much of a controversy."

Was it a case of good cop, bad cop? "I think Albaugh might have got ahead of himself a little," Conner said, laughing. "Then McNerney took it on as the bad cop. At the end of the day, I think they were in total agreement. I think it might have just been a little bit of a mistake on Jim Albaugh's part. Look, I love Jim. I thought he was a great guy. I don't think he totally thought it through at that point, but it worked out fine."

Given the experience and risks Boeing clearly knew about with the Charleston 787 site, why would it take the risk of creating a greenfield site for the MAX? The factory was humming along at a high production volume. The skillset that that the IAM had was long-standing and efficient.

"You wouldn't," remarked Conner. "I completely agree it just made no sense, but McNerney put that little hint of doubt out there. The union goes, 'Holy shit, these guys may be crazy enough or stupid enough, either one, to do something different.' That was the only thing that was ever said, and the union contacted us about doing a deal. They contacted me about doing an extension to the current deal. I said, 'Okay, but we got to address some healthcare costs on this deal.' That's what we did. We got to a deal, no problem. It was really, I would say, one where I felt like 'Wow, what a great win-win.'"

Airbus's gamble had paid off. By forcing Boeing's hand into re-engining the 737 instead of launching a new airplane, Airbus now was the leader and Boeing the follower. Airbus didn't have to commit billions of dollars to a new airplane program. It was one of Leahy's most satisfying wins. It was one of Albaugh's most disappointing defeats.

18

Grounding

"The FAA announced a comprehensive review of the 787's critical systems."
—FEDERAL AVIATION ADMINISTRATION PRESS RELEASE,
JANUARY 16, 2013

BY JANUARY 2013, 50 787-8 DREAMLINERS had been delivered to airlines across the globe. The airplane's service, since introduction on October 26, 2011, had largely been trouble-free. Then on January 7, an empty JAL 787-8, parked on the ramp at Boston's Logan Airport, caught fire. The lithium-ion battery, it would later be determined, overheated, and the fire began. A thermal runaway between battery cells caused the fire to propagate. It took 20 minutes to put the it out. A near-disaster had been averted.

The flight arrived nonstop from Tokyo at 10:15 a.m. Eastern time. All 184 passengers and crew deplaned. A mechanic in the cockpit discovered the smoke emerging from the electronics bay, filling the cabin. The airport fire department personnel had to use infrared equipment to find the source of the smoke and flames. During the event, the battery exploded, causing a flare-up. Had the fire occurred during the 15-hour flight, in all likelihood the aircraft would have been lost and everyone aboard killed.

A March 2012 safety study by Airbus concluded that an in-flight fire may go out of control in eight minutes, and the airplane would need to land within 15 minutes. The study was done as part of an annual safety conference sponsored by Airbus. The presentation pointed to a few minor cargo-hold fires in Airbus aircraft, all of which had been controlled.

The JAL fire initially prompted quick inspections out of prudence by Japan and other airlines. United, which had six 787s in service, reported the next day that everything appeared fine. Given the history of the 787's design and production problems, the test-flight fire and some other niggling issues, a caution flag was raised. But at this point, regulators had little reason to be overly concerned.

All that changed a week later when an ANA 787 made an emergency landing shortly after take-off. Instruments alerted the flight crew to a battery anomaly. The crew declared an emergency, turned around, landed and evacuated the 137 people on board. Smoke was later confirmed to have come from the lithium-ion battery, but there was no fire.

CHAPTER 18 **GROUNDING**

The FAA was quick to act, immediately grounding the 787. Its order only applied to US-registered aircraft (just six, all at United), but regulators elsewhere quickly followed suit. All 50 aircraft then in operation were parked. "As a result of an in-flight Boeing 787 battery incident earlier today in Japan, the FAA will issue an emergency airworthiness directive (AD) to address a potential battery fire risk in the 787 and require operators to temporarily cease operations. Before further flight, operators of US-registered Boeing 787 aircraft must demonstrate to the Federal Aviation Administration (FAA) that the batteries are safe," the FAA said in a press release. "Last Friday, the FAA announced a comprehensive review of the 787's critical systems with the possibility of further action pending new data and information." The FAA's swift action would stand in stark contrast to its belated grounding of the 737 MAX six years later.

The A350 XWB was a few months away from beginning flight testing when the 787 was grounded. It, too, was designed with lithium-ion battery power. However, the 787 had only one, recharged by a powerful generator that sometimes overcharged and overheated the battery. Airbus designed the A350 for two batteries and two charging systems. This way, overcharging and overheating, at least in theory, was avoided.

In response to the 787 battery problems, Airbus said that it would instead use nickel-cadmium batteries for an indefinite time until investigations were completed and safety assured. The 787's battery was designed and produced by a Japanese company. The root cause of the incidents remained a mystery while Boeing worked on a fix.

Some believed the battery was overcharged and overheated. Some believed the cells were too close to each other and didn't have enough protection to prevent thermal runaway in the event of a failure. Whatever the root cause, Boeing's fix was to design a box to contain a fire and a tube to vent the smoke overboard through an outlet in the belly. In other words, the solution was to contain a fire and not prevent one.

Conner, by now BCA's CEO, went to Japan in February to apologize to ANA and JAL for the incidents. The move was not unprecedented, though highly unusual. Apologies are important in the Japanese culture. In 1985, Boeing had offered a formal apology to JAL and Japanese families of victims after a 747 crash in which the aft pressure bulkhead blew out. After a harrowing 32 minutes in which the pilots tried to control and land the tail-less airplane, they ran out of space and the plane, with 520 people on board, crashed into Mount Takamagahara, 62 miles from Tokyo. Only four people survived. Boeing had repaired the bulkhead years earlier, which was cracked from a hard landing. The accident investigation concluded the repair was faulty.

With two 787s experiencing battery events at two Japanese airlines, Conner and the Boeing team held a press conference in Japan to extend apologies. They claimed there had been no fire in the ANA incident, and everything had occurred according to plan. These assertions appeared to be at odds with the known facts. The NTSB and Japanese were still investigating. But there was no question Boeing's press conference was contrary to the policy that parties to an investigation weren't to make statements ahead of a formal hearing. The NTSB criticized Boeing for its public actions and nearly kicked it out as a party to the investigation.[62]

The safety board didn't issue its report until December 2014. Even then, the root cause of the battery events could not be established.[63] The NTSB criticized the level of oversight the FAA exercised over Boeing. Television news channel *CNN* wrote, "The FAA allows Boeing and other qualified manufacturers to use their own employees to confirm that new aircraft components meet safety regulations. They follow specific FAA guidelines and submit to regular checks by FAA officials. Experts say more and more of that self-checking oversight is moving further down the supply chain to subcontractors. NTSB investigators recommended that both the FAA and Boeing 'develop or revise processes to establish more effective oversight' of suppliers," in this case, the battery maker. It was a theme that would reemerge in 2019, following the grounding of the 737 MAX.

The 787 was grounded for 123 days. The previous grounding of a commercial jet had been the DC-10 for five weeks in 1979, following a crash in Chicago of an American Airlines flight. The 787's troubles weren't over. On July 12, 2013, just two months after the 787 returned to service, an Ethiopian 787 parked at London Heathrow caught fire.[64] This time, the fire was in the top of the cabin in the aft end of the airplane. An investigation determined that wiring to the emergency locator transmitter, which sends a signal in the event of a crash, was pinched, causing an electrical short and fire. It was unrelated to the battery issue but coming so soon after the 787 returned to service, it was another black eye.

Six months later, a year and a week after the Boston fire, JAL discovered white smoke and a leaky battery cell on another 787-8, this one at its hub at Tokyo Narita. The airline voluntarily grounded its 787s for further inspection. The airplane was undergoing maintenance at the time. No passengers or crew were on board.

Airbus largely kept quiet about the 787's problems. There is an unwrit-

---

62. https://www.seattletimes.com/business/boeing-faulted-by-ntsb-for-comments-on-787-fix/

63. https://www.cnn.com/travel/article/boeing-787-dreamliner-investigation-report/index.html

64. https://www.forbes.com/sites/grantmartin/2013/07/12/more-trouble-for-the-boeing-787-as-another-dreamliner-catches-fire-in-london/#e36a85d287fa

ten rule that one manufacturer doesn't criticize the safety of a competitor's airplane. For the most part, this is followed, although salesmen have been known to touch on the topic quietly while making sales calls.

Airbus slipped, however. Bregier, then CEO of Airbus Commercial unit, told journalists in January, shortly after the 787's grounding, that Airbus had the back-up plan to use NiCad batteries if necessary. "I'm not going to give any lessons to Boeing," Bregier told *Reuters*. "At the same time, I don't have to take any either, when I think we have done well and have a plan, which allows me to have aircraft flying with batteries that don't catch fire."[65] It was a rare breach of industry decorum.

While Boeing was going through these latest tribulations, Airbus was planning a new attack to counter the 787. Having dropped the A350-800, Airbus had a product gap. The 787-8 had no modern competition in what would later become known as the middle of the market (eventually known as MOM). Sales of the A330 had been unexpectedly strong since the 787 was launched. Even so, the A330 was aging. Despite promoting the airplane as economically competitive with the 787—with highly generous assumptions for the A330 and overly negative ones for the 787—outside independent analysis concluded that, at best, it was a wash. Internally, Airbus officials knew better, too. The far cheaper capital cost of the A330 kept the airplane competitive.

In light of the A320neo's success, Airbus naturally looked at re-engining the A330. "The 330ceo was not going to last, because the 330ceo was so far behind in its economics against the 787 and the 350s," Rao admitted years later. "It was on a different planet compared to the 787s and 350. If we hadn't done the neo, the 330 line would have finished four years ago," he elaborated in 2019. "By doing the neo, it was its last development to squeeze a few more sales out of the aircraft. It wasn't a very expensive development, and we got enough for a launch."

Airbus's public stance was it would sell upwards of 1,000 A330neos. A former Rolls-Royce salesman at the time scoffed, predicting no more than about 400 orders. (Rolls-Royce supplied the engines on the A330neo.) Rao, after he retired, pretty much agreed. "I think the original business case was 500 aircraft, but they won't get that far," he said in a 2019 interview. "As long as you can sell a 330neo at nine-abreast seating, it will beat the pants off 787-9 if you don't need the range on a lot of missions." But the A330 was designed for eight-abreast coach seating. Adding a ninth seat squeezed the customers, resulting in a poor passenger experience.

Rao is currently a consultant to airlines on fleet planning. As a buyer,

---

65. https://www.reuters.com/article/us-airbus-a350-batteries/airbus-says-it-has-a-plan-b-for-a350-jet-batteries-idUSBRE91006F20130201

he has a new perspective. And now, he receives marketing pitches from Boeing. Sales of the A330neo languished for the first several years; Rao admits Airbus fell down selling the airplane. "I don't think the marketing would take the blame for it, but I don't think we pushed hard enough when the 330neo was launched. Even internally, it was seen not as good an airplane as Airbus normally produces. But it could have been, and maybe it still will be."

In 2020, a Boeing executive dismissed the 330neo out of hand. By their analysis, Airbus would have to sell the airplane for $50 million to make it economically competitive with the 787, he said. But Boeing is known to exaggerate, and an independent analysis concluded the figure was closer to $65 million—a price that was well below the $85 million Airbus was selling the 330neo for at the time.

Airbus's prime motive for launching the A330neo was to pressure the pricing on the 787, Rao and Leahy said after they retired. "We knew there'd be a little bit of cannibalization on the A350, but it also hurts the 787," commented Leahy. "We could go after the 787 from two sides. If you want the all-new clean sheet of paper airplane with a 6,000-foot cabin and a 0.85 Mach cruise speed, with good economics, you'd go with the 350 and the all-new wider fuselage, etc., etc. If you want very similar economics but you cruise at 0.82, maybe 0.81, you have the higher cabin altitude, you have the old fuselage, but good economics, you go with the A330neo. The economics on paper look pretty damn good. Why spend all the extra money? That's the argument that we had."

Airbus and lessors who ordered the A330 argued the large customer base and aging fleet supported the A330neo business case. There were more than 100 customers with more than 1,000 airplanes in service. But many of these customers already ordered the 787, reducing or eliminating the likelihood of ordering the 330neo to do the same mission. Other than a cheaper price and commonality, there isn't a lot to recommend the 330neo, even with its 787-vintage engines and newer wing. The basic A330 systems and technology date to the late 1980s. In some respects, the A330neo is to the 787 as the 747-8 is to the A380. And airlines preferred newer to older.

By the end of 2019, Airbus received orders for 337 A330neos. Not all of these would be delivered, given the weak customer quality and, from 2020, the havoc created by COVID-19.

19

The X-Factor

"The A350-1000 drove the 777X."
—**JIM ALBAUGH,** BOEING COMMERCIAL AIRPLANES CEO
WHEN 777X STUDIES WERE UNDERWAY

WHEN AIRBUS LAUNCHED THE A350 XWB IN 2006, it finally had a competitor to the 777-300ER in the 350-1000. The -1000, with 350 passengers, was slightly smaller than the -300ER's 369, in the advertised configurations then used on the Airbus and Boeing websites.

Boeing had an outstanding year in 2012 selling the 777 Classic; 196 were booked, including 44 from Emirates, but Boeing recognized the A350-1000's threat to the -300ER. Airbus touted the A350-1000's new engines, composites and aerodynamics, and noted its airplane was 40 tons lighter than the -300ER. Officials claimed that, on a comparable mission, the -1000 was 25 percent more fuel efficient than the -300ER. Boeing quibbled with the precise number but conceded it was in excess of 20 percent. It was clear Boeing had to do something.

The 777, along with the 737, had been a mainstay of BCA's profits for years. Declining 747 demand prompted development of the 747-8, but it was a sales dud. Boeing took forward loss charges against this program. Albaugh, Carson and others admitted the 777-300ER cannibalized the 747.

Boeing had to respond to the A350-1000. But, like Airbus with its muddled A350 response to the 787 because of other troubled development programs, Boeing's hands were tied, too. The 787 and 747-8 programs were delayed and went billions of dollars over budget. Now, Boeing also had the 737 MAX development on its plate. It also was two years into development of the KC-46A USAF refueling tanker. The last thing it needed was another new airplane program. So, officials decided to develop a derivative, dubbed the 777X. "X" indicated the aircraft was a concept. It would serve to distinguish the new derivative from the original 777 design, which was dubbed the "Classic" by the media and analysts (much to Boeing's annoyance).

"The A350-1000 drove the 777X," said Albaugh. "The 350 was a big airplane that could fly a long way, and it was all composite. We looked at the economics of the 777, and we had to make it more efficient. The way to make it more efficient was a composite wing and the bigger wing. We could have continued to build the all-aluminum 777, but we would have had to severely discount it in order to win in the marketplace."

Boeing quickly ruled out a composite fuselage or an entirely new design. "I don't think we looked at that a lot, but derivative airplanes served the company pretty well. I think that right on the heels of having done the 787, and the issues associated with it, the more conservative approach that it is a better airplane than A350-1000, and the derivative was much less risk," added Albaugh.

At the time, in 2013, Boeing just had gone through the 787 grounding. There was still a backlog of 787s parked around Everett awaiting rework or, in the case of the Terrible Teens, subject to protracted sales efforts and ultimately loss-making discounts. Adding the 777X to the work was either going to be a high-risk new airplane, or a low- (or at least lower) risk derivative airplane. A derivative would also cost billions of dollars less than a new airplane design.

The design and development of the 777X was straight-forward, without the debate, options and indecision that surrounded the 737 MAX. Controversy erupted over where the factory for the new airplane's composite wings would be built and where the 777X's FAL would be located.

The Classic was assembled in Everett. It made all the sense in the world to assemble the 777X there, too. But the need for a new composite wing factory presented McNerney with another opportunity to beat down the IAM 751, as well as hold up Washington state for more tax breaks. It was McNerney's last hurrah in the war on labor, which began with the 2009 decision to put the second 787 FAL in South Carolina. Boeing announced it was going to compete the final assembly site and wing factory across the U.S. The union went ballistic, and state officials cowered.

The legislature quickly passed a bill providing about $8.7 billion in tax breaks over 20 years to the aerospace industry. It was a straightforward extension of the 2003 tax breaks provided for the 787—and which the WTO later found violated its rules. The U.S. appealed the finding to the WTO appellate body but lost. Boeing asked the legislature in early 2020 to withdraw the 787 tax breaks, but those for the 777X, based on the 787, remained in place.

The IAM 751 membership was less pliant. For starters, IAM 751 members officials doubted Boeing was serious about relocating the 777 FAL somewhere else. After the MAX FAL threat, they also were in no mood to go through another round of demands from Chicago to cut health and pension benefits just two years later. But Boeing was serious.

This time around, McNerney was adamant that 751 had to give Boeing relief on the level of funding of the health plan and on the pension fund. "We had this massive pension situation," recalled Conner, who succeeded Albaugh in 2012 as CEO of BCA. "Our pension obligation was $80 billion. It was worth more than the company at that point. It was something that had to be addressed."

CHAPTER 19 THE X-FACTOR

Conner wanted the Composite Wing Center (CWC as it was now known) and the FAL to be in Everett. "We were working with the union leadership at both the International and the Local. I discussed the union negotiations with them. We weren't successful in getting to do the second 787 here, but the respect that we had for each other, I think, was very strong."

Under the IAM's structure, "International" refers to the headquarters operation. "Locals" are the district chapters. IAM District 751 is the Puget Sound (and some other areas) "Local" chapter of the union. District 837 is the Local that represents Boeing's St. Louis workers, and so on. Under the IAM bylaws, International can (and has) overruled Locals in labor negotiations throughout the decades. This became a huge fight between 751 and International as 777X negotiations proceeded.

Conner called the respect "particularly" strong with IAM International because they realized that "We were really trying to get to a position that helped the company and employees, everybody involved, and we're just trying to figure out what to do best. Unfortunately, we had to make decisions about where to go because we couldn't get to a deal" on the 787.

When the MAX came along, the Local and Boeing figured out a solid solution for everybody and passed it very easily. "The 777X comes along, we're working primarily with the International guys because they see this as something that needs to get done," Conner said. "Unfortunately, it got sprung on the Local guys, and in retrospect, I don't think the International guys brought the Local in enough to get that thing through the first time. They didn't give themselves enough time to do it." Boeing bypassed the Local because, Conner said, the International drove these things anyway.

Open warfare broke out between 751 and International. The Local's board voted 18 to 10 to oppose the deal International negotiated. Local leadership and its media team were sidelined by the International. Nevertheless, Tom Wroblewski's pique hit the public domain at a meeting. He called the contract proposal "crap," tore it up and vowed to see if he could cancel the vote—and return to the bargaining table. International overruled him on all counts.[66]

Boeing management, as it had done in the past, completely misread the mood of the union, thinking jobs would trump dismay over the givebacks. Instead, the members were angry at Boeing for what they perceived as a take-it-or-leave-it ultimatum directed at the IAM International, the Local leadership (whom they understandably believed were complicit); the timeline; the terms and conditions; and the element of surprise.

On November 13, the membership rejected the contract by 67 to 33 percent. It was a stunning rebuke by the membership to everyone else in-

---

[66]. Some within the IAM 751 called Wroblewski's move a stunt. They said, in reality, the Local president was quietly supporting International's effort.

volved. Conner issued the Boeing response: "We are very disappointed in the outcome of the union vote. Our goal was two-fold: to enable the 777X and its new composite wing to be produced in Puget Sound, and to create a competitive structure to ensure that we continue market-leading pay, health care and retirement benefits, while preserving jobs and our industrial base here in the region. But without the terms of this contract extension, we're left with no choice but to open the process competitively and pursue all options for the 777X."

In an interview for this book, Conner said that after that first vote, he got personally involved. "I spent a lot of time with the Local union business reps. I spent a lot of time in trying to explain the situation," especially the pension. Conner said Boeing offered to provide financial advisors to assess and explain the pension revisions. He said the union leadership wasn't explaining how the 401(k) and the pension benefits would work together. Conner was swamped with emails. He answered each one.

"I tried to explain to people, I wouldn't be doing this, I wouldn't even be asking the membership to do this if I didn't think this was the right thing for Boeing and the members." Conner remembered. "We were to put ourselves in a position where one, we can maintain our competitiveness, and two, that we can keep growing Puget Sound."

Conner acknowledged that the union leadership and membership saw the demands as a takeaway. "Yes, there was no question about that. But the way pensions were accounted, it was a massive anchor on our ability to reinvest in new products." Boeing wanted to change the pension from a defined benefit plan to define contribution. It was, Conner said, a different form of pension.

Boeing issued a Request for Proposal (RFP) across the country for the wing factory and FAL. States lined up to bid for the business. The company outlined three scenarios:

SITE SELECTION

Scenario 1:

- Wing Fabrication & Assembly, Body Assembly, Final Assembly & Delivery
- Start of facility construction no later than November 2014
- Production start July 2016

Scenario 2A:

- Wing Fabrication & Assembly
- Start of facility construction no later than November 2014
- Production start July 2016

CHAPTER 19   THE X-FACTOR

Scenario 2B:

- Body Assembly, Final Assembly & Delivery
- Start of facility construction no later than June 2015
- Production start January 2018

Boeing set a goal for the 777X EIS in 2020.

PRODUCTION

According to the RFP, production was to begin in July 2016 or January 2018, depending on the site selection scenario chosen. The RFP raised interesting points:

- If production began in July 2016, this represented a four-year timeline to the 2020 EIS.
- If production began in January 2018, this represented a two-and-a-half year timeline to EIS.

"Production" was undefined in the RFP, but typically this means components, not just final assembly. Given a 2020 EIS, it seemed that Scenarios 1 and 2A were more likely than Scenario 2B, but it all depended on how "production" was ultimately defined by Boeing. According to the RFP, the facilities needed to have a production capacity of 10.4 aircraft a month. The 777 Classic was being produced at a rate of 8.3 per month, although Boeing was known to have studied a rate of at least nine per month. Boeing basically wanted the winner to build the CWC and FAL free to Boeing.

A production capacity of 10.4 aircraft per month for the 777 was an odd request, considering the history of the Classic's production rate. Either Boeing was wildly optimistic about the future of the X, or it had in mind other airplanes eventually sharing the buildings. Boeing and GE Aviation publicly claimed a market demand of 1,200 airplanes for the X. However, insiders forecast the demand between 700 and 900. (By 2020, even this seemed wildly optimistic.)

Despite inclusion of the CWC in the RFP, Boeing already was clearing the site where the CWC building would be located. This and other actions tied to the CWC convinced some within 751 that Boeing's threats and RFP were nothing more than scare tactics designed to influence the membership vote.

While Boeing was shopping for a new site, IAM International and Boeing decided to force a second vote on District 751. On December 21, *The Seattle Times* broke the story. District 751 leadership and members were outraged. Not only was International interloping again, a large number of members were already on vacation for the Christmas–New Year's holidays. The vote was scheduled for January 3, the first day back for many from vacation.

Their absence meant most would not have time to assess a revised contract offer, members and 751 leadership complained.

"Because of the massive takeaways, the union is adamantly recommending members reject this offer," the leadership wrote. "Members need to look at the facts of the economic destruction they would live under for the next 11 years—without any opportunity to change those economic proposals or any other provision of the contract. And all of this comes as Boeing is experiencing record profits and backlogs, not to mention the $10 billion stock buyback the Boeing board approved just this last week." The latter move, and its timing, was yet one more example of Boeing's insensitivity to or disregard for optics.

When January 3 came around, the 751 membership voted 51-to 49 percent to accept the contract. There was a huge sigh of relief throughout Puget Sound and in Olympia, the state capitol. Boeing committed to build the CWC and FAL in Everett. Twelve days later, Wroblewski quit as president of the Local, effective January 31. The union leader cited health reasons.

McNerney's long war with the unions, which began in 2008 with the 57-day strike by 751, was over. He hadn't busted the union, but it was neutered. The defined benefit pension was gone. Union members had to pay a portion of their health insurance premiums. Wages were adjusted, and the contract was extended to 2024. There would be no strike for another decade.

While the labor war drama was playing out, Leahy, his sales team and the top executives engaged in their own combat with Boeing. Leahy, as usual, led the charge. The only way Boeing was able to reduce the seat-mile economics sufficiently was to add 40 more seats to the 777-9, Leahy asserted. The A350-1000 was so much lighter that the 777-9 couldn't hope to match the economics without adding a lot more seats, he claimed.

As for the 777-8, despite the Boeing rhetoric that this model was more efficient than the closely sized A350-1000, Leahy said poppycock. The -1000, he claimed, was economically more efficient than both 777Xs.

Independent analysis bore Leahy out. And, when airlines began their analysis, they largely agreed.

The 777X was formally launched in November 2013 at the Dubai Air Show. The "Big Three" Middle East (ME3) airlines—Emirates, Etihad and Qatar—announced orders for more than 200 777Xs. (Lufthansa was the first airline to order the 777X, the model -9, earlier in 2013, but the program wasn't launched until the ME3 orders were announced at Dubai.)

Boeing touted that the 777-9 had significantly more efficient cost on a seat-mile basis than the A350-1000. It was an entirely unfair comparison. The -9 had between 40 to 60 more seats than the -1000, so of course the seat-mile cost was better. But the lighter -1000 beat the -9 on trip costs. This, too, was unfair. The -1000 didn't compete with the larger -9. Airbus didn't have a direct competitor to Boeing's 425-passenger airplane. This was why Air-

CHAPTER 19 THE X-FACTOR

bus studied the A350-2000. "One day, they will build it," Leahy said recently.

Boeing also promoted the 777-8 as more efficient than the -1000. This was a fairer comparison, as these were roughly the same size. (The 777-8 capacity was 350 passengers to the -1000's 369.) But the -8 was a significantly different airplane, too.

Designed as an up-gauged replacement for the 301-passenger 777-200LR ultra long-range airplane, the 777-8 had an advertised range of 8,730nm. The -1000 then was less than 8,000nm. (Changes a few years later boosted the advertised range to 8,700nm.) The 777-8 is heavier than the -1000 and, despite Boeing's claim that it's more economical than the -1000, independent analysis concludes otherwise.

The 777-8 is a highly niche aircraft for ultra long-haul routes, a requirement for only about five percent of the markets. In the history of commercial aviation, similar planes, dating back to the Douglas DC-8-62 right through the 777-200LR, didn't sell more than 100 models. Net of cancelations, there were, in 2020, only about 35 orders for the 777-8.

By 2020, seven years after launch and the original targeted EIS date, the global market had changed. Deliveries of the 787 and A350 were well underway, with hundreds of each in service. The 737-8 MAX entered service in 2017; it could fly eight-hour missions. The A321LR and XLR were capable of 10-hour flights. These options further fragmented the service need to route passengers to hubs that connected to the 777-9. Route fragmentation was the very foundation of the 787 business case, which undercut the A380 and 747-8. Now, it undercut the business case for the 777X.

More than 70 airlines were active operators of the 777 Classic, before COVID-19 grounded the world's fleet. Boeing sold more than 1,500 Classics over the life of the program. The A330ceo, 787 and 747 programs come close among wide-body airplanes, with 1,486, 1,510 and 1,571 sales, respectively—the latter over more than 50 years. But by 2020, only eight airlines ordered the 777X.[67] At its peak, Boeing recorded 344 orders. By 2020, this dropped to 304 by 2020 because of cancelations—and some of these were iffy.

Initially, the ME3 airlines accounted for more than 70 percent of the 777X orders. These airlines—Emirates, Etihad and Qatar—signed up for 150, 60 and 25 orders, respectively. Lufthansa, the first airline to place an order, committed to 20 firm orders, plus options. Cathay Pacific Airways ordered 21, but this was part of a deal in which Boeing bought back 747s. Emirates eventually reduced its order to 115. Clark, Emirates' president, said even some of these might get canceled in favor of the 787. Etihad ran into financial problems and said it would take only six of the 25 it ordered. As

---

67. There also was one unidentified customer, believed to be an airline, also in the Middle East.

finances worsened, those close to the carrier indicated Etihad didn't even want these.

Cathay Pacific deferred its order to 2025 and beyond, following the COVID crisis. But its orders became suspect before the pandemic because of the democracy movement upsetting local air travel demand. What's more, Lufthansa was becoming squishy on its order before the pandemic, though it wasn't expected to cancel.

There is no question the 777X was the final blow to the 747-8 and A380, both of which were already dying programs. The future of the 777X may be similar to the 747 or A380—in other words, a plane too big for a changing market.

With sales stalled, cancelations coming in and a changing marketplace, the future of the 777X began to rest with the potential of the 777-8F, the third model conceived for the line. The new-build freighter market is a miniscule but important niche compared to passenger airplane demand. It's one that Boeing has "owned" since the 707.

Boeing offered a new-build freighter for every 7-Series airplane except the 787. Airbus offered a new build freighter for the end-of-life A300-600R and the A330-200. The A330F was a disappointment; only 41 orders were recorded. (This is the basis of the A330 MRTT refueling tanker, however, with additional sales.) Airbus killed development of the A330-900F in post-COVID cost reduction. In 2021, Airbus began showing airlines and lessors an A350F concept that generally met with favorable response.

With the program termination of the 747-8F set for 2022, the 777 was the star of Boeing's freighter line. There were 254 orders for the 777-200LRF since the first in 2005 through August 2020. This compares with 233 767Fs from 1993 through August 2020 and 390 for the 747 over the entire life of the program, starting with the first orders in 1966. There were 138 orders for the 747-8F. Development of the 777-200LRF cannibalized the 747-8F.

The 747-8F had great volume space, but the economics no longer worked, a Boeing insider admits. "The name of the of the game going forward is twin engines. Even if you take the metal-wing 777 Freighter, you'd have to get to 80 percent of an 8F load before you can start being in the economics of the 777 metal wing. How often do you operate at 80 percent? That's why there are a limited number of folks who fly the 747-8F today vs. the 777F. In terms of the numbers, it just makes more sense."

The 777-8F, if and when it comes about, nevertheless faces its own challenges. The freighter is slightly longer than the 777-8 but shorter than the -9. The fuselage lengths are:

- 777-300ER: 239.75 feet
- 777-8P: 224 feet
- 777-8F: 227.5 feet
- 777-9:   246.75 feet

On its face, having three fuselage lengths on the 777X assembly line seems unnecessary. Why not simply build a freighter version of the 777-8P? The choice came down to favoring payload or range, said a former Boeing salesman who was assigned to the X program. A freighter based on the -8P maximized payload; a slight stretch maximized range.

If Boeing wants to retain its leadership in the freighter sector, it has no choice but to launch the -8F. Standards published in 2017 by ICAO, the International Civil Aviation Organization, limiting emissions means the 777-200LRF and 767-300ERF won't comply—and production must cease from 2028.

In an era of e-commerce, a freighter tends to max out by volume before weight, favoring range, but Boeing hasn't been able to line up a launch customer for the 777-8F. Absent an active freighter program, the future of the 777X has a very dark cloud over it.

20

Smashing a Bug with a Sledgehammer

"The CS100 could bring down Boeing and the entire U.S. aerospace industry."

—BOEING, IN ITS 2017 TRADE COMPLAINT
TO THE U.S. DEPARTMENT OF COMMERCE

IN JANUARY 2016, THE FIRST A320neo WAS DELIVERED to the first operator, Lufthansa. The same month, the first flight of the 737 MAX occurred. In February, Air Canada ordered 45 CS300s from Bombardier. In April, Delta ordered 75 CS100s, and Air Baltic converted options for seven CS300s to a firm order. It was a great start to the year for the Canadian manufacturer. These three deals had to be done at low prices to finally give sales a new, dramatic boost. Bombardier took a $500 million "onerous contract" charge against these transactions, believed to be mostly associated with the Delta deal.

These C Series deals would bring the wrath of Boeing down upon it. Although Albaugh initially dismissed the threat of the C Series and vowed to compete by dropping the price on the 737-700, Bombardier proved to be more than a passing irritant.

Bombardier was, by 2016, struggling to win orders for the C Series, a full eight years after launch. The airplane had run $2 billion over budget, and it was two years late entering service. Stressed by the cost overruns; the simultaneous development of the new Learjet and the latest Global corporate jet models; declining sales of the Q400 and CRJ regional airliners; and problems in the train division, Bombardier was in serious financial trouble.

Bailouts came in the form of more than $2 billion from the Quebec Provincial government and the quasi-governmental Quebec Pension Fund. The order from Air Canada, which previously favored the Embraer E190 [E1], for 45 CS300s was a strong shot in the arm. In exchange, Air Canada leveraged the federal government's desire to save Bombardier and the C Series in order to release the airline from obligations for Western Canada jobs, dating to its take-over of bankrupt Canadian Airlines International.

Delta provided the boost to the program Bombardier needed. The Air Canada deal, while an important blue-chip airline, was seen by many as a "house" deal prompted by the government. Delta, on the other hand, was a straight-up transaction driven by commercial terms.

CHAPTER 20 **SMASHING A BUG WITH A SLEDGEHAMMER**

Earlier, Bombardier missed selling the C Series to United when Boeing swooped in at the last minute, selling 25 737-700s. Embraer offered the E195-E2 in competition with Bombardier. At the time, Bombardier and Embraer thought Boeing sold the 737-700 to United for about $24 million per airplane. United said this figure was wrong, and Boeing, understandably, declined comment. Years later, another Bombardier official suggested the price was $23 million.

Whether it was $23 million, $24 million or some other number in this range, Boeing dropped the price to rock-bottom to block Bombardier from gaining entry at one of the world's largest airlines and in the lucrative U.S. market. But this deal wasn't just for the 737-700. United was a big customer for the 787. In 2015, it placed its first order for the 777-300ER, at a time when Boeing was struggling to bridge the production line between the 777 Classic and the 777X. Over the course of the next couple of years, Boeing returned to United to fill more -300ER orders.

The 737-700 deal included some nexus, never specifically described, to other Boeing deals. It's believed that Boeing lowered the price of 787s and also granted more pricing concessions for the 777. All the aircraft were powered by GE or CFM engines. Some concessions on pricing and/or maintenance contracts also were possible. There probably also were contract provisions to swap the -700 order for the MAX. Swaps are not uncommon in contracts, and it wasn't too long before United swapped to the 8 MAX. Later still, these aircraft were swapped for the 9 MAX.

Whatever the Boeing deal, John Slattery, the CEO of ECA, cried foul. He could not compete with the government "subsidized" C Series, he complained. Although Embraer didn't compete for Delta's business—the airline sought only used E190s as part of its RFPs—Slattery's market intelligence heard that Bombardier offered Delta "a very low price," as it did with Air Canada. He pointed to Bombardier's $500 million onerous contract charge as proof.

Boeing responded to Delta's RFP by offering a combination of E190s it took as trade-ins from Air Canada and 717s. It did not offer new 737-700s or the 737-7. When Delta ordered the 75 CS100s, with options for 50 convertible to the CS300, Boeing nevertheless had enough of Bombardier. At long last, Boeing recognized the threat the C Series presented to its smallest jetliners. It wasn't as if Boeing wasn't warned. In an opinion column published in March 2005, an analyst wrote that Bombardier's proposed airplane would be a threat to the low end of the single-aisle market.[68]

---

68. The prediction was premature. The article pointed to the original C Series 2005 concept, the one that Bombardier Commercial Airplanes president Gary Scott concluded wasn't good enough and shelved. The redesigned version, the one that

In 2019, Conner said that its analysis concluded Bombardier had contracted with Delta to sell the CS100 for a mere $19.6 million, including credits (or about $23 million, excluding credits, according to filings with Commerce). Boeing filed a price-dumping trade complaint in April 2017 with Commerce, shortly after Donald Trump was sworn in as U.S. president.

Trump, who made unfair trade one of his signature campaign issues, previously criticized Canada as an unfair trading partner in the areas of milk and soft wood, among others. Shortly after he took office, Trump slapped 20 percent tariffs on wood imported into the U.S. This especially affected the Pacific Northwest, which benefitted from logging in British Columbia. Trump also renounced NAFTA, the North American Free Trade Agreement, of which Canada, the U.S. and Mexico were signatories.

Conner said Boeing—having fought Airbus over illegal subsidies off-and-on since 1992 and constantly since 2004—only saw another government-subsidized airplane program coming from a bailed-out manufacturer "dumping" airplanes into its core U.S. market. Whatever the merits of the Boeing complaint, which many debated, Boeing went over the top in its citations. In a classic case of using a sledgehammer to smash a bug, the complaint painted a picture of looming calamity if Bombardier went unchecked.

Boeing claimed that the price of $19.6 million (a figure Bombardier and Delta each said was "millions" low) for the CS100 would migrate to the CS300, which competed directly with the 737-700 and 737-7. This would put pricing pressure on these airplanes, which in turn would depress prices on the 737-800 and 737-8, Boeing's lawyers wrote in the complaint. The 737 was Boeing's top moneymaker, accounting for some 40 percent of the profits. If the 737 profit margins were cut sufficiently, Boeing's lawyers claimed, The Boeing Co. would fail and drag down the entire U.S. aerospace industry. It was a preposterous scenario. Critics were quick to roll their eyes and jump on the arguments.

By 2017, the 737-700 was no longer a big seller in the 737NG portfolio. Airlines migrated to the larger 737-800 and -900ER. Even Southwest, the largest operator of the -700, swapped its remaining orders for the -800, and only a few -700 orders remained on Boeing's books. The -800 and -900ER were being superseded by the 8 and 9 MAXes. Boeing already had a backlog of more than 3,000 MAXes, the fastest-selling airliner in Boeing's history.

Furthermore, Bombardier teetered on bankruptcy until the government bailouts and even now had only a CCC credit rating to Boeing's AAA. Boeing posted nearly $100 billion in revenues, while Bombardier was less than 20 percent of this. The amount of cash Boeing paid in stock dividends and buy-

---

finally went into production, didn't come along until 2008. https://www.seattletimes.com/opinion/look-out-boeing-here-comes-bombardier/

CHAPTER 20 SMASHING A BUG WITH A SLEDGEHAMMER

backs could have bought Bombardier many times over; its stock price was lucky to hit C$2 (approximately US$1.59), and its market cap was peanuts.

As a matter of principle, a subsidized competitor, Boeing, probably was on solid ground for a complaint before the WTO. But the Airbus WTO process already had taken 13 years. By 2021, the WTO had disposed of all but a few details in appeals—17 years after the complaints were filed. No resolution would be forthcoming any time soon if Boeing and the USTR went to the WTO. Brazil filed a complaint with the WTO. Four years later, no action had been taken.

The Commerce complaint could be resolved in a matter of months. Bombardier officials were gobsmacked by the complaint since Boeing hadn't competed for the Delta deal with a new airplane. Industry observers agreed. Furthermore, Boeing was in the middle of a campaign at Delta, trying to sell the 737-10 MAX and competing with Airbus, which offered the A321neo. Up to then, Delta had not ordered either the MAX or neo. It had ordered the A321ceo and 737-900ER, however, so neither Airbus nor Boeing was thought to have an advantage. Why, many asked, would Boeing risk antagonizing Delta in the midst of this competition?

There were several theories. One was that Boeing looked long-term and simply wanted to kill the C Series. Two sources close to Boeing's thinking, separately and in virtually identical language, told *Leeham News* that if Boeing denied Bombardier the U.S. market, with the largest potential, Bombardier would have to kill the program.

Gary Scott, the former president of Bombardier Commercial Aviation and a former career Boeing employee, was long gone from both companies by the time the complaint was filed with Commerce. But knowing Boeing as he did, he suggested Boeing was sending a message to China, as did a retired Boeing officer also watching from the outside.

One theory suggested that Boeing was fronting for Embraer, which had no standing in the U.S. to file a complaint because it was a Brazilian company. This picked up steam when news broke the following October that Boeing and Embraer were discussing a merger.

Conner dismissed these theories. Boeing at the time felt it was competing in a world against subsidized Airbus and Bombardier, with China and Russia also being state supported. "We didn't do anything on Airbus until they were off and running and totally up to speed," Conner said. "Bombardier was just another extension of governments supporting businesses that weren't necessarily viable on their own, using pricing and subsidies to reduce pricing to win market and establish themselves in a non-competitive fashion."

There was concern within Boeing that the complaint against Bombardier involved Delta. The concern was not confined to Longacres, however; Chicago shared the worries. "I think [CEO] Dennis [Muilenburg] and team felt it was important to establish that kind of a precedent around further subsidized manufacturers coming into the marketplace," said Conner.

BOEING LOSES DELTA

Delta ultimately selected the A321neo over the 10 MAX. There was a lot of speculation that the trade complaint, which was still underway when Delta made its mainline jet decision, tipped the scales to Airbus. Delta and Conner say this wasn't the case.

An officer at Delta said the competition slightly favored the MAX. But part of Delta's business model is a heavy emphasis on licenses to perform maintenance, repair and overhaul for its own fleet, and also for third parties. Delta said P&W was willing to expand its MRO deal already in place for the C Series GTF engines to the A321neo. CFM, the sole-source provider for the engines on the MAX, was unwilling to grant Delta the terms it wanted. So Delta chose the A321neo.

Conner took a larger view. "This [complaint] wasn't about Delta. I think the Delta guys knew that. The rumor mill had it that Ed [Bastian, the Delta CEO] was supportive of trying to do a Boeing deal. I think he felt like they had become unbalanced in their fleet."

Conner said he told the Delta people at the Commerce hearing that the complaint was about unfair, subsidized competition. It was an argument Delta should have understood. At the time, Delta was leading the charge against Emirates, Etihad and Qatar being unfairly subsidized. Delta also led the charge to kill U.S. Export-Import Bank financing of Boeing airplanes to these three carriers. Just as Boeing got mugged in Delta's Ex-Im campaign, Delta was innocently standing on the street corner when Boeing drove by to gun down Bombardier.

"I think it was sending a message to everybody," Conner posited. "Whenever you do things, think about the bigger, broader picture like this and on the world stage. I think maybe that was a consideration at that point." This begs the question, why hadn't Boeing filed a trade complaint with the WTO against China for subsidizing the ARJ21 and C919? Conner said there hadn't been competitive sales where there had been visibility on pricing. All the C919 sales have been "directed" sales, he remarked. Conner didn't think the United deal was involved in the decision to file the Commerce complaint, although Boeing referenced the deal in its filings. "It was the dumping [at Delta]" that drove the decision to file the complaint, Conner said.[69]

---

69. In 2021, the EU and U.S. agreed to a five-year standstill of the 17-year WTO complaint between them over the Airbus and Boeing subsidies. Part of the agreement was that the two countries would finally join to begin looking at the subsidies

CHAPTER 20 SMASHING A BUG WITH A SLEDGEHAMMER

Leeham News was told by a former United executive in September 2019, long after the United deal, that the C Series had been nothing more than a stalking horse to suck Boeing into a low-priced offer. United officials never intended to buy the C Series, he said. At the time, the 737-700 was the desired airplane all along. But another United official, directly involved in the events, said the C Series wasn't a stalking horse. Boeing's global deal simply presented a better overall transaction. United later swapped the -700 order for the -8 MAX and still later swapped this order for the -9/10 MAX as priorities shifted.

BOEING'S MISSED OPPORTUNITY

During the Commerce proceedings, news emerged that Bombardier approached Boeing about buying the C Series program before Boeing filed the dumping complaint. Conner confirmed this years later. Boeing thought the airplane was a good, solid design. But it competed with the 737-7, and the systems and cockpit design didn't fit with Boeing's product line. It was more compatible with Airbus than with Boeing.

"We looked at it very seriously," Conner said. "I commend Bombardier. They put together a really good machine. But it wasn't a $19 million or $20 million machine. I know what they did to get a foothold, but the Canadian government kept them alive throughout this whole process. They took the subsidies and put it into a campaign and prices that weren't even in the realm of reasonable."

As the complaint wound its way through Commerce, the industry was stunned when Airbus and Bombardier announced a deal, whereby Airbus would acquire 50.1 percent of the program for US$1. Bombardier would pay for construction of an FAL in Mobile and cover up to $700 million in losses. It was the sweetheart deal of the century. Bombardier was shopping the program; Conner and Boeing knew it. But "in my wildest dreams did I think they would do it for what they did? No," Conner recalled in 2019.

Under the U.S. process, the complaint was first filed with the International Trade Commission, or ITC, to determine if there were grounds to proceed to Commerce. The ITC agreed that it at least merited further investigation. Bombardier was resigned that it was going to lose at Commerce, especially under the Trump administration's anti-Canada, anti-trade policies. And it did.

But the proposed tariff was a shock to everyone involved. At Boeing's urging, considered by observers to be typical Boeing overreach, Commerce announced a levy of 292 percent. This, of course, would render it impos-

---

the Chinese government gave its aerospace industry, including COMAC, which was developing airplanes directly competitive to Airbus and Boeing.

sible to import the C Series into the U.S., thus achieving Boeing's desired outcome of killing the U.S. market for the airplane.

From there, the case went to the U. S. Court of International Trade (CIT) to determine if Boeing suffered "harm," a required element to allow the tariff to be imposed. Observers concluded that the CIT would almost certainly rule in Boeing's favor.

Thus, the industry was stunned again when the CIT ruled against harm. Not only that, it was a unanimous 4–0 ruling. Bombardier was off the hook. In 2019, Conner acknowledged that the CIT's ruling of no harm to Boeing in the Delta deal was true. "But this was more about the future. If we had been allowed to provide a proposal, maybe that would have been a different story. But we complied with the RFP."

Bombardier's sale of the C Series program to Airbus reset the competitive landscape. By 2016, market demand for the smallest Airbus and Boeing jets, the A319neo and 737-7, was virtually non-existent. Boeing delivered 1,128 -700s. Airbus delivered 1,486 A319ceos, but only a few dozen each of the MAX 7 and A319neo were ordered. The "heart of the market" clearly had moved up to the A320 and 737-800/8.

Nature abhors a vacuum. So does aviation. Airbus and Boeing didn't see a big market for the 100- to 150-seat sector. Embraer's E-Jet was in this sector, and Bombardier, needing to replace the aging CRJ design, took the leap with the C Series. Although Bombardier forecast a 20-year demand of 7,200 airplanes in this sector—a forecast some considered wildly optimistic—the C Series nevertheless was the only new design.

For Alain Bellemare, the ex-United Technologies executive brought in to save Bombardier, selling control of the C Series to Airbus could have been bittersweet. "Bittersweet? I think that it's a proud moment. It's a real proud moment. Think about that," he said when asked about the deal at the groundbreaking in Mobile by Airbus for the new A220 assembly line.

"In 2015, people were asking me about the future of the program. We are here four years later, and nobody's talking about that. The backlog is solid. You've got Delta, you've got JetBlue, you've got AirBaltic, you've got Air Canada, you've got Swiss and you've got Korean in the backlog," Bellemare said "Now, we're building or expanding our global footprint by building right here in the U.S., which is a huge market, a huge market. We're getting closer to customers because now we have the volume to be able to do that. Also, it shows that it's a great aircraft. It is the best aircraft. I've been saying that for four years straight. There's nothing else even close to it in the 100- to 150-seat class, nothing, nothing."

Did Bombardier have to do the Airbus partnership to really give it the boost that it needed? "We had to. It's clear," admitted Bellemare. "We didn't have the balance sheet to support this growth. Time will prove that this is going to create tremendous value for everybody."

CHAPTER 20   **SMASHING A BUG WITH A SLEDGEHAMMER**

Well, not everybody. Bombardier remained in such bad shape that it couldn't live up to its end of the partnership in covering program losses for the next several years, nor fund the construction of the Mobile FAL. Airbus eventually bought out Bombardier's remaining shareholding in the partnership and, in 2020, the remaining C Series-focused parts and supply business. Bombardier sold the Belfast wing manufacturing plant to Spirit Aerosystems, which wanted to diversify its exposure to Boeing.[70]

Enders, who rejected an offer for the C Series in 2015, grabbed it this time. It was a 180-degree change. The sweetheart deal Bombardier offered Airbus to take majority ownership of the program was too good to pass up. "It didn't transpire [in 2015] because I felt that was more feeling than on data," Enders recalled. "I felt that it was not the right time. There were still too many risks on that program. It hadn't been certified yet. There was no customer feedback. Obviously, there were considerable development costs.

"There were perhaps additional costs, which I think Bombardier grossly underestimated. When talks leaked out, I used that as an opportunity to say, 'No, let's stop that.' It's too risky. We have enough risk. At the time, we were in the early days of a 350 ramp-up and the A400M jet," said Enders. Airbus also had just decided to launch the A330neo. "We had our hands full, and we said we don't need to stumble into another financial disaster," he pointed out.

In the summer of 2017, Enders got a call from Eccleston. "Tom, I had a call from the Canadian Ambassador here in Washington," he said. Canadian officials wanted Airbus to talk with Bombardier about buying the C Series. "Well, that's strange," Enders thought. "I don't think it will lead anywhere, but if the Canadian government asked us to look at it again, we cannot be rude and say, well, we won't, so we will talk to them. But I don't think it will amount to anything."

Enders and his strategist, Patrick de Castlebajac, met Bombardier CEO Bellemare and his advisor, Henri Coupron (who was a former Airbus executive) in Paris. Enders put an offer on the table: $1 for 50.01 percent of the program, assumption of costs for the next few years and money to build an FAL in Mobile. Bombardier's reaction was, you can't be serious. But instead of rejecting it, they followed through. There was zero risk to Airbus.

By September, the Airbus board greenlit the deal. Canadian politicians in parallel made it clear that they were fully supportive. "Stupid Boeing had opened the barn doors for us on this one as well," Enders said. "They treated Bombardier very arrogantly. Bombardier went to Boeing. They sent

---

70. Unrelated to Airbus, Bombardier separately sold the Q400 program to Canada's Longview Partners, the CRJ program to Japan's Mitsubishi and its train division as well, shrinking to only its corporate jet business.

them away. I think it was only then, probably, the Canadian government picked up the phone and called us."

As for the agreement to build an FAL in Mobile, Enders said this was triggered by Boeing's trade complaint with Commerce. "If the Boeing complaint hadn't existed, I think that putting the C Series into Mobile would have been a non-starter politically," he elaborated in 2019. "I don't think that Bombardier would have suggested that. With that complaint, it's made a lot of sense. Still, these were difficult discussions with the Canadian side. It was blatantly obvious that this could be a solution."[71]

When word leaked in October 2017 that Boeing was negotiating to take over Embraer, many concluded this was in reaction to the Airbus C Series deal. And some concluded the E2 jets didn't fully solve Boeing's gaps at the low end of the market.

---

71. In the trade complaint, Boeing actually pointed to A320s assembled at the Airbus Mobile plant as U.S.-made, in contrast to the Hamburg- and Toulouse-assembled airplanes. And when the Trump administration slapped tariffs on Airbus aircraft imported from Europe, the Alabama-assembled airplanes were initially exempt, despite the fuselages, wings and other major components coming from Europe for assembly in Mobile.

21

The Boeing-Embraer Joint Venture

"It certainly cleared the decks in terms of who to partner with."
—**RAY CONNER,** FORMER CEO OF BOEING COMMERCIAL AIRPLANES

DID AIRBUS PROMPT BOEING to do the Embraer transaction? Conner says, not really. But for Embraer, the deal clearly was the motivator. Boeing had been in discussions with Embraer for "quite some time around different ways to partner. The relationship with Embraer went back years," he said.

In fact, Embraer was geared up to partner with Boeing on the development of what was known as the NSA, or the New Small Airplane, in 2011 when Boeing launched the MAX instead. Initially, Boeing wanted to buy Embraer's commercial and defense units. Push-back from the Brazilians revised this to creating a JV for ECA and, eventually, a second JV just for the KC-390 multi-role tanker transport.

The commercial JV, which would be named Boeing Brasil-Commercial (BBC), would be 80 percent owned by Boeing and 20 percent owned by Embraer. Boeing got the right to name the board and management. Slattery, CEO of ECA, was picked as the CEO of BBC.

Sixty percent of Embraer's services unit—that portion supporting the E-Jets—also came with the JV. The KC-390 JV was a 51 to 49 percent ownership split in favor of Embraer, but Boeing would be in charge of marketing the airplane worldwide. Boeing agreed to pay, in cash, $4.2 billion for ECA. A special dividend of more than $1 billion would be paid by Embraer to its shareholders out of these proceeds.

Boeing and Embraer touted the deal as competitive to the A220 strategy. Embraer had a new family of commercial airplanes to bring to Boeing: the E2-Jets. As a group, these slotted in nicely, on paper, below the 737 family. By then, Boeing had refined the 7 MAX slightly, increasing the passenger capacity from 126 (two-class) to 138 to boost sales. In doing so, the 7 MAX became a shrink of the 8 MAX, instead of a re-engining of the venerable 737-700. From a production standpoint, the -700 was sufficiently different from the 737-800 (and therefore the 7 MAX from the 8 MAX), adding complexity and costs to the final assembly. By making a shrink of the 7

MAX, commonality was increased for production—but design optimization suffered.[72]

The E2 family included the 76-seat E175 E2, the 105-seat E190-E2 and the 122-seat E195-E2 (two class). The 7 MAX was barely selling in its original form. The redesigned, slightly larger 7 MAX (derisively called the 7.5 MAX by some) did no better.[73] This left a big gap between the 122-seat E195-E2 and the 175-seat 737-8. By contrast, the A220-100 seated 110 passengers, the A220-300 seated 135 to 149 passengers (as did the A319neo) and the A320neo seated 160 passengers (two class).

The Boeing-Embraer messaging about the E2 slotting in perfectly below the 737-7 was marketing hype, and the E2 wasn't even the top reason for doing the deal. Randy Tinseth, vice president of marketing at the time, told a closed-door conference in Seattle in September 2018 that the reasons Boeing wanted Embraer were, in order, the services business, the engineering talent, the KC-390 and finally, the E-Jet. One of the attendees promptly shared these reasons with *Leeham News*.

Conner, when told about this in 2019, swapped the priorities slightly. The engineering resources came first and the services second. "I'd say the E2 was at the bottom," Conner confirmed. "What we were thinking about were possibilities of the future." The future was, at the time, the NMA. Conner was impressed with Embraer's technical and engineering capabilities.

"Embraer's got good engineering resources and are able to do things at a lower cost," he said. "I liked how they were able to design and produce airplanes at a relatively less expensive way than we were able to—and in a more efficient way. They do a good job. They are very capable." Discussions between the two companies over how to cooperate had been going on for years, Conner added.

In 2017, the E175-E2 was stillborn, due to restrictions of the U.S. pilot contracts called the "Scope Clause." Scope limits the seats, the number of airplanes that can be operated by U.S. airline regional partners and the weight (size) of the airplanes. It was the latter that created the problem for the E175-E2: Its weight exceeded the 86,000 lb. limit by about 2,000 lbs. And the unions weren't willing to change.

The E195-E2 and the E190-E2 became the viable E2 jets, but the market

---

72. Boeing faced a similar production mismatch between the 787-8 and the 787-9/10, which it would finally begin addressing in 2018.

73. It wasn't until 2021, after the MAX grounding was lifted, that the 7 MAX got a sales boost from Southwest. The carrier ordered 100 with the prospect of more to come. Albaugh had it right when he said there were essentially no other customers for the 737-700, the forerunner of the 7 MAX. So far, only Southwest, WestJet and a start-up Canadian airline are identified customers for the airplane.

outside the U.S. favored the E195-E2 by a wide margin over the E190-E2. This left Boeing with the potential for "a family and a half" after the E-Jet integration.[74] Conner downplayed the conventional wisdom that Boeing pursued the JV because of the Airbus-C Series deal. "I'm not sure the C Series deal was the action to move it forward. It certainly cleared the decks in terms of who to partner with."

Insiders at Embraer had a different view. Slattery recognized it was going to be very difficult for an independent Embraer to compete against a C Series campaign as part of the Airbus family of airplanes. Well after the Embraer-Boeing tie-up was announced, but long before the hoped-for regulatory approval by the EU, Slattery was competing for an order from JetBlue, a launch customer of the E190. JetBlue wanted to replace the jet, which proved disappointing, largely over costly GE CF-34 engine maintenance. The airline deferred the last batch of orders indefinitely.

Slattery offered the E195-E2. Bombardier, owning the C Series program when the sales campaign started, offered the CS300. Industry sources believed Embraer was ahead of Bombardier as a decision neared. Slattery certainly thought so.

The Airbus-C Series acquisition became effective July 1, 2018. Within days, Airbus swooped in and offered to up-gauge an outstanding A320neo order to the A321neo on favorable terms as part of a deal if JetBlue ordered the newly renamed A220-300 (the CS300). The airline agreed, ordering 60 A220s with a like number of options. Airbus also got its A321neo order as well. There was nothing the frustrated Slattery could do about it. Once Embraer Commercial became part of Boeing, The Boeing Co. would be able to pony up a similar "global" deal with 7-Series airplanes.

Conner's ranking of Embraer's engineering talent ahead of the services business is especially important because 2017 data from SPEEA, the engineering and technicians union at Boeing, indicated that over the next five to 10 years, there would be more than 5,000 employees who would be hitting retirement age.

Embraer needed Boeing more than Boeing needed Embraer, however. The E2 program was all but wrapped up from an engineering standpoint. Slattery hoped to launch a new turboprop program for a 70- to 90-seat, two-member family in early 2019. However, by the end of the year, he still hadn't closed the business case—something with a familiar ring as Boeing struggled to close the business case for the NMA.

Slattery said he needed the turboprop program to keep his engineers busy. The expectation had been that Boeing would need these engineers to

---

74. John Slattery vociferously defended the E175-E2 and claimed it had a viable future in the joint venture.

help on the NMA, backfilling the SPEEA retirements. The March 13, 2019, grounding of the MAX, following two accidents five months apart of brand new airplanes, killing 346 people, upended the NMA timeline. Decisions for Authority to Offer the NMA in early 2019 and launch the program by the end of the year were put off indefinitely.

The MOU, signed when Boeing and Embraer announced the JV in early 2018, provided Boeing Brasil with the responsibility for future airplanes in the 100- to 150-seat sector. This meant legacy Boeing would do everything from 180 seats and up, though Brazil could and would participate in development and supplying the NMA.

At a June pre-Farnborough Air Show briefing at Embraer headquarters in Brazil in 2018, Slattery waxed optimistic to the assembled crowd of international journalists. "We're now going through the process of antitrust immunity. We are making solid progress on that front, but those timetables are dictated by the various regularities in the different jurisdictions. We are working to their timetables. I would say that that engagement has been very positive. Our team has been very forthright in presenting all the information that's required to the various authorities around the world. That process is ongoing, and we will continue for many months to go."

Slattery explained that Embraer was going through that process of carving out ECA from the larger corporation—the people and the infrastructures across the globe—and identifying what would stay with Boeing Brasil-Commercial or remain in Embraer. "The guidance we got to the marketplace and our internal plan continues to be one where we see this transaction closing by year-end," Slattery said.

International regulatory approval was swift for Airbus and Bombardier. After all, Bombardier was all but bankrupt. In fact, the approval process was completed a month ahead of schedule. Embraer had little reason to believe a long process was in the cards for the Boeing JV.

Slattery outlined benefits to Embraer during the same briefing. "We have 75 operators of the E-jets in 50 countries today. Boeing has over 400 operators of the 737 platform and even more operators when you add in the wide-bodies on top of that," he said. "We need to get access to some of those customers. It's so difficult to get in front of airlines if you're not an incumbent or provider with them already. The first obvious place to get synergies is to try and figure out how best the sales teams will work after closing in presenting an offering to airlines that will frankly give airlines more flexibility than they have beforehand."

Slattery also said Boeing's heft with the supply chain would be able to cut production costs of the E2. In addition, he told journalists that Boeing Brasil would have a role in the Boeing NMA. "Our engineering capability is a key part of the Boeing Brasil-Commercial and a key attractive feature to The Boeing Company when they ran the ruler over the opportunities.

CHAPTER 21 **THE BOEING-EMBRAER JOINT VENTURE**

My vision is that Boeing Brasil-Commercial will add significant value on the engineering front to Boeing as they require of us, whether it's on the NMA R&D or other platforms. We can add real value to Boeing when they want us on various packages and other vertical integrations, like our landing gear shop, for example."

Slattery's optimism about winning global regulatory approval for the JV proved misplaced. Of the 10 jurisdictions that had to grant anti-trust approval for Boeing and Embraer, all did so on a timely basis, except the EU. There was widespread suspicion the EU was dragging its feet in retaliation for the Trump administration's trade war with the EU, generally, and by placing import tariffs on Airbus aircraft, specifically. EU officials denied this, but privately, Embraer officials got hints this was the case.

The EU demanded Embraer produce hundreds of thousands of pages of documents for deals going back 20 years—far more than the other nine governments required. Some in the EU argued Embraer's tiny E-Jets, which didn't compete with Airbus or Boeing airplanes except tangentially, provided a pricing discipline for the Big Two that would otherwise be absent if ECA became part of Boeing.[75]

It was a preposterous suggestion, which only lent credibility to the theory that the EU was dragging its feet in retaliation to the Trump administration. Even as Embraer produced an increasing mound of documents for the EU, officials demanded more and more. It was not hard to conclude politics, not anti-trust, were truly responsible for the delay. There was, however, no getting around that, with the effective exit of Bombardier from the small jet market and the potential disappearance of ECA into Boeing, the Big Four would become the even Bigger Two.

When Bombardier launched the C Series, it turned out to be a "disruptive" airplane. Airbus followed with the A320neo. Boeing countered with the 737 MAX, and Embraer, last to the party, followed up with the E2 family.[76] Slattery's pet project, the turboprop, wasn't going anywhere. Embraer was looking at a new turboprop since at least 2015. With the launch of the E2 in 2013, Embraer's product development was effectively barred by market conditions from going any bigger for the next new airplane.

This meant that an "E3" turboprop, below the E2 sector, was the alternative. However, in 2015, executives were cool to the idea. Development cost was about the same as a jet, yet the turboprop market over 20 years

---

75. One former BCA CEO told the author that he informed Embraer that if it designed the E2 to compete directly with Boeing, he'd kill them through pricing the new airplane out of the market.

76. Russia's Irkut launched the MC-21, a competitor to the neo and MAX, but it really wasn't triggered by the C Series.

was only between 2,100 and 2,500 airplanes. At the time, Bombardier was still in the turboprop business with the Q400—albeit having squandered its backlog, market share was only about 15 to 20 percent. ATR had the rest.[77] ATR was 50 percent owned by Airbus which could, if it wanted, provide financing and other support for development of a new design. The Italians, who owned the other 50 percent through Finmecannica (now Leonardo), wanted to develop a new airplane to replace the aging ATR 42/72. But Rao of Airbus, who was then chairman of ATR, and Bregier, the CEO of Airbus Commercial, were opposed.

Rao said the numbers for a new turboprop simply didn't work. The cost to develop one could not be overcome by the engine technology and superior economics then available to provide substantial economic gains for the airlines. They would then have to pay a sharply higher price than the amortized ATR could be bought for. Utilization couldn't be significantly increased, either. So, the return on investment to ATR or to the airlines simply wasn't there, Rao said. Bregier was much more cold-blooded. With 80 to 85 percent of the market share, he said there was no need for ATR to do something better than the 42 and 72.

Those early turboprop studies went nowhere for the next few years. By late 2017, Slattery was hot to trot, but this issue was no longer Embraer's call alone. Although legally Boeing couldn't call the shots about what Embraer did, Slattery knew they couldn't launch a new airplane program with a financial commitment of up to $2 billion while the Boeing JV was pending.

At one point during the next 18 months, Slattery told the media Embraer couldn't afford the program without Boeing money, but this was for public consumption—and to put pressure on the EU. Slattery's patience was running out with the EU dawdling. He gave several interviews with international press, complaining about the EU's pace and demand for documents.

The first E2, the E190, entered service with Norway's Widerøe, the largest regional airline in Scandinavia, on April 24, 2018. The first E195-E2 followed the next year with Azul. Sales of the E2 family were disappointing. The E190-E2 was a "tweener" airplane at 108 seats. Although cash-operating costs of the 195 are about eight percent greater than the 190, the revenue potential with 14 more seats (13 percent) was much greater. The 175-E2 didn't sell at all outside the U.S. and the order for 100, from SkyWest Airlines, within the U.S. was conditioned on Scope being relaxed. Accounting rules required Embraer to remove these orders from its backlog.

Slattery repeatedly promised that sales of the 175-E2 would be forthcoming outside the U.S., but as December 31 passed to January 1, no sales came

---

77. For purposes of this discussion, the Chinese and Russian turboprops, strictly home-market airplanes, are excluded.

in 2018 or 2019. Sales of the 190-E2 were anemic, and sales for the 195-E2 stalled. The CEO claimed the market was waiting to see the Boeing JV close before ordering. There was probably some truth to this. The market waited for the C Series deal with Airbus to close and once it did, the orders flowed in. The comparison was not strictly even-up, however. The market had real doubts about Bombardier's ability to survive and service the C Series in the future. Few doubted Embraer's ability to survive without Boeing.

There was nothing Slattery could do about the EU's demand for more information other than comply and fume about the repeated delays.

22

Last Gasp

"We weren't happy about that."

TOM ENDERS, AIRBUS'S CEO, ON THE COLLAPSE
OF THE EMIRATES AIRLINE A380 AT THE 2017 DUBAI AIR SHOW

THROUGHOUT 2016 AND INTO 2017, Airbus and Boeing each had challenges to deal with. The first A320neo, with the P&W GTF engine, was delivered in December 2016. There was little to indicate at the time that the GTF was going to be a disastrous entry into service. CFM engine delivery delays also affected the A320neo program. A350 production lagged, too. The A350 FAL in Toulouse in mid-2016 had 40 aircraft in different states of readiness, but very few were delivered. Of the 50 A350 delivered to customers, only nine were handed over in the first five months.

In May 2017, the 737 MAX was five months away from first delivery to Malindo Air, a unit of the Lion Air Group. Boeing heralded the timing as the long-awaited return to performing on schedule after the three-and-a-half-year delay of the 787 and a two-year delay of the 747-8. True, the MAX was overbudget, but compared with the two twin-aisle jets, the extra $2 billion or so was pocket change.

Still, delays of the CFM engines and a snafu in the supply chain parts delivery would cause headaches for Boeing. There certainly was no hint in 2018–19 of the disaster to come with the MAX. Operations were generally good and economics met promises, unlike the early 787s.

Airbus continued to have the overhang of the bribery investigation and the disruptions within. The engine problems on the A320neo would cause huge headaches for Airbus and its customers. At one point, Airbus built around 100 A320neos that were stored all over the Toulouse and Hamburg airports, parked without engines.

"We have been making gliders for some time now," Williams candidly noted in the May 2016 pre-Farnborough Air Show briefing. It would be quite a while before engine deliveries caught up with airframe production, but these were problems that would work themselves out over time. The main shows revolved around the future of the A380 and 747-8.

Airbus officials were reluctant to give up on the A380. The airplane was

CHAPTER 22 LAST GASP

viewed by many within the company as the most prestigious aircraft in the commercial product lineup. The A380 didn't have the sleek, elegant lines of the Boeing 747. In fact, it was rather dumpy and blunt. But technically, the A380 was a very good aircraft, even though its engines were a half generation out of date as soon as the airplane entered service in 2008. And its very size was controversial from the day it was conceived.

Enders occasionally acknowledged that if the A380 was filled to 80 percent capacity, it was a great moneymaker. Less than that, it was a difficult business case for the airlines. Using a fairly standard 550-passenger configuration (some airlines were under 500), an 80 percent load factor equaled 440 passengers. On a 777-300ER, 80 percent of the typical 365-seat layout meant an airline had to fill 292 seats. This made a big difference in the airline's risk profile in off-peak seasons or for thinner routes. Additionally, while the A380 had lower seat-mile costs, its trip costs were substantially higher than the -300ER.

Emirates used the A380 on some counter-intuitive routes (like Dubai to Manchester, England), but to fill the airplane, it had to offer deeply discounted fares. This ran counter to long-held practices of having the right size airplane for a particular route. Yet Emirates developed its business plan around the A380, an Airbus official once said.

China was a market Airbus was counting on to be a big customer, but the government, which placed or had to approve all airplane orders, only okayed a grand total of five A380s. These were assigned to China Southern. As Airbus China President Laurence Barron noted, the Chinese airlines—like most of their Western counterparts—were afraid of not being able to fill the behemoths.

When Boeing launched the 777X program, the larger of the two models, the 777-9, was conceived with a nominal 425 seats. (Since then, this has increased to around 450.) The -9 economic projections showed it to have better or, at worst, the same seat-mile costs as the much larger A380 but with trip costs that would be at least 10 percent better. The lower passenger capacity meant less risk for the -9 compared with the A380, although many airlines still viewed the -9 as too big.

It was against this backdrop that Airbus began developing ideas to lower the seat-mile cost and improve economics. Giving the A380 economics that would be competitive with the 777-9 required new engines. Given the poor sales, neither Rolls-Royce nor Engine Alliance was excited about the idea of developing a new engine, or even adapting an existing one that was more advanced than the Trent 900 or GP7200 to create a neo.

This was Clark's preferred option. He didn't want to order more A380s unless Airbus committed to the neo. Airbus and the engine makers didn't want to commit to the neo unless there were other customers besides Emirates—and there weren't. So, Airbus set about a series of band-aid solutions to improve economics. The A380-plus concept was unveiled at the 2017 Paris Air Show.

Having met with success by installing Sharklets (vertical wing extensions that blended into the wing in a smooth curve) on the A320 family, Airbus proposed this for the A380. These would reduce the fuel burn by four percent, the company said. The airplane's range could be increased by 300nm to an advertised range of 8,500nm. Reductions in maintenance costs would add to the operational savings.

In an effort to improve the seat-mile costs, Airbus proposed a coach section with 11 seats abreast instead of 10 to cater more to the cheap-seat crowd rather than the premium jet-set. Coupled with galley and lavatory reconfigurations, and other changes to the cabin, this would add 80 seats to the A380.

All in, Airbus forecast a 13 percent reduction in seat-mile costs. The seat width wouldn't be any worse than the competing 777s, but a single photo by a reporter at the annual aircraft interiors conference in Hamburg ridiculed the 11-abreast plan. The cabin wall's curve in the mockup allowed little foot room for the window-seat passenger.

The engines remained the insurmountable problem, however. Rolls-Royce and Engine Alliance didn't want to invest in more than nominal Performance Improvement Packages, or PIPs. Neither saw a business case for major PIP investments. The A380-plus met with yawns from the market—and no takers.

Nevertheless, unwilling to throw in the towel, Leahy and his sales team focused on winning a program-sustaining deal from Emirates. It was a tall order—and a last gasp. Enders, in a 2019 interview a few months after he retired, was frank in the reliance on Emirates to keep the A380 line alive. "It was always clear that the backing of Emirates was essentially called a survival problem. For some time, I hoped that we could land perhaps a big order in China because that was the potential that we really hadn't been able to tap. Five aircraft to China. Imagine that."

"The airlines were reluctant to purchase the product. It frightened them, I think," Barron said. The airplane was too large. "[China] didn't work. Then Emirates pulled the rug from under the program. Who would have thought in the first place that they would ever order more than 100 380s? Without Emirates, this program would have been dead in the water years before."

In 2017, Leahy and Enders thought they had Clark lined up for an order of 36 A380s, to be announced at the Dubai Air Show in November. The press release was written, and the room at the air show was set up for the announcement. An announcement by Boeing and Emirates was scheduled to follow Airbus in the same room.

CHAPTER 22 LAST GASP

At the appointed time, the Airbus communications team was ready, but there were no Airbus executives entering the room—only Boeing and Emirates. One Airbus communications person on the scene thought, Boeing must be going first. Emirates and Boeing announced an MOU for 40 787-10s. Then they left.

It was a huge embarrassment for Airbus and for Leahy, a public humiliation, as *Bloomberg* wrote, and there was nothing but mystery as to why the deal fell apart. "The halt came so swiftly that Airbus PR executives who were already in place for a double-signing ceremony ... found themselves awkwardly among the audience as Boeing walked away with the sole Emirates order, worth $15 billion," *Reuters* wrote in its November 19, 2017, report of the event.

The events were still sensitive and embarrassing two years later. In an interview in October 2019, Enders claimed he didn't recall why the deal fell apart. Leahy wouldn't comment, and Clark declined multiple requests for an interview. But two people familiar with the events said Clark's superiors at Emirates, including Sheikh Ahmed bin Saeed Al Maktoum, wanted better pricing from Airbus and Rolls-Royce than either was prepared to give; a guarantee the program would continue for 10 years; and an investment in an A380neo. None of the parties was willing to provide these guarantees, and the deal collapsed.

Although Airbus finished the air show with 500 orders and commitments, largely on the strength of a deal Leahy achieved with four airlines in which IndiGo Partners was an investor, all eyes had been on Emirates and the A380 deal. The IndiGo deal would have been a nice retirement package for Leahy, but headlines at air shows are often driven by expectations. The expectations of an A380 deal were huge. So were the negative headlines, followed by scores of stories questioning the future of the program.

Leahy, ever persistent, was not through, however. On January 18, 2018, Sheikh Ahmed Al Maktoum and Leahy signed an MOU for those 36 A380s. Airbus agreed to keep the program alive for 10 years, but there was no neo, no plus and no engine PIPs. In fact, there were no engines selected at all. It was the last deal Leahy would sign for Airbus. Over the course of the next year, Clark was unable to come to agreements with Rolls-Royce or Engine Alliance to improve the engines to his satisfaction. Airbus was unable to find any more customers. By February 2019, Airbus decided to throw in the towel.

Enders, now a lame-duck CEO ahead of his retirement April 1, announced the last A380 would be delivered in 2021. Incoming CEO Faury would have a clear deck. Emirates canceled most of its 36-airplane order, replacing it with an MOU for A330neos and A350-900s. (The neos would be dropped when Emirates firmed up and expanded the A350 contract at the 2019 Dubai Air Show.)

THE CASE FOR FAILURE

Why did the A380 fail so badly?

- There's the Boeing theory: Airbus simply made a colossally bad product decision.
- There is John Leahy's theory: The engine makers flimflammed Airbus by developing engines for the A380 that proved to be a half generation behind those they were secretly designing for the Boeing 787.
- Production delays severely hurt the entry-into-service timing, and with it, demand.
- The SARS health epidemic depressed demand, and then the 2008 financial crisis killed demand for large aircraft.
- The A380 was a decade too soon.
- Boeing's highly touted theory of market fragmentation proved correct. The twin-engine wide-bodies, beginning with the 767, then the A330, 777 and 787, would split the market. Even this understated the market fragmentation theory.

DECLARING VICTORY FROM THE JAWS OF DEFEAT

It was in May 2019, less than two months after Enders retired, that Airbus held its annual pre-air show press briefings. Airbus already wrote off billions of euros with the program. The A380 had been hoisted on the WTO petard, still a thorn in the side, right up to the point where President Trump levied tariffs on Airbus airplanes because, in part, the WTO found Airbus and the EU hadn't cured the A380 subsidies.

The German government was still owed $600 million for the launch aid for the behemoth. Airbus said it had no intention of repaying the loan. It also said terminating the program meant the U.S./Boeing complaints about the A380's financial assistance were moot.

At the Innnovation Days dinner, Faury declared that despite the sales and financial failures of the A380 and the big launch aid package from Germany that was going to go unpaid, the program had been a success. Journalists in the room looked at each other and murmured, "Is he nuts?" Here's how Faury explained his declaration. The A380 was an industrial if not a sales success because, in 2006, problems in final assembly exposed the cultural and industrial mismatch between the French and German plants where the A380 was produced and assembled.

Lessons learned from the A380 debacle were applied to the A350 production, then in its infancy. Production was smooth. Processes emerging from the A350 program have been applied to the greater Airbus. There were nearly 900 sales of the A350. This transformation is what Faury meant when he said the A380 is a success for Airbus.

As Faury explained his reasoning, he wasn't wrong. Without the A380, he said much later, there wouldn't have been an A350.[78] One Airbus official was more succinct. Without the A380, Airbus, he said, would have "fucked up" the A350. But it was a classic case of trying to make a silk purse out of a sow's ear.

STRUGGLING TO KEEP THE 747-8 ALIVE

Even as Airbus struggled to save the A380 program, Boeing finally gave up on the 747-8I, the passenger model. Carson said Boeing debated internally in 2008–2009 whether to launch the -8. Back when the 777-300ER program was launched, entering service in 2004, Boeing knew internally that this was the beginning of the end of the 747. Some argued then to discontinue the airplane. Others said the prestigious airplane was too valuable to give up.

The freighter, with its unique nose-loading door, was needed in only five percent of the service, and the value proposition of the big freighter was declining. The twin-engine 777-200LR was cheaper to buy, cheaper to operate and, in most cases, better sized for the demand. All too often, loads are directional anyway. With the huge amount of belly capacity in the 777-300ER, A330-300s and forthcoming neos, the 787 and the A350s, the 747-8F was a hard sell, but it wasn't impossible. As long as Boeing was going to build the 747-8F, it didn't cost that much more to develop and build the 747-8I passenger model.

Still, the 8I was, as Conner called the Sonic Cruiser, a "tweener" airplane. It fell between the 777 and the A380. Had Boeing not encountered two years of delays with the -8, it might have had better sales success given the two-year delay of the A380. Boeing, however, squandered this in the overhang that the 787 debacle had on the 747-8 development and EIS.

In February 2009, *The Everett Herald*, *Flight Global* and *Leeham News* each reported that Boeing was reviewing the program. "Boeing is reassessing the viability of the 747-8I," *Leeham News* wrote. "But we are told this reassessment is a full program analysis that includes whether to continue development of the freighter, with production at a slower rate than originally envisioned; to cancel the passenger version; or to cancel the program entirely." Cancelation was unlikely once the program was underway, and Boeing ultimately continued.

In its 10-Q filing with the SEC for the second quarter of 2016, Boeing acknowledged the end was on the horizon. "Lower-than-expected demand for large commercial passenger and freighter aircraft, and slower-than-expect-

---

78. Enders has a different view. In an interview for this book and with the benefit of hindsight, he thinks Airbus made a mistake proceeding with the A380.

ed growth of global freight traffic have continued to drive market uncertainties, pricing pressures and fewer orders than anticipated. As a result, during the second quarter of 2016, we canceled previous plans to return to a production rate of 1.0 aircraft per month beginning in 2019," Boeing wrote.

Boeing wrote off $1.19 billion in the quarter. It previously wrote off $885 million and $70 million during the second half of 2015 and the first quarter of 2016. "If we are unable to obtain sufficient orders and/or market, production and other risks cannot be mitigated, we could record additional losses that may be material, and it is reasonably possible that we could decide to end production of the 747," wrote Boeing. The company gave up on the -8I but limped along with the freighter at a rate of one-half per month until July 2020, when it announced the last one would be delivered in 2022.

23

The Alphabet Airplane

"This is a marketplace that intrigues me."
—**BOEING SALES EXECUTIVE JOHN WOJICK,** JULY 2014

THE MULTI-BILLION DOLLAR, HIGH-STAKES GAMBLE Airbus and Leahy played to force Boeing into re-engining the 737, instead of launching a new, clean-sheet airplane to replace it, paid off. Leahy's win at American—and Boeing's decision to launch what would eventually be named the 737 MAX—established the single-aisle market for at least the next 15 years. It cemented Airbus's lead over the 737.

The MAX name initially received lukewarm reception in the industry. According to insiders, CEO McNerney asked BCA executives what the brand options were for the re-engined aircraft. There wasn't a really ear-catching suggestion. MAX ultimately was derived from MAXimum efficiency, MAXimum range and MAXimum economy, the insiders said.

The following year, in 2012, Boeing began looking at what might replace the 757. The 757 was designed in the 1970s as a replacement for the 727. The first orders were received in August 1978. The first service was on January 1, 1983, with Eastern.

The 757 initially was offered in only one model, the -200, with standard two-class configuration of 180 to 200 passengers. In the single-class, high density of the day, it could seat 239 passengers. A smaller -100 model never proceeded. The later, larger -300, with 243 to 280 passengers, entered service in 1999 with charter specialist Condor Airlines. Only 55 -300s were sold out of the total production run of 1,049.

The 757-200's initial advertised range was about 3,200 miles. It was intended principally as a U.S. domestic airliner. ETOPS, the extended over water range certification for twin-engine airplanes, had yet to be approved.

It was a hot rod of an airplane. The 757's big wing allowed it to get off hot-and-high airports and short runways with full loads. Economics, for the day, were impressive, far better than the 727-200A. However, by the end of the 1990s, the 757 was fading. The cost of fuel was climbing, and the 757 was becoming more expensive to operate. Overhauls for the Rolls-Royce and P&W engines were expensive. More to the point, Boeing stretched the 737-800 into the -900, a 189-seat, two-class airplane. While slightly smaller than the 757-200 and with less range, the -900 did most of the U.S. domestic missions performed by the 757 for less operating cost. When Boeing refined the -900 into the longer-range -900ER, the model gained more flexibility and further ate into the 757's market. For airlines, not only were cash operating costs less expensive, the -900ER was priced about $20 million less than the 757.

From Boeing's perspective, the 757 became costly to produce. While the 737 production line in Renton had been modernized with greater automation and efficiencies, the 757 production line in the same building had not. One Boeing official said that assembly costs rose to the point where Boeing lost money on each 757 delivered.

Then 9/11 happened, and this was the death knell for the 757. Customer concentration was in the U.S., with American, Delta, Northwest, United and UPS (for the freighter version) as the principal operators. America West and Continental also were users. With U.S. carriers hardest hit by post-9/11 turn downs, demand for the 757 dried up. The final 757 rolled off the assembly line in 2004, delivered to a Chinese carrier.

Between 2001 and 2011, Boeing developed a twin-aisle concept that ultimately became known as the "New Lite Twin," or NLT. Early concepts were patented in the U.S. Patent Office. It also spurred discussions within Boeing about an airplane to replace the 757 for the MOM. Over time, NLT migrated to NSA. Depending on the era and context, NSA represented New Small Airplane and, mistakenly, New Single-Aisle Airplane.

For Boeing, losing its exclusivity at American to Airbus, with the A321 a major part of the Airbus deal, was "when it sunk in that the 737-900ER was not gaining traction, and we were conceding market to Airbus," says a former Boeing employee. "We were going to concentrate on the 737-800 and the new airplane [the 8 MAX] as the heart of the market. It also prompted discussions of the NMA, at least in the early stages."

NMA stood for New Midmarket Airplane, the name that eventually succeeded the moniker MOM. Boeing frequently shifted its informal names over the course of an airliner's conceptual evolution. For example, NLT and MOM, two meanings of NSA and NMA at various times, all referred to the same airplane development. The alphabet airplane in many respects was symbolic to the challenges Boeing would have trying to develop the business case. Boeing just couldn't make up its mind.

Boeing officials described MOM as above the 737 (which, at the time, stopped with the 737-900ER/9 MAX) and below the 787-8. With Conner's concept of a 757-like replacement, the MOM was logical. However, as the concept evolved more into a 767 replacement and once the 10 MAX was launched, the definition became muddled.

Sales of the 787-8 were poor after the initial launch sales surge. From a production standpoint, there wasn't much commonality between the -8 and the 787-9/10. Boeing acknowledged the profit margin on the 787-8 fell well short of the larger siblings. Forward planning saw reduced production of the -8 to one a month by 2020.[79]

The NMA's 767 heritage meant the NMA-7—the larger of the two models—encroached on the 787-8's capacity. Range, at 4,500nm, was substantially below the 7,200nm range of the -8, but an independent analysis of airlines schedules revealed that only 35 percent of the operations were 5,000nm or more. This meant the NMA-7 could do most of the missions operated by the 787-8. The remainder could be covered by the 787-9.

The NMA-6, the 220-seat model, was conceived to be above the 737-9. With the launch of the 210- passenger 737-10, the NMA-6 now would overlap on the -10. The NMA-6's range of 5,000nm was far greater than the 10 MAX's 3,200nm. But if Boeing succeeded in operating costs for the NMA-6 that matched the mediocre 10 MAX, the NMA-6 would be a far more flexible and capable airplane.[80] Regardless, the 9 MAX and the 10 MAX proved to be small band aids on a big wound. Following the 2013 program launch of the 777X, Boeing began to openly discuss the prospects of a 757 replacement.

At the July 2014 Farnborough Air Show, *The Wall Street Journal (WSJ)* interviewed John Wojick, Boeing's head of sales at the time. "This is a marketplace that intrigues me," the newspaper quoted Wojick. "We're trying to figure out how big that marketplace really is, how efficient the airplane really needs to be … and, if you ask me, I think we can address that marketplace a lot more efficiently" than the A330neo launched the year before, the newspaper reported.

Wojick, the report continued, envisioned a 200- to 300-seat airplane with a range of 5,000 nautical miles, capable of flights of about 10 hours. "Boeing's potential options include putting new wings, engines and a longer body on its single-aisle 737, shrinking the body of its Dreamliner, or starting from a clean sheet of paper, he added," *The WSJ* reported.

Boeing also considered restarting the 757 line, which was discontinued in 2005—the tooling was retained and in storage. Also considered was re-engining the 757. In other words, Boeing was looking at all options, as was its practice.

By 2015, the "757 replacement" became the 767 replacement. Instead of

---

79. The 787-8's lack of production commonality with the -9/10 was due to all the redesign required for the -8 in the early days. Boeing would eventually migrate the aft fuselage from the -9/10 to the -8 to make production more common, while reducing costs on the -8. Once the COVID-19 pandemic took hold in 2020, Boeing undertook further studies on how to increase commonality, reduce costs and make the -8 more attractive.

80. The 10 MAX was designed specifically with Ryanair in mind.

starting a new family of airplanes at about 180 seats, which was the plan in 2011 for the NLT 737 replacement, the MOM and NMA upsized the concept to begin with a two-member family at 225 seats, eventually going up to 270 seats. The range grew to 5,000nm for the "797-6" and 4,500nm for the "797-7." The ovoid, composite fuselage was the same concept as the NLT. It was key to matching the single-aisle CASM.

Airbus predictably dismissed the economics target, but independent analysis concluded that the 797-6 composite airplane could match the A321neo economics. Only a stretched A322, with 12 more seats, a new wing and a new engine, would preserve the Airbus advantage. Boeing also had to have production costs that matched a single-aisle airplane. On earnings calls and in interviews, Muilenburg, appearing at investors events sponsored by Wall Street aerospace analysts, began saying production was important to the NMA business plan.

Muilenburg wasn't specific, but potential customers were told by Boeing that the NMA plan included producing the airplane at a rate of 20 to 30 a month. This was well below the 737 rate but substantially higher than any previous twin-aisle airplane rate. It was also a rate that could not possibly be sustained by the projected market demand, but this wasn't the point.

The goal was to combine advanced manufacturing processes—from BCA's 7-Series airplanes and the military T-X jet trainer and MQ-25 unmanned aerial vehicle—into one commercial airplane for the first time. The NMA's medium-rate production was expected to lay the groundwork for high-rate production and de-risk the entire process. At least one airline was told of a production concept in which the fuselage would be halved longitudinally to stuff the systems and then mated in final assembly.

Boeing defined the "addressable" MOM market sector as 4,500 airplanes. Airbus and others believed the NMA market was really only 2,100 to 2,400 airplanes with an EIS 2025, of which Airbus wanted to grab at least half if the NMA was launched in 2018.[81] Internally, Boeing also knew the market was about 2,100 airplanes, multiple sources said. The 4,500 number was for public consumption. Albaugh confirmed the 2,100 figure in an interview for this book.

The business case for a two-member family, with 2,100 sales split between Airbus and Boeing, was iffy at best. But had Boeing looked at it as a three-member family, like the original NLT plan, the demand would have ballooned to more than 9,000 airplanes. The business case would have been a slam dunk. Boeing did not respond to questions posed for this book on this point (or any other).

---

81. Every year Boeing delayed a program launch meant Airbus would sell more A321neos, eroding the lower end of the MOM sector.

CHAPTER 23 THE ALPHABET AIRPLANE

Concurrent with the debate over the business case for the NMA and the size of the market, Muilenburg launched Boeing Global Services, or BGS. Combining Boeing Commercial Aviation Services from BCA and a similar support unit at Boeing Defense, Space and Security (BDS) into a new business unit, Muilenburg saw BGS as a profit center that could achieve margins neither BCA nor BDS could reach.

Price competition at BCA was under steep pressure from Airbus. Pricing at BDS was also under pressure. Winning the KC-X tanker contract in 2011 required Boeing to sharply drop its price from the second round. CEO McNerney acknowledged that the 2011 tanker contract award wasn't going to be profitable by itself. Over time, he predicted, future tanker orders and services contracts would make the program a financial success.[82]

Initially, Muilenburg and others said the NMA business case was a stand-alone prospect. In other words, Boeing wanted the business case to rise or fall on selling airplanes at a profit. BGS contracts, they said, weren't required to support the business case.

Stan Deal, the newly named CEO of BGS, said in an interview at the 2017 Farnborough Air Show that tying services to NMA sales contracts wasn't necessary to close the business case. A year later, however, the tune had changed. In another interview with the same reporter at the Paris Air Show, Deal said tying services to sales was now important to the business case.

Leahy, Enders and others claimed they had the MOM covered with the A321neo and the A330-800. It was wishful thinking. The A321neo, as originally launched in December 2010, was better than the A321ceo and certainly a replacement for the 757 in non-ETOPS operations. But as a transatlantic airplane, it fell short. The range simply wasn't enough.

In January 2015, Airbus launched the A321LR with an order from Air Lease Corp. The LR has an advertised range of 4,100nm, 100 more than the 757. In practice, flying westbound across the Atlantic (the prime market target), while allowing for required potential holding time and alternates, meant as much as 20 percent of the range of most airplanes, including the neo, was trimmed from the advertised range.

The A321LR, while better than the standard neo, still wasn't enough. So Airbus revised the design again as the XLR version with 4,700nm advertised range. This sub-type was launched at the Paris Air Show in June 2019 with a planned EIS in 2023. Once again, ALC was a launch customer.

The A300-800neo (the re-engined version of the A330-200ceo) was so much airplane that, despite new engines and a new wing, it simply would

---

82. A series of technical and production issues with the KC-46A caused Boeing to take $5 billion in charges on the early contracts, a worse performance than expected.

not be economically competitive with the NMA-7 (797-7). Independent analysis concluded the A330-800 would fall short in cash operating costs by double-digit percentages. The plane simply was designed for a different mission.

The NMA-7 concept had a range of 4,500nm. This meant that the A330-800, while similar in capacity, would haul around tons of dead weight given its range of 7,500nm to 8,150nm. The NMA's technology would be years ahead of the A330-800 as well. The 330neo still had a metal fuselage. The wing was an improved design, but the fuselage and systems dated back to the late 1980s. The Rolls-Royce Trent 7000 engines were essentially the 787's Trent 1000 but with bleed air instead of non-bleed air. This technology dates to the early 2000s.

Boeing's analysis of the A330neo, when compared with the 787, concluded that Airbus had to sell the 330neo for $50 million to offset the 787's better economics. Setting aside the inherent Boeing bias in any such analysis, the fundamentals were spot on. Of course, Airbus couldn't do this. Nor could it expect to cut the price of the A330neo to a point that would offset the huge double-digit economic advantage the NMA would have over the A330, which was substantially higher than the 787 vs. the A330.

Airbus wasn't fooled by its own public rhetoric about the A330-800 covering the top end of the MOM, however. Officials played the game, also played by Boeing, to sow doubt in the market about a competitor's new airplane concept. Analysts remained skeptical of the NMA.

On the third quarter 2015 earnings call October 21, Ron Epstein of Bank of America Merrill Lynch asked Muilenburg about the market potential. "We still see that as a niche market but an important one, and we're having conversations with our customers," Muilenburg said. "We see today that that market space is largely served by our 737 MAX 8 and 9 family and on the upper end, by the 787, and we think that in large part serves that market space." The MAX 9, he added, served "some of those needs that are in that, more the middle of the market segment. So, for the near term, we see our current product line as being the right answer for that segment."

A year later, on the third quarter 2016 earnings call, analyst Myles Walton asked about Boeing's plan to fill the space between the MAX and the 787. Muilenburg responded, "We have a number of options for satisfying those needs. Those include continuing to deliver on our current airplanes, getting the 737 MAX and the full family of the 7, 8 and 9 delivered, and continuing to ramp up the 787 and satisfy the customers' future needs with that family. That could be the end outcome here that we simply deliver on those two programs as currently defined. We're also continuing to look at a potential additional stretch of the MAX."

This stretch, in fact, would proceed in the form of the 10 MAX. The airplane was sized directly across from the A321 in passenger capacity. While the range of the standard A321neo and the 10 MAX were about equal, the neo had much better airport performance. With the shorter landing gear, the 10 MAX had only a 6.5-degree rotation on take-off (the 9 MAX had a 7.5-degree rotation), much less than the 321. The 321neo worked better off shorter runways than the 10 MAX—and was better in hot or hot-and-high environments.[83]

Longer term, Muilenburg told Walton, "We're continuing to look at the so-called middle of the market airplane options in that space. [We're] having very productive dialogue with the customer, firming up our opportunities there. If we were to go with that new airplane, that would be more in the 2024, 2025 entry-into-service range. On the other hand, an additional stretch of the MAX could be done more around the end of this decade, just to give you a sense for the timing there. And it's a realistic possibility that we could do both. We have the capacity and the ability to do both, and the timeline and phasing of those would allow us to do both. We're looking across that whole range of solutions, and over the next several months, we'll work through our decision process."

Muilenburg suggested that a decision on the MOM airplane might be months away. In fact, the studies would drag on and on, largely because Boeing couldn't close the business case. He was also clear that the MOM airplane program would be sequential to the 777X and not concurrent, keeping R&D costs level. This was key to maintaining shareholder value.

"None of this would be a significant change to our R&D profile over the next five years, so we're steady from that standpoint, and all of that fully supports our plans to grow cash year-over-year," Muilenburg told Walton. Keeping R&D spending in check and maintaining shareholder value were only two of the myriad factors in the NMA planning. Costs were naturally another, but this extended beyond the NMA itself.

In February 2016, Conner told employees during one of the leadership's periodic internal meetings that production costs of existing airplanes needed to be trimmed in order to produce sufficient margins to invest in new airplanes, like the MOM aircraft. Conner said Boeing had a "killer product line," but he also touched on a fundamental problem that, ordinarily, executives were loath to admit: Boeing's market share was poor.

"The challenge is really about driving the cost to the point where we can compete very aggressively to go win our share," Conner told employees. "Forty-six percent backlog share is not where we need to be. Thirty-seven percent on the single aisle is certainly not where we need to be. We've got to get that up, and we've got to go win—and win in the marketplace."

---

83. For all the shortcomings of the 10 MAX, the added capacity made it more attractive to airlines than the 9 MAX, despite the latter's longer range.

Throughout 2017 and 2018, Boeing still hadn't decided whether to proceed with the NMA. Efficient and advanced production remained a key component to the business case.

On the third quarter 2018 earnings call, Julie Johnsson of *Bloomberg* hit the nail on the head—although her question was rather benign—when it came to production. "Greg, you mentioned that Boeing now selectively is taking sort of longer-term market opportunity into account when it looks at a business case for products like T-X and MQ-25. Does that mindset and that sort of strategic outlook carry over to the NMA and if it does, how [do] you go about ring fencing risk and costs?"

The T-X and MQ-25 are defense programs that are the prototypes of the advanced manufacturing so important to the NMA, or—as it would turn out—Boeing's next new airplane in the absence of an NMA program. "I'd actually say the MQ and T-X are really more looking at it like we typically do and you would on a commercial-type opportunity, so it's really the reverse of that," said Greg Smith, CFO of The Boeing Co. "Having said that, there's a lot of things that we're doing on these programs that Dennis indicated that we're looking at about how does that make us more efficient and more productive on the NMA, and how does it de-risk the NMA business case. We've had NMA teams, and we've had 787 teams over on T-X. We've had T-X teams over on NMA and on 787."

Three days after this earnings call, Lion Air flight 610, a new 737-8 MAX, crashed into the Java Sea 13 minutes after take-off. Initially, Boeing dismissed the accident as probably pilot error. As it turned out, this accident was the beginning of a chain of events that, in addition to killing a total of 346 passengers and crew when a second 737-8 MAX crashed the following March, killed the NMA.

What exactly was the NMA? This is a very good question. Publicly, the concept evolved from a 757 replacement to a 767/A330 replacement (along with 757s and other aircraft). It was described as a 225-seat, 5,000nm range NMA-6 and a 270-seat, 4,500nm range NMA-7. It was an ovoid twin-aisle fuselage, composite design. At least this is what Boeing said publicly, but it wasn't this simple, if "simple" can be applied to any airplane program.

Boeing was unusually tight-lipped about the NMA. Whether this was because the business case couldn't be closed, or because officials wanted to keep Airbus in suspense, is speculation. It probably was for these and other reasons. But here's what was in the market from suppliers, airlines, lessors and via insiders at Boeing who were willing to share limited information:

- There was consensus that Boeing decided the NMA would be composite, but there was a team studying the metal fuselage option. At various times, the preference appeared to go back and forth. However, Boeing could not get the economics needed from a metal fuselage to give the airlines a twin-aisle airplane at single-aisle costs.

CHAPTER 23 THE ALPHABET AIRPLANE

- The airplane morphed from a 757-size aircraft to a 767-200/300 size.
- Rolls-Royce, P&W and GE (CFM) spent a lot of time and money studying engines for the NMA and, in fact, submitted proposals. Rolls-Royce eventually dropped out, but P&W and GE went forward. Boeing wanted healthy nine-figure financial contributions from the engine makers ("pay to play"). The level to play was never publicly revealed, of course, but sources indicated it was in the vicinity of $250 million. This figure was never confirmed.
- There was consensus that while the airlines wanted a choice of engines, the business case (already iffy) could support only one. Boeing insiders suggested GE or CFM would be the winner, though P&W disputed this. GE and CFM had a decades-long relationship with Boeing, and at the time, P&W was engrossed in the GTF reliability debacle on the A320neo. Relations between P&W and Boeing were also poor, dating to its withdrawal from the 787 engine competition.
- Boeing publicly stuck steadfastly to a timeline with a 2025 EIS until well into 2019. Few believed it. For one thing, the engines would not be ready until 2027-2029. The reason Rolls-Royce dropped out was because, the CEO said, it could not meet Boeing's desired timeline. Rolls-Royce's own Trent 1000 debacle required billions of dollars to fix technical problems, providing replacement engines and paying customer compensation. This might have had as much to do with it as anything else. Boeing insiders indicated that internally, Boeing Chicago knew full well that 2025 was a pipedream, and 2027, or even 2029, was more realistic.

There was some noise that Boeing was favoring a single-aisle design. In most quarters, this was discounted. A single-aisle NMA, it was argued, would essentially be a clone of the A321neo. But this was a disservice to the technology advances from the 1980s design of the A320 family, any advancements in the GTF or CFM LEAP, or the availability of new engines by 2025 when Boeing kept suggesting the NMA would be ready to enter service. Furthermore, this description over-simplified the situation.

"The NMA got bigger and became more niche-oriented," Conner said in 2020. "The idea originally would be more 757-like. It could have been a little bit bigger, with transatlantic range. What I was proposing when I became CEO was, let's look at doing an airplane that sits above the current MAX family. It could have been a little bigger and that's how you would start a new family of aircraft. The new single-aisle family."

Embraer would participate in the design of the new airplane. Later, it would take on the task of replacing the 737-700/7. There would be a common flight deck between the two families. "Ultimately, you would replace the 737-8 and -9 last," Conner said. "You would start your production systems so you could slowly build it with what became the NMA."

Conner said Boeing played with a twin-aisle design, but it would have been in the single-aisle market. "It went through a lot of iterations," he said. "There were all kinds of things going around. It didn't need to be a single aisle. It could have been a twin aisle. It was more about where it sat in terms of seat count."

Conner acknowledged that talking about a 230- or 250-passenger airplane, similar in seat count to the 757-300, meant a long airplane. "That's why we were talking about a twin aisle." But, he said, "at the end of the day, it became more like a 767. It actually became more of a 787-3." When American forced Boeing's hand in July 2011, Conner said Boeing was vacillating between a twin- and a single-aisle design.

It's been widely told that Boeing was taken by surprise about the pending Airbus-American deal, and that McNerney made a hasty decision to launch the re-engined 737 instead of the new airplane. Leahy and Eccelston still believe this to be the case.

Conner has a different view on just how surprised Boeing was—or should have been. At the time, he was leading Boeing's supply chain. In May, a little over two months before the American order was placed on July 20, Conner and Horton were playing golf. Horton, the president of American, told Conner that American was in talks with Airbus.

Conner said he reported the conversation to Boeing's salesman for American, Marlin Dailey. Discussions continued through the Paris Air Show in June, he added. "I told [Dailey] because Tom Horton grabbed me at [an industry event]. He told me the whole thing. They all said, hey, guys, we're talking. That was in May. Tom was very up front about it. I don't think Marlin and team believed it, but it was happening."

Within a month after the big order, Dailey was reassigned and Conner returned to sales in August. "I came back to sales when Marlin flamed out," said Conner. In addition, he recalled that while McNerney made the decision to launch the MAX for American, "the decision was being discussed quite a bit during that period of time. Albaugh was pinging a lot of people trying to get their thoughts."

A few airlines and lessors acknowledged Boeing talked about a single-aisle NMA in 2019, but this was in the context of the MAX grounding. Some of the lessors reported that Boeing asked if lessors would be willing to swap half their MAX orders for a new, single-aisle NMA. One major U.S. airline confirmed that Boeing discussed a single-aisle concept.

Although Boeing was tight-lipped, the idea that it could launch a twin-aisle 767 replacement and then a single-aisle 737 replacement was not unknown. In other words, this would be the 757-767 scenario from 1982 to 1984. Or as Robert Spingarn, the aerospace analyst with Credit Suisse, called it, the "two-tube strategy."

There are those within Boeing who swear this was the long-term strategy Chicago was considering, but did Boeing really want an orphan "NSA" and a twin-family NMA-6/7? It didn't make sense. And for the very few key suppliers in the know, this wasn't the path Boeing was talking about. These suppliers, in very private conversations, said an "NMA-5" would be another member of the twin-aisle NMA-6/7 family. It would be the same fuselage, if shorter, and directly fall within the 737-9 class. Still, it would not be a shrink in the classic definition. A new wing and smaller engines would be required to obtain maximum efficiency. The same fuselage technology and systems would provide commonality across a three-member family that an orphan and twins would not, especially production commonality. At least one airline also was aware of this concept.

Boeing, as noted, was unusually tight-lipped, even with suppliers. Many complained that they were in the dark, inhibiting their ability to make strategic plans or even respond to Boeing with good information about their ability to work on an NMA. Several suppliers complained in conversation—and a few to reporters—that Boeing demanded they not only sign a non-disclosure agreement before attending the few supplier meetings Boeing held. Boeing also demanded that they buy "a pig in a poke" (as one supplier put it) by agreeing to cutting costs in advance. Even then, they weren't guaranteed a role on the NMA.

Airbus officials asked why would Boeing launch a new airplane in 2020 for an EIS of 2025 at a cost of billions of dollars, when major new technology was around the corner in the 2030 decade? It was the same argument, in identical language, that Airbus used in putting down the idea Boeing would launch a new airplane to replace the 737NG, while Toulouse worked to maneuver Boeing into launching a re-engined 737 instead. This argument was déjà vu all over again.

By early 2019, Boeing still had not greenlit the NMA and that illustrated the difficulty in closing the NMA business case. Also, Asian airlines wanted more belly cargo capacity than the ovoid fuselage design allowed, so there remained some customer pushback as well.

The longer Boeing waited to launch the NMA, the more the market narrowed as Airbus sold more A321neos—especially once Airbus launched the A321LR and A321XLR. Why didn't Boeing take the leap? It was recognized within Boeing that the NMA was supposed to be the transformative production airplane for the future, but there was strong resistance in Chicago.

It was well known within finance circles, and within Chicago, that CFO Smith was opposed. "I hate that fucking airplane," he was colorfully quoted as saying. Lead director David Calhoun was also said to be opposed. He was quoted as believing the NMA was the wrong airplane at the wrong time. Neither Smith nor Calhoun agreed to be interviewed for this book, and they did not respond to written questions.

Furthermore, for a board of directors obsessed with shareholder value, institutional investors were broadly opposed to any new airplane program on the theory that a spike in R&D costs would eat into stock buybacks and dividend payments. It didn't matter that Muilenburg vowed that R&D spending would remain more or less level as spending wound down on the 777X.

Albaugh, who was gone by 2013, nevertheless looked back on the era from his vantage point in 2019. "I think the 787 family is a pretty good one. I have to think—this is just me speculating—that if they don't do the middle-of-the-market airplane, and I think there's a good reason not to because I think the market is finite, that the better play would be a new small airplane."

Another consideration was directly related to the time between launch and EIS. Muilenburg repeatedly said Boeing was "protecting" a 2025 EIS, even as the decision to launch kept moving to the right. Launch-to-EIS was taking seven years or more as planes became more sophisticated. Boeing rolled the dice and planned a four-and-a-half-year timeline for the 787. This, of course, was blown to hell by the design and industrial delays.

As Boeing put off a launch decision while protecting the EIS, the timeline for the NMA publicly kept shrinking until it was about five years—a little more than the original timeline for the 787. Reducing certification time was important to the NMA, and part of its business plan relied upon drastically cutting this. As it would soon be revealed, the certification process would become a critical component to the MAX.

Throughout the years of Boeing's indecision, Airbus aggressively said the A321neo and A330-800 covered the MOM. However, it was clear the customers weren't buying the idea. Although sales of the A321neo took off, especially with the evolution of the LR and XLR versions, the A330-800 has been one of the worst sales duds of all time. It doesn't cost Airbus much to shrink the A330-900 into the smaller -800, but the range of more than 8,000nm and the weight of the airplane simply makes it a poor competitor to the proposed NMA-7. Through June 2021, only 15 A330-800s were ordered.

In 2021, it turned out that the NMA might not be dead after all. *Aviation Week* magazine reported in February that a three-member NMA family remained under study by Boeing. This was a change to the previous two-member family concept. It also marked a return to the original three-member concept favored in 2011 by Bair and Albaugh. Until the pandemic was under control, however, and Boeing's finances were on the way to recovery, no decisions could be made.

24

Grounding

"Safety is our top priority."
—**MANY BOEING OFFICIALS** AS THE MAX CRISIS UNFOLDED

AT 6:20 ON THE MORNING OF OCTOBER 29, 2018, 31-year-old Bhavye Suneja, the captain of Lion Air Flight 610, and co-pilot Harvino[84] lined up the five-month-old Boeing 737-8 MAX on the runway of Jakarta's international airport for a flight to Pangkalpinang. Flying time was generally just 70 minutes.

Twelve minutes after take-off, the two pilots, six flight attendants and 181 passengers were dead. It was the first fatal accident of the 737 MAX, which entered service in May 2017 with Lion Air affiliate Malindo Air. The flight plunged into the Java Sea at high speed, disintegrating on impact. The fact that the plane crashed into the sea delayed recovery of plane, victims, and the important FDR and CVR.

Recovery of the FDR and CVR on land-based accidents usually quickly provides investigators an initial read of the basic facts of the accident. Lion Air's flight JT610's FDR was recovered November 1. (JT is Lion Air's two-letter IATA code, identifying the airline in schedules and on-air traffic control radars.) The FDR was badly damaged from the impact, but investigators were able to recover 69 hours of flight data over 19 flights. Analysis began on November 5. The CVR would not be recovered until January 19.

The FDR and radar tracking from the Jakarta control tower, and brief radio communications from the flight, indicated control problems. The flight's altitude was erratic, ascending and descending sharply and at a high rate of speed. Boeing immediately blamed the Lion Air pilots. While Boeing was roundly criticized for its quick finger-pointing, this was not unusual for Boeing or even the industry.[85]

In the case of Lion Air, suspecting the airline came naturally. Its safety record was poor and the EU, at one point, banned the airline from flying to the EU. Before and after JT610, pilots landed a few airplanes in the wa-

---

84. The co-pilot used only his last name.
85. Airbus has been quick to blame pilots in crashes of its aircraft, too.

ter rather than on the runway. Still, in this case, the captain of JT610 flew for the airline for more than seven years and had a little more than 6,000 hours of experience. More than 5,100 hours were on various models of the 737. The co-pilot had more than 5,100 hours under his belt with nearly 4,300 hours on various 737 types.

Despite suggesting the Lion Air pilots were responsible, within a week Boeing was quietly reassessing a software program called Maneuvering Characteristics Augmentation System, a mouthful more easily referred to as MCAS.

Simply put, MCAS pushes the nose of the 737 MAX down when the software detects a stall is imminent. The software accepts readings from an angle of attack (AOA) sensor that tells how high or low the nose is. The 737 has two sensors, but MCAS was only tied to one of them.[86] This would become a critical issue as investigations unfolded.

MCAS software ran in the background, much as many programs do on a home computer. Most consumers are unaware of background programs and even if they are, awareness doesn't mean much. Boeing thought MCAS, as a background program, wasn't something pilots needed to know about. Engineers believed that once triggered, the system would help the pilots avoid a stall. If triggered erroneously, engineers thought the event would be like runaway trim. Handling runaway trim, while not common, is also not something so out of the ordinary that pilots can't handle it efficiently. Boeing figured it would only take four seconds to recognize the event and take corrective action. Later analysis concluded that if it took pilots 10 seconds to recognize the problem and react, they'd, in all likelihood, lose the airplane. (It takes about 15 seconds to read this paragraph.)

Boeing also wasn't concerned about MCAS being tied to one sensor. In millions and millions of flight hours on the 737, AOA sensor failure occurred only a handful of times. None led to a fatal crash. If in VFR conditions, a pilot only had to look out the window to orient himself. But Boeing—and the FAA—quickly recognized that Lion Air revealed a flaw in these assumptions. It turned out JT610 pilots weren't aware of MCAS, and this became a cause *célèbre* in the coming weeks and months.

On November 7, 2018, the FAA issued an Emergency Airworthiness

---

86. The entire MAX crisis saga is well beyond the scope of this book. Reams of stories have been written in newspapers, and some TV specials aired. Congressional testimony in the U.S. House and Senate, with documentation, was generated. Thousands of pages of investigative documents also have been generated. A book about the MAX crisis is being written and others probably will be. This chapter focuses on the impact to Boeing and, by extension, to Airbus as well as Embraer, which became collateral damage.

CHAPTER 24 GROUNDING

Directive (a big deal in aviation lexicon), listing corrective procedures if MCAS erroneously activated. The procedures were for a Runaway Stabilizer, just as Boeing thought. "This emergency AD was prompted by analysis performed by the manufacturer showing that if an erroneously high single angle of attack sensor input is received by the flight control system, there is a potential for repeated nose-down trim commands of the horizontal stabilizer," the FAA wrote. "This condition, if not addressed, could cause the flight crew to have difficulty controlling the airplane, and lead to excessive nose-down attitude, significant altitude loss and possible impact with terrain."

This was the crux of the problem. When activated, MCAS could repeatedly push the nose down under certain flight control settings (flaps up). The strength of the system was such that a pilot could not overcome it. If the airplane's speed was too high during an event, pilots could not manually trim the horizontal stabilizer with the trim wheel in the cockpit.

As the investigations eventually revealed, failure by pilots to properly set flaps and reduce speed contributed to the accidents. At one point, Muilenburg stepped up and said Boeing had responsibility in the Lion Air and subsequent Ethiopian accidents. A few days later, he reverted to blaming the pilots, too. He was severely criticized, but in truth, he wasn't wrong. The pilots did contribute to the accidents, but those who lay the blame principally on them also went too far.

With the FAA's Emergency Airworthiness Directive, every MAX operator was notified of the procedures in case MCAS activated again. The presumption was that if MCAS erroneously activated, the procedures would allow the pilots to fly through the event. Sure enough, it did, but the plane crashed anyway.

On March 10, 2019, Ethiopian Airlines flight ET302 took off from Addis Ababa, the capital of the country. Six minutes later, the plane crashed. All 157 on board were killed. The plane never got higher than some 800 feet, and it nosed over into the ground at approximately 500 mph.

The captain was Yared Getachew. Although just 29 years old, Getachew had been flying with Ethiopian almost nine years. He had more than 8,100 flight hours, including 1,417 on various 737 types. He had been flying the MAX for about nine months. The first officer was Ahmed Nur Mohammod Nur. At 25, he recently graduated from the airline's flight academy. He had only 360 hours, including some 200 in the 737.

The radar-tracked flight profile captured by Flight Radar 24 and other trackers was somewhat sketchy given the remote part of the world, but it was generally similar to the JT610. A series of climbs and descents and varying speed caused many to suspect MCAS was involved.

As with Lion Air, some immediately pointed fingers at the Ethiopian pilots, although Boeing was not among them. Having been alerted to the Lion

Air accident and the FAA Emergency AD, surely, most thought, the Ethiopian pilots knew what to do—and did it incorrectly. Some specifically pointed to the young co-pilot as proof positive the flight crew was inexperienced and at fault. It wasn't that simple, of course, but it would take some time to recover the FDR and CVR for analysis.

China's FAA equivalent, CAAC, immediately grounded the MAX. Nearly 100 were in operation in China, more than in any other country. Regulators in other countries followed suit, while Muilenburg reportedly called President Donald Trump to implore him to order the FAA not to ground the MAX. The FAA said it would not be stampeded by other regulators into grounding the airplane. The FAA, a statement said, was data-driven.

After the European Union Aviation Safety Agency (EASA) and Transport Canada received more data confirming the initial indication of flight profile similarities between JT610 and ET302, the FAA finally followed suit and grounded the MAX on March 13, three days after the accident. The contrast to its rapid action in grounding the 787, within hours of the ANA battery incident, couldn't be starker—and nobody died in the JAL and ANA battery events.

Families and friends naturally blamed Boeing, as did others, including a number of American politicians looking to score political points. The airlines involved did, too. They were anxious to avoid responsibility on their part. The pilot unions at American and Southwest blasted Boeing for not informing them about the existence of MCAS. The union at United, however, suggested that a lack of training by the two accident carriers was to blame.

On March 27, 17 days after the Ethiopian accident, Boeing held a press briefing. Mike Sinnett, the vice president of product strategy and development, was the lead briefer. "The first thing I want to say is what MCAS is and what MCAS isn't," Sinnett began. MCAS, he said, is a function that was added to the airplane because the airplane has larger engines, they're bigger in diameter, and they're mounted a little bit further forward on the 737 MAX than they were in the 737NG. "MCAS is a function that was added to the 737 MAX to ensure that it has consistent handling qualities with the 737NG."

Sinnett explained that when Boeing went from the 737 Classic (the -300/400/500 series) to the 737NG (the -600/700/800 and later the -900/ER series), a function called the Speed Trim System was added. This system on the 737NG, at elevated angles of attack, provides automatic, horizontal-stabilizer motion to ensure that when the pilot pulls on the control column, there's a constant, increasing gradient of force per inches of displacement on the column.

"When we went to the 737 MAX and went to certify that airplane, because of the different pitching characteristics at elevated angles of attack between the MAX and 737NG, we expanded that speed trim control law that existed on the NG to operate at higher angles of attack, to continue to give you a linearly increasing gradient of column force for displacement, as you went through those elevated angles of attack. That's what the MCAS function is designed to do," Sinnett explained. Although in previous briefings Boeing referred to MCAS as an anti-stall system, by now officials avoided this description.

After a lengthy technical description of how speed trim works, options the pilots have and memory reactions to events, Sinnett got to the point of MCAS. "On the 737NG and on the 737 MAX, a speed-trim function can provide automatic input, and on the 737 MAX, at additional angles of attack, the MCAS function provides that input," he explained. "Flight crews can always override that at any time with a switch that's under their thumb or with the manual trim wheel."

Sinnett explained that while the AOA sensor and the sole-source access of MCAS to one sensor later became a focus of the ensuing debates, MCAS relied on a number of systems to work. The pitot probe on the front of the airplane measures total air pressure. Total air pressure measures airspeed, and it goes into the calculations that MCAS uses. The AOA position from an angle-of-attack vane on the front of the airplane is another.

The pitot and AOA data are provided to the Air Data Inertial Reference Unit (ADIRU). The ADIRU processes that data, calculates the Mach number that the airplane's flying at and provides that data to the flight control computer.

Sinnett came to the key points. MCAS, he said, does not operate when the autopilot is engaged, and it does not operate when the flaps are extended. "In order to operate, the trailing edge flaps need to be up, and the autopilot needs to be turned off. The flight control computer gets that data from the airplane. If these conditions are met, the function inside the flight control computer goes to the table, and it looks up the angle-of-attack and Mach number, and if required, it sends a command to the horizontal stabilizer trim motor, which will then move the horizontal stabilizer in the position that's commanded by the function MCAS. Once that movement happens, that movement is transmitted to the flight deck through the stab trim control cables, and those trim wheels that I mentioned earlier turn on the flight deck."

As data was analyzed from the two accidents, investigators found that flap positions varied from up to extended as pilots tried to troubleshoot their way out of the events. They also discovered that in the case of the Ethiopian accident, because the event began almost as soon as the flight took off, thrust remained at take-off power instead of throttling back. This helps account for the very high rate of speed at impact.

In the Lion Air accident, the captain was initially flying through the event, while the co-pilot went through the Quick Reference Handbook

(QRH) trying to find something that, in the end, wasn't there. After paging through the book without success, the captain turned control of the plane over to the co-pilot and began looking through the QRH. It was then that control of the airplane was lost, and Lion Air plunged into the Java Sea. Pilot actions and inactions would become the focus of two former officials of the NTSB as they later dissected the accidents.

At the March 27 briefing, Sinnett revealed that Boeing was making three "big changes" to MCAS. "The first big change, and probably the most important, is that we compare data from the left and right angle-of-attack sensor full time. When the flaps are up, in other words, in a situation where MCAS would be armed, we compare the inputs from those two angle-of-attack indicator sensors. If those inputs vary by more than 5.5 degrees, the system will inhibit MCAS and the entire speed trim function for the remainder of that flight," he said. "An indicator light will show on the flight deck, indicating to the flight crew that the speed trim system has failed, and this combination of things will eliminate the chance of erroneous data ever causing an MCAS activation."

Sinnett said the second change removed the repetitive activation of MCAS. In the two accidents, MCAS repeatedly engaged in an on-off-on type of event. In Lion Air's case, where the flight reached an altitude of more than 5,000 feet and lasted 12 minutes, MCAS activated about two dozen times. ET302 was airborne only six minutes and never got higher than some 800 feet. The number of activations was less, but, at a much lower altitude, just as deadly.

"If MCAS is activated in a non-normal situation, it will only be activated one time for each elevated angle-of-attack input," Sinnett went on to say. "This means that if the airplane goes to a high angle-of-attack, MCAS will operate. It'll give the pilot nice, smooth control forces as he pulls linearly through the force curve. The nose, as the pilot recovers, will come down. At that point, once you're at a normal angle-of-attack again, the system will reset so that if during the rest of the flight the pilot has another elevated angle-of-attack situation, MCAS will continue to operate. However, if for some reason an angle-of-attack vane gets stuck in a high position, the system will detect the inconsistency between the two inputs, and it would not operate a second time."

The third major change, Sinnett explained, is that in a situation that is the presence of unknown unknowns, "meaning things that we haven't even imagined no matter how hard we try, there's no situation in which more stabilizer input can be provided by the MCAS system than there is control column authority for a pilot's response. The control column will always be able to override MCAS inputs with sufficient maneuvering capability that the airplane can still climb. These are very important changes. In addition,

CHAPTER 24 GROUNDING

the pilots continue to always have the ability to override MCAS and manually control the airplane with the trim switch that's under their thumb."

Based on previous groundings, most believed the MAX would be grounded for only a few months. Certainly, Boeing seemed to believe this. Muilenburg often suggested soft, early timelines when the MAX would return to service (RTS).

It wasn't to be. As Boeing discussed the MAX grounding, the fixes and the RTS, Muilenburg and all subordinates, right down to the corporate communications team, echoed the refrain, "Safety is our number one priority," and Boeing worked for the "safe return to service" of the airplane. These phrases became a broken record—and as information emerged about the development, engineering and production of the MAX, the phrases became platitudes.

Boeing and the FAA came under a myriad of investigations: criminal probes from a federal grand jury and the U.S. Department of Justice (USDOJ); the Inspector General of the Department of Transportation; and the inevitable Congressional hearings. As the probes unfolded, investigators, the media and politicians learned that engineers and assembly line workers at Boeing were under great pressure to keep costs down and meet the delivery schedule. After the out-of-control programs with the 787, 747-8 and the very low bid on the KC-46A, Boeing needed to demonstrate to its customers—and to Wall Street—that it could produce an airplane on time and on budget again. This pressure, especially as it related to cost control and appeasing Wall Street, became one of the many focuses of severe criticism. Many concluded that Boeing cut costs at the expense of safety.

Any airplane program is under cost and schedule pressure, and the MAX was no different. Internally, there was intense debate and disagreement in some quarters over decisions and design direction. But it would be a stretch to conclude that controversial decisions in the name of cost cutting and keeping on schedule were made without regard to making a plane less safe. In the end, there was nothing in it for Boeing to deliberately make an unsafe airplane.

Rather, mistakes came from a sense of "it never happened before," "the AOA sensor almost never failed," confidence that the MAX was, after all, basically just a modified and more modern Next Gen aircraft, the reliability of which was 99-plus percent, and so on. Call it arrogance or complacency, carelessness or even recklessness, but suggesting intent and criminal intent is a hard case to make.

The investigations revealed embarrassing shortcomings at Boeing. Emails from test pilots flying simulators revealed a disdain for the FAA. Other emails revealed disdain from one set of engineers for decisions made. Documents revealed what some characterized as a wholesale handover of certification responsibility and oversight from the FAA to Boeing. This, too, became a pointed focus of criticism.

An internal review by the Department of Transportation would later clear the FAA's approach. The fact of the matter is that government agencies, including the FAA, routinely assign responsibilities to the companies and industries they regulate. This has been going on for decades. Part of the reason is that Congress doesn't authorize budgets for the agencies to hire their own experts. While the Acting FAA Administrator Daniel Elwell made this point before the House hearing, members of Congress weren't about to accept responsibility for under-funding the FAA for decades.

Furthermore, the FAA simply didn't always have the scientific knowledge required. When Boeing developed the all-composite 787, the FAA didn't have the requisite knowledge for this level of composites or for the first use of lithium-ion batteries. It imposed "special conditions" Boeing had to meet as development progressed, but the agency relied heavily on Boeing throughout.

The FAA testified that while Boeing did oversee internal development of the MAX, ultimate certification authority always rested with the agency. However, the investigations revealed that the relevant FAA personnel weren't told Boeing redesigned MCAS from a less aggressive response to an AOA event to a more aggressive one that dramatically increased the power and initiated a repetitive action. The FAA agreed to MCAS "1.0." It didn't know about MCAS "2.0." The FAA agreed to remove any mention of MCAS from the flight manuals, denying pilots any knowledge of its existence.

Boeing's failure to tell the FAA of MCAS 2.0 was yet another point of intense criticism. Keith Leverkuhn, the general manager of the MAX program, wasn't informed, either. Nor was Conner, by then the CEO of BCA. The first Conner heard of MCAS was in connection with the Lion Air crash. Certainly, the MCAS redesign would not have made its way to Muilenburg in Chicago. (However, Chicago was the recipient of emails from employees outlining overarching concerns about shortcomings in the MAX program, the investigations would later reveal.)

Boeing's tough labor union, the IAM 751, objected when Boeing proposed in May 2019 laying off 900 of its inspectors in favor of automated processes. Predictably, Boeing viewed the automation as more efficient (and as a cost-cutting measure).[87]

While FAA delegation of authority to Boeing was nothing new in principle, few would question the handover went too far. And in 2017, Boeing asked Congress to "streamline" aircraft certification, which at the time

---

87. https://www.usatoday.com/story/news/nation/2019/05/06/boeing-inspection-job-tech-crashes-outcry-737-max-poor-quality/3650026002/

CHAPTER 24 **GROUNDING**

could take 14 months.[88] As far back as 2004, unions and critics warned of shifting oversight from the FAA to Boeing.[89]

As part of its business plan for the NMA, Boeing wanted to shorten the certification timeline further. An outgrowth of the Congressional hearings was legislation tightening FAA oversight and certification. The impact affected certification of the 777X, and that blew up the dream of shortening the certification of the NMA, or whatever Boeing's next new airplane will be.[90]

The hits just kept on coming for Boeing and the FAA. Initially, Boeing kept producing the MAX, albeit at the rate of 42 airplanes per month instead of 52 at the time of the grounding. Boeing clearly anticipated a short grounding. By January 2020, about 450 MAXes were produced and stored in four locations in Washington state, one in California and one in Texas. The previous month, Boeing announced production would be suspended in January.

Muilenburg came under fire for Boeing's responses, becoming Boeing's public face of the crisis. His problem had as much to do with style as substance. Muilenburg is your stereotypical engineer: dispassionate. Statements expressing condolences were devoid of emotion. The only time this public veneer broke was during one of the Congressional hearings. Muilenberg met with families of the victims shortly before the day's hearing began, and the emotion of the experience finally emerged in his voice.

At a press conference in April 2019 following Boeing's annual meeting, a month after the grounding, Muilenburg was visibly angry and defensive. He cut the 30-minute press conference short after 15 minutes. He came across as highly scripted. There was a sense that Muilenberg was robotic in his demeanor.

On October 11, the board of directors took Muilenburg's position as chairman away. Shareholders, dominated by institutional investors typically aligned with the board, refused to do so in April. But by October, the board clearly was frustrated with Muilenburg's performance and failed promises about RTS. Lead Director David Calhoun was named chairman. Boeing put

---

88. https://thehill.com/policy/transportation/319723-boeing-urges-congress-to-streamline-aircraft-certification-process

89. https://www.politico.com/story/2019/03/21/congress-faa-boeing-oversight-1287902

90. The MAX certification controversy had the opposite effect. Certification of the 777X clearly was delayed, although by how much is uncertain. Technical issues with the 777X's huge GE engine caused about a nine-month delay. The COVID-19 pandemic froze any interest by customers to take delivery. EIS, originally planned for late 2019 or early 2020, now is targeted for late 2023. Early customers don't think EIS will happen until 2024 or even 2025.

the best face on the move, of course, citing the ability for Muilenburg to focus on RTS while Calhoun took other duties off his hands, but it clearly was a demotion.

Calhoun started becoming the face of Boeing in televised media interviews. In contrast to Muilenburg's stiff, scripted style, Calhoun was relaxed and appeared to talk in a casual manner. There was even a sense of candor that was lacking in Muilenburg's approach. It was a welcome change. However, in short order, Calhoun stepped in it three times that made it clear he needed a bit of scripted discipline. Calhoun in CNBC interviews, for example, expressed strong support for Muilenburg.

On October 22, the board canned McAllister. Reports were ambiguous about whether McAllister resigned or was fired, but Wall Street sources made it clear the move was not voluntary and came as a surprise to McAllister.

Because McAllister became CEO of BCA in November 2016, well after the first flight and several months before EIS, the root decisions of the MAX's development were already cast in stone. However, his invisibility was a problem. Customers were calling Chicago complaining about the lack of contact, hand holding and compensation from BCA. McAllister's interaction with the FAA also was a question mark.

The customer complaints weren't universal, however. Gary Kelly, the CEO of Southwest, appeared on CNBC and, when asked, gave an endorsement of the ousted McAllister. Kelly complimented Southwest's interaction with him. Asked about Muilenburg, the ever-polite Kelly was terse, if brief. The absence of support for Muilenburg was telling. Given Southwest's status as a loyal Boeing customer that had ordered, over the decades, more 737s than any other airline or lessor, Kelly's clear rebuke of Muilenburg had to be stinging to Chicago.

Deal, the CEO of BGS, was named to replace McAllister. An affable personality, he set about repairing customer relations and internal employee morale. However, over the next year, Deal avoided press interviews. Throughout his first 16 months as BCA CEO, he gave no interviews.

Muilenburg clearly was on borrowed time, even if Boeing public relations said otherwise, and his tone-deafness was on full display at the Congressional hearings. Aside from the momentary break in demeanor after meeting with the families, Muilenburg reverted to form as the ice-cold, scripted and repetitive CEO he'd portrayed since the MAX crisis began.

Asked why he hadn't suspended his compensation, Muilenburg said that was a decision of the board—completely ignoring the option that he could request a $1 a year salary or suspend it entirely. After roundly being criticized, a few days later he did just that. (His stock options remained intact, however.)

The House hearings were so hostile that Muilenburg actually gained

CHAPTER 24 **GROUNDING**

sympathy in a few quarters. Some House members were clearly shooting for the sound bites. On the Senate side, while there was no shortage of grandstanding, the Upper Chamber clearly was more interested in getting to the bottom of what happened than their colleagues in the House.

The hearings were damning for Boeing and the FAA. Back in the office, Muilenburg continued to make predictions about when recertification could be expected. By December, the FAA had had enough. In a blistering rebuke, the new administrator, Steve Dickson, once more criticized Boeing for pressuring the FAA, reiterated there was no timeline for recertifying the MAX and assured the FAA staff he had their backs.

On December 23, the board fired Muilenburg. Calhoun, serving as non-executive chairman since October, was named president and CEO, effective in mid-January. The delay was needed so he could exit other business commitments. CFO Smith was named interim CEO; long-time director Larry Kellner was named chairman.

The firing came as a surprise to Muilenburg, a Wall Street analyst told a reporter, based on information he received from Chicago. In January, after assuming the top spot, Calhoun was asked in a TV interview about the support he articulated for Muilenburg in October and November. Muilenburg, Calhoun replied, had the support of the board right up till the moment he didn't. It was a remarkable statement.

The fired CEO may have given up his salary, but he still walked away with $62 million in previously earned stock awards and compensation. The "Golden Parachute" drew outrage in some quarters, especially from the crash victims' families.

The choice of Calhoun to lead Boeing out of its crisis drew skepticism. He had been on the board since 2009, including 2011 when MAX was launched. He was on the compensation committee. He supported cost cutting and shareholder value, two elements that came under scrutiny in the MAX crisis, and he was the lead director. Many viewed Calhoun as an insider who was part of the problem. But not Calhoun himself. When asked about this on his first media call after assuming office on January 13, Calhoun said he was like a movie goer with a front-row seat, but he wasn't an insider. Wall Street, media and critics hooted at the claim.

In an interview with *The New York Times*, Calhoun confounded some institutional investors with his criticism of Muilenburg. "Mr. Calhoun has become more willing to openly criticize Mr. Muilenburg. He said the former chief executive had turbocharged Boeing's production rates before the supply chain was ready, a move that sent Boeing shares to an all-time high but compromised quality," the newspaper reported.

"I'll never be able to judge what motivated Dennis, whether it was a stock price that was going to continue to go up and up, or whether it was just beating the other guy to the next rate increase," Calhoun said. He added later, "If anybody ran over the rainbow for the pot of gold on stock, it would have been him."[91]

Once again, Wall Street hooted. After all, the board approved buybacks and dividends, and Calhoun was part of these decisions. The board was fully behind returning 100 percent of free cash flow to shareholders. Blaming Muilenburg for boosting the stock price and supporting the board objectives of buying back shares and increasing dividends was, to say the least, poor form. Calhoun needed some scripting after all.

It was clear Muilenburg's firing had become necessary. Kevin McAllister, who succeeded Conner as CEO of BCA, also had to go, despite being late to the party. McAllister had been invisible in the public responses to the crisis and customers were complaining he wasn't around to meet with them, either. During the 787 grounding, Conner had been the public face of Boeing.

"This is all about how you handle a situation," said a former Boeing official. "We've had lots of crashes, and we've had lots of things. If you go back in time and you think about Japan Air Lines Flight 123 [the 747 in which the aft bulkhead blew out], we stepped up and took responsibility for that and moved on. We made all the changes to the 747 that we needed to do. This is about you couldn't do anything about Lion Air, but you probably could have done something about Ethiopia."

The former official doesn't think the situation was handled properly from the very beginning. "Everybody wants to go back in time and say, it's about culture. It was never about a culture. We made some mistakes. Airplanes are complex, and you're going to make mistakes. Sometimes you'll make mistakes, or sometimes you catch them and fix them. There was a succession of decisions that were made that were inappropriate. There's no question about that."

In the wake of the MAX accidents and groundings, many charged that the MAX was driven by a cost-conscious board of directors. A former Boeing official believes the board must accept responsibility. "I don't think the MAX decision was a bad decision," he said. "I think it was a decision that was not driven necessarily by the board. It was more driven about getting the airplane as quickly as possible. The airplane is a great airplane. Did we screw it up? Did we make mistakes? Absolutely, we made mistakes. There's no question about that. Did we mishandle the crashes? There's no question about that. Is the airplane a bad airplane? No, it's not a bad airplane. Did we not have a solution for the A321 and what that airplane could be in terms of all its ability to grow? No question about that. To me, that's what we didn't address. I don't think that MAX was a bad decision.

---

91. https://www.nytimes.com/2020/03/06/business/dealbook/boeing-calhoun-muilenburg.html and https://www.nytimes.com/2020/03/05/business/boeing-david-calhoun.html?searchResultPosition=4

"Here's where I would say, 'Now, wait a minute. This is the same board that hired Kevin [McAllister], that hired Dennis [Muilenburg], and then the same board fired them because they said that they didn't handle things correctly. And now, this is the same board that put themselves in charge.'" That's the question that people needed to ask, the official said. "Where's the board? This is the classic situation. Where does board accountability come into play here?"

Another Calhoun statement in the same *Times* interview raised eyebrows and went directly to a critic's point. Asked about the task ahead, Calhoun replied, "It's more than I imagined it would be, honestly. And it speaks to the weaknesses of our leadership." It also speaks to the weak oversight and complacency of the board of directors and Lead Director Calhoun.

Despite criticism, Muilenburg was exactly right: a series of factors contributed to the accident, and Boeing's actions and inactions, as well as the FAA, are at the head of the list. Which makes the full-throated defense of Boeing and even the FAA, by a former crash investigator and a former board member of the NTSB, puzzling.

In a series of podcasts dedicated to the MAX crisis and the Lion Air crash, former NTSB investigator Greg Feith and former NTSB Board member John Gogolia exonerated Boeing, blaming the airline, pilots and Indonesian regulators.[92] They said they based their conclusions only on the facts, not on media reports or testimony before Congress. In multiple podcasts, they noted they were not paid by Boeing, nor did Boeing pay for a trip in December 2019 to get a briefing, meet Boeing engineers and Muilenburg, and fly a simulator. In one podcast, they criticized Muilenburg for accepting at least some responsibility for the accidents and not defending Boeing more.

Feith doubted pilot knowledge of MCAS would have saved the airplanes at Lion Air or Ethiopian. Training, the two said, was key. Goglia and some U.S. pilots pointed out that recovering from MCAS was similar to runaway trim recovery. This was Boeing's basic thought process as well.

"It would have saved the day in this if it had been used by the flight crew," Goglia said. Indeed, on a Lion Air flight on the same airplane the day before, pilots encountered an MCAS activation and followed procedure to fly their way out of the problem. (One of the problems JT610 faced was that the previous crew or airline didn't inform the JT610 crew of the incident.)

"Are there issues with the airplane?" Feith asked on a podcast. "Yes. Are they as dramatic as has been portrayed in the media?" Goglia and Feith didn't think so, based on the facts and circumstances they reviewed.

Dissecting the Indonesian report of the Lion Air crash made it clear "the airplane was flyable, and it was flying for better than 11 minutes before it

---

92. https://www.flightsafetydetectives.com/e/fly-the-way-you-train-train-the-way-you-fly/

crashed. It was flying under control of primarily the captain, and then control was lost by the first officer," Feith said. "The facts speak toward pilot issues, not product issues. Does there need to be a review of regulations, which were written in the 1950s? Yes. Does there need to be an overhaul and start with a clean sheet of paper? No."

Feith criticized the Indonesian investigators for failing to probe areas and ask questions that he and Goglia said should have been pursued. "It starts with the maintenance issues and the installation of a bad AOA vane," Feith said in one podcast. The previous crew "performed the procedures that were necessary to handle that unreliable air speed ... It didn't take any extraordinary skills and got the airplane down in one piece." The question is, did the report of that event get to the engineering group and was a proper fix made?

Goglia added that the accident aircraft was not airworthy. Maintenance failures were involved. Additionally, Feith pointed to US Airways' Captain Chesley "Sully" Sullenberger's successful landing in the Hudson as an example of what experience and training means in an emergency.

Yet in Congressional testimony about the MAX, Sully said he struggled to recover from an MCAS-induced event in a simulator. "I can tell you firsthand that the startle factor is real, and it's huge," he testified. Sully later said, "The startle factor ... absolutely interferes with one's ability to quickly analyze the crisis and take corrective action." The current system of aircraft design and certification failed, he added.

While Feith and Goglia say that the Lion Air and Ethiopian crews should not have been overwhelmed by the plethora of cockpit warnings, Sully testified that he could see how they could have been, even knowing what was going to happen in his own MAX simulation.

The Ethiopian flight had a 60-degree difference with the other AOA, Feith noted. The crew had been trained to the new procedures from Boeing through the FAA Airworthiness directive. "The stick shaker goes off. It had nothing to do with MCAS," said Feith. "As soon as flaps came up, MCAS was triggered. The crew knew the airplane wasn't standing on its tail. They could look out the window, and they had the artificial horizon. The auto throttles were still engaged at take-off power. All they had to do was turn the auto throttles off and pull the throttles back. That's called airmanship. That's called being a pilot."

Just nine days after the Ethiopian accident and seven days after the FAA finally grounded the airplane, Sully wrote, "Our credibility as leaders in aviation is being damaged. Boeing and the FAA have been found wanting in this ugly saga that began years ago but has come home to roost with two terrible fatal crashes, with no survivors, in less than five months, on a new airplane type. To make matters worse, there is too cozy a relationship between the industry and the regulators. And in too many cases, FAA employees, who rightly called for stricter compliance with safety standards and more rigorous design choices, have been overruled by FAA management, often under corporate or political pressure."

In a report June 19, 2019, National Public Radio (NPR) cited Sully's testimony before Congress: The MAX "automated flight control system on the 737 Max was fatally flawed and should never have been approved." The head of the American pilot union also was critical of Boeing.

"Daniel Carey, president of the Allied Pilots Association, noted Boeing's strong safety record generally," NPR reported, "but he criticized the aerospace giant for making 'many mistakes' in order to reduce costs, while still developing the MAX plane so that it would feel as much like the previous version of the 737. 'Boeing designs and engineers and manufactures superb aircraft,' Carey testified. 'Unfortunately, in the case of the MAX, I'll have to agree with the Boeing CEO [Muilenburg], they let the traveling public down in a fatal and catastrophic way.'"

Carey told the committee that the MCAS flight control system, which was designed to prevent an aerodynamic stall, was flawed in that it had a single point of failure without redundancies. In the case of both the Lion Air flight in Indonesia and the Ethiopian plane, a single AOA sensor provided faulty data to the system, so the MCAS forcefully and repeatedly pointed the nose of the plane down when it shouldn't have. "A huge error of omission was the fact that Boeing failed to disclose the existence of the MCAS system to the pilot community around the world," Carey continued. "The final fatal mistake was therefore the absence of robust pilot training in the event of an MCAS failure."

Feith and Goglia, without naming names, criticized a "famous pilot" who said he would have difficulty flying through MCAS. This "famous pilot" shouldn't be in the cockpit, Feith said in a later podcast. There were no bells and whistles causing confusion in the Lion Air cockpit, the two said. Only the stick shaker and trim wheel could be heard—along with pages of the QRH being turned. The captain and copilot were speaking in normal voices, they said. When "one of the famous pilots" flew the simulator and said he couldn't handle it, "get out of the airplane," Feith said on the podcast.

Their defense of Boeing and the FAA contrasts with regulators from Europe and Canada and some pilot unions—American, Southwest and British Airways, among them—who criticized the certification process, linking MCAS to one AOA sensor and Boeing's approach to the system's design. Ironically, Lion Air asked Boeing for simulator training for the MAX. Boeing said it wasn't necessary.

As the FAA neared recertification, it issued a proposed procedure for pilots to follow in the event of an MCAS activation. Pilot unions for Southwest, American and others complained the procedures were too complex.

Even though Feith and Goglia exonerated the roles of Boeing and the FAA as contributors to these two accidents, they didn't entirely let them off the hook. "Boeing has a long way to go, because they have issues internally that they are starting to fix," Feith said. "It's evolutionary. It's not going to happen overnight. It's the same with the FAA. They aren't clean in all of this."

In January 2020, Boeing entered into a Deferred Prosecution Agreement (DPA) with the U.S. DOJ to end the criminal probe. (This was similar to the action taken by Airbus in connection with its bribery scandal.) In a press release, Boeing outlined the agreement:

"The DPA contemplates that the Company will: (1) make payments totaling $2.5 billion, which consist of (a) a $243.6 million criminal monetary penalty; (b) $500 million in additional compensation to the heirs and/or beneficiaries of those who died in the Lion Air Flight 610 and Ethiopian Airlines Flight 302 accidents; and (c) $1.77 billion to the Company's airline customers for harm incurred as a result of the grounding of the 737 MAX, offset in part by payments already made and the remainder satisfied through payments to be made prior to the termination of the DPA; (2) review its compliance program for implementation of continuous improvement efforts; and (3) implement enhanced compliance reporting and internal controls mechanisms. Under the terms of the DPA, the criminal information will be dismissed after three years, provided that the Company fully complies with its obligations under the DPA. Of the payments described above, $1.77 billion has been included in amounts reserved in prior quarters for 737 MAX customer considerations. The Company expects to incur earnings charges equal to the remaining $743.6 million in the fourth quarter of 2020."[93]

When dissecting the verbiage, Boeing only had to pony up an additional $743.6 million in cash. Some were quick to point out that Boeing faced a criminal cash penalty of $244 million. Airbus paid more than $4 billion in penalties, including more than $500 million to the DOJ—and neither safety nor fatalities were involved.

---

93. https://boeing.mediaroom.com/news-releases-statements?item=130799

25

Scandals

"We unearthed a crushing body of evidence."
—SEN. JOHN McCAIN, NOVEMBER 19, 2004[94]

AIRBUS AND BOEING SLUGGED OUT THEIR COMPETITION through sales campaigns and product strategy for decades. However, there was another element over the same period that deeply affected both companies: scandals.

Boeing's tanker scandal of the early 2000s led to changes with the chief executive officer that had ramifications for the development of the 787. The competition to win the contract to replace the aging fleet of USAF KC-135s dragged on for nearly 10 years—and resulted in billions of dollars in write-offs from the extraordinary low-bid contract awarded Boeing.

Airbus's bribery scandal dogged the company for almost a decade. This led to a wholesale housecleaning of the executive ranks and, fairly or not, scores of others. A series of DPAs between Airbus and authorities in three countries resulted in record fines.

Finally, the 737 MAX scandal caused immeasurable damage to Boeing's reputation and bottom line. Although the legal outcome of a criminal investigation resulted in a DPA, the culpability buck stopped with two test pilots and a financial slap on the wrist.

The impacts of the three scandals will be felt by the two companies for decades to come.

BOEING'S TANKER SCANDAL

September 11, 2001, was a beautiful day across the U.S. There was nothing to hint that there was going to be anything wrong. But between 8:46 a.m. and 10:03 a.m. Eastern time, four Boeing airplanes operated by American and United airlines were hijacked by terrorists. Two were flown into the two 110-story World Trade Center towers in New York City. One was

---

94. https://www.defense-aerospace.com/articles-view/verbatim/4/49262/mccain-exposes-usaf-role-in-tanker-lease.html

flown into the Pentagon in Washington, D.C. Another was crashed by terrorists into a field in Pennsylvania when heroic passengers tried to take back the airplane. It never was clear if the fourth airplane was headed to the White House or the Capitol, but the destination was Washington, D.C.

The FAA ordered the U.S. skies closed to all air traffic. Domestic airliners were instructed to land at the nearest suitable airport. International flights were diverted to non-U.S. airports. U.S. airlines were grounded for four days before service resumed. Up to then, it was the only time all air transportation in the U.S. was halted.

Airlines in the U.S. were especially hard hit. Federal aid was granted to some, but scores of young, "new-entrant" carriers collapsed and went out of business. Several of the major airlines declared bankruptcy. Some successfully reorganized. Others eventually ceased operations. BCA was faced with scores of requests for delivery deferrals. Brand new airplanes went from the assembly lines straight into storage for what, at that point, was an indeterminate amount of time. As some airlines went bankrupt, they sought revised contract terms. As others ceased operations, Boeing was left with white-tail airplanes. It was a scenario that would repeat itself 20 years later with the COVID pandemic.

Airbus was not immune. In 2001, Airbus's market share in the U.S. was less than today, but it, too, got requests to defer or cancel airplanes.

"During the aftermath of 9/11, every airline and leasing company was in chaos," Leahy recalled. "Everyone wanted to cancel all aircraft in backlog. This would have caused chaos in production at Airbus." Although Leahy helped some airline operators with deferrals (not cancellations), he took a much harder line with lessors. They were the financial intermediaries. They made a lot of money in the good times, so Leahy believed that they needed to help in the bad times.

The teams from both sides spent weeks negotiating and trying to find a solution between Airbus and a few key lessors, such as GECAS and ILFC. The lessors knew Leahy was granting deferrals and some cancellations to airlines, but he and Scherer took a hard line with lessors.

Henry Hubschman, CEO of GECAS, called Leahy on his cell phone. He said he needed to cancel all his orders. Leahy responded, "Henry, we're all in this together and you have a better credit rating than Airbus. So, sorry. We'll try to help you place the aircraft, but you must take them." Hubschman hung up the phone, but GECAS took the aircraft, some of which were parked for a long time.

Even Leahy's good friend, Steve Hazy, ran into resistance. Finally, Leahy and Hazy had enough of their ILFC negotiations, which were going nowhere. One evening in Toulouse while Leahy's wife, Grace, was preparing dinner, Leahy's cell phone rang. "Hello, Mr. Leahy, this is Hank Greenberg [CEO of AIG, ILFC's parent]. Sorry to bother you, but we need to talk." He then explained the dire situation of ILFC and their urgent need to cancel substantial amounts of aircraft in backlog. Greenberg was disappointed that Hazy and Leahy were not able to find an equitable solution. Leahy predictably responded that AIG was stronger financially than Airbus ... and "we are all in this together."

Greenberg continued to argue about the need to cancel and the importance of AIG. Leahy was polite but would not budge. Finally, Greenberg gave an ultimatum. "If you do not agree to this cancelation, I will never speak to you again." The implication was clear. There was a long pause. Leahy once again said he was sorry, but he would not change his position. Greenberg hung up the phone. ILFC remained one of Airbus's largest customers, but to this day, Greenberg never spoke to Leahy again.

In 2001, the U.S. market encompassed the world's dominant demand for airliners from Airbus and Boeing. Boeing was especially hard hit as orders dried up, and airlines deferred deliveries. Boeing executives were clearly worried about the impact of 9/11 to the airline industry, along with all stakeholders. But they had worries closer to home, driven by their own duty to protect the corporate health of The Boeing Co., its employees, shareholders and the entire supply chain whose own livelihood was so interwoven with Boeing.

The Boeing Co. was then divided into two main subsidiaries (and a whole bunch of smaller ones): BCA and Integrated Defense Systems (IDS). BCA officials had to scramble to deal with airlines that wanted to cancel or defer orders, orders that fell away with bankrupt airlines, the loss of cash flow from these factors and production disruption with scaled-back rates at the 737/757 factory in Renton and the wide-body factory in Everett, where the 747, 767 and 777 were built. The financial disruption was enormous. At IDS, with a response to Al Qaeda only days away and signs emerging that any military action would soon expand to Iraq, government orders would ramp up. But BCA needed help.

Boeing thought there was an obvious answer, one that would help BCA, IDS and the U.S. military. The USAF had a large fleet of KC-135 aerial refueling tankers, based on the commercial 707 platform designed in the 1950s. While the oldest models had long since been retired and the later ones had been modernized, including some with more fuel-efficient and reliable CFM56 engines, the last KC-135 came off the assembly line in 1966. By 2001, the youngest KC-135 was 35 years old—older than some of the servicemen piloting the aircraft. Many tankers were much older.

Boeing proposed leasing 100 new tankers, based on the 767-200ER airframe, to the USAF for 20 years. It was an unusual idea, but not unprecedented. Boeing once proposed creating tankers based on the 747 platform and leasing them to the USAF. The idea went nowhere, but this demonstrates it wasn't a new one.

There were many problems with leasing. One of them was that Boeing suggested there could be commercial application for the tankers at the end of the 20-year leases or well into the 2020s. However, the 767-200ER, on which the KC-767 was based, was not the preferred choice for a cargo airplane; that was the larger 767-300ER. Another: Retiring the 20-year-old tankers assumed the USAF would be ready (and have the funds) to replace them.

Nevertheless, the idea wasn't ridiculous. Airbus later arranged a lease of the KC-330 with Britain's Royal Air Force. A private company, Omega Air, converted a 707 and a DC-10 to tankers and leased them to the U.S. Navy on an as-needed basis.

Boeing's proposal quickly worked its way through the USAF. Darleen Druyun was the head of the USAF's acquisition program and approved the deal. A short time later she was offered, and accepted, a high-level job at Boeing. CFO Mike Sears, who came over from McDonnell Douglas, made the job offer.

The tanker deal was agreed to in May 2003. By the following September, Arizona Sen. John McCain, a self-proclaimed watchdog of government waste, scrutinized the transaction as too costly to the government. The $26 billion deal equated to a lease of $260 million per airplane, compared with a purchase price of $150 million. McCain thought the deal was a bad one, way too expensive, a bail-out for Boeing post-9/11 (arguable, but a stretch) and smacked of illegality.

The senator waged a dogged campaign against the Boeing deal throughout 2004. In November, McCain entered a statement into the Congressional Record eviscerating Boeing, the USAF and the Pentagon. "The rider was in fact the result of an aggressive behind-the-scenes effort by The Boeing Company, with considerable assistance from senior USAF procurement official Darleen Druyun and others," McCain said. "Through the hearings and investigations that followed, we unearthed a crushing body of evidence on how much a folly the proposal actually was." He also accused the parties of a host of improprieties and of conspiring to discredit him. McCain's statement was nearly 4,500 words or nine pages long.

By December, the USAF froze action while investigating all the elements of the procurement, including the roles of Druyun and Sears, to determine whether any corruption was involved. It turned out that Druyun inflated the price of the Boeing tanker and also had passed on to Boeing confidential information on the competing Airbus A330 MRTT bid. Shortly before McCain's statement, she pled guilty to a variety of charges and went to jail for nine months, beginning in January 2005. Sears was fired and went to jail for four months. Boeing paid a fine of $615 million for this and another defense-related scandal. Condit resigned in December 2003, succeeded by Stonecipher.

In the next round of procurement, McCain urged the Pentagon to search for competition to Boeing. The only competitor capable of offering a large

CHAPTER 25 SCANDALS

jet transport to compete with the KC-767 was, of course, Airbus. Boeing's bitter archrival had designed a tanker based on the A330-200, a larger aircraft than the 767-200ER. The KC-135 was the first jet tanker for the USAF. Boeing designed the B-47 and B-52 bombers that became the backbone of the Strategic Air Command.

With the A330 having all but killed the passenger 767 and with airlines reeling from 9/11, Boeing needed the USAF order. But the leasing deal amounted to a boon for Boeing; a straightforward purchase obviously would have made more sense for the taxpayer. McCain and others believed robust competition between Airbus and Boeing would lead to a better deal for taxpayers.

The idea of Airbus supplying the USAF with such a high-profile airplane, especially in lieu of Boeing, amounted to blasphemy among some U.S. elected officials, Boeing employees and even some persons in the Armed Services. Airbus came from nowhere in 1974 to capture 50 percent of the mainline commercial airplane market by 2005. McDonnell Douglas not only had exited the commercial airplane market but was now part of Boeing. Many blamed Airbus's success on government subsidies, complaining that Boeing didn't get any and was disadvantaged as a result.

There is no doubt that Airbus had government support. The French, German and Spanish governments invested heavily in Airbus, subsidizing early programs. But many European aircraft programs since World War II had significant government support. Still, they were commercial disasters. The Concorde is probably the prime example.

In 2004, the U.S. renounced the 1994 trade agreement governing subsidies to commercial airplane development, and the U.S. Trade Representative, at Boeing's behest, filed a complaint with the WTO, charging that Airbus received illegal subsidies.

There are those in many circles who believe Boeing initiated the complaint to divert attention from its tanker scandal. Airbus and its parent, EADS as it was then known, were and are firmly convinced this was the case. Only Boeing principals know whether this was the motive, but it doesn't matter: The subsidies truly were considered unfair competition by Boeing, and officials were determined to put an end to them.

Boeing's parallel strategy was clearly to tarnish Airbus in the coming tanker competition. Without turning this into a detailed examination of the subsidy issue, Boeing certainly succeeded in Congress in ripping Airbus to shreds. Over at the USAF, however, there were other dynamics involved.

Airbus, which through the EU filed its own trade complaint with the WTO against subsidies Boeing was alleged to have received illegally, teamed with Northrop Grumman Corp. (NGC) to front the tanker bid, called KC-X, in 2005. This was an entirely new arena for Northrop. NGC built drones, fighters and ships. It was into cybersecurity, and it was a contractor to Boeing on some of the latter's defense programs. Proposing to become the integrator on an airplane the size of the A330, for a system for which it had no experience, was cheeky. Because of its long-standing relationship with Boeing on defense programs, many observers were surprised NGC would team with the hated Airbus.

The 2005 tanker fight became mean and nasty, very quickly. It was clear very early on that Boeing's communication team was out for blood. They attacked Airbus for its illegal subsidies; its inexperience in building tankers; for illegal subsidies; inexperience in building refueling booms; for illegal subsidies; being French; for illegal subsidies; tying up with Northrop, which also didn't know anything about building tankers; for illegal subsidies; proposing a "greenfield" assembly site in Mobile; for illegal subsidies; and the Mobile workforce being incapable of building tricycles at Christmas.

Boeing was obsessed about the subsidies. As an after-thought, Boeing also said the KC-767 was a pretty good airplane. Except it wasn't all that good: Only eight were built, there were flight control flutter and structural issues, all were delivered late and large write-offs were taken for the losses incurred.

For its part, Airbus and Northrop guffawed over biting cartoons by J. D. Crowe of the *Mobile Press-Register*. Crowe drew the Boeing tanker, which used the fuselage from the 767-200ER, wings from the 767-300ER and the cockpit of the 767-400 and labeled it the Frankentanker. Another cartoon mocked Boeing's tricycle characterization of the Mobile labor talent.[95]

The USAF, by all appearances, tried to stay above the fray. However, it emerged that the USAF changed the parameters of the procurement in a way that favored the Northrop-EADS KC-330 offering. They thought it appropriate to give EADS credit for the extra capabilities of their aircraft, which, of course, in any rational analysis, it was. When the time came to announce the contract, Boeing, its employees and supporting members of Congress gathered for a celebration, anticipating the win. Northrop, EADS and Airbus were consigned to losing.

Thus, when the USAF gave the contract to the Northrop team, everybody—on both sides, in the media, consultants, everybody—reacted with shock and disbelief. Many believed the KC-330 was a far better choice than the troubled KC-767, but its French heritage was universally viewed as fatal to its prospects.[96]

---

95. Former Defense Secretary Robert Gates, in his memoir titled *Duty* about his time as secretary of defense for presidents George W. Bush and Barack Obama, sharply criticized Boeing, Northrop Grumman and Airbus for their tactics in the tanker fight.

96. Northrop, Airbus and some others said the KC-330 was the better airplane because it was a decade newer in technology, and it had much longer range and refueling capability than the KC-767. Given that the Pentagon was planning war

CHAPTER 25 **SCANDALS**

In the routine debrief by the USAF about why it had lost, Boeing learned for the first time that the service gave the KC-330 extra credit for its greater range, cargo payload, on-station loitering time and refueling capacities. These extra credits had not been outlined in the competitive documents. Boeing officials cried foul. The company protested, and the protest was upheld. The competition would have to be re-run a third time. The USAF returned to the drawing board, so to speak, and recast the specifications to what is known as Technically Acceptable, Lowest Price, or TALP. While TALP may not be the best way to equip the war fighter, this approach is not unknown.[97]

This, essentially, eliminated what were the KC-330s' greatest advantages. Only if the bids were within one percent of each other would the extra attributes be credited. Northrop took one look at the TALP approach and said, "No, thanks." The A330 list price was more than the 767-200ER, and operating costs were higher. What's more, the very participation of Northrop added to the total contract price to account for its own services, costs and profit. Northrop said it would not partake in the next round.

After taking a deep corporate breath, EADS and Airbus decided to compete again, this time with EADS North America as the prime contractor.[98] In

---

scenarios in the Pacific against China (something not known publicly at the time), the long "legs" and greater loiter time gave the KC-330 a key advantage. Also, Boeing's KC-767 program for the Italians and the Japanese (eight airplanes in all) was a disaster. Design issues leading to flutter problems on the airplane itself and the refueling boom for the Italians, as well as issues with sub-contractor Alenia in Italy, combined to make the program years late—and subject to a huge cost overrun and financial write-off. This was the plane Boeing offered the USAF in the 2005 competition, and it was a dog enveloped in high risk. One of the reasons the USAF cited awarding the contract to Northrop was the risk factor in the Boeing tanker. It should be noted however, that the airplane Boeing offered in Round Three of the tanker competition was a somewhat better airplane than it offered in Round Two.

97. Frank Borman was CEO of Eastern Airlines and the former commander of the Apollo 8 Space Mission, the first one to orbit the moon. When Borman was trying to persuade the powerful and militant Machinists Union to go along with a variable wage plan, a grizzled member asked Borman why they should follow someone dumb enough to sit atop a rocket built by the lower bidder. Borman laughed along with everyone else. Source: *Countdown*, by Robert Serling.

98. The reason EADS teamed with Northrop in the first place was that, in 2005, EADS North America was just establishing a footprint in the U.S. and had little exposure in the way of Defense contracts. NGC, on the other hand, was highly experienced in working with the Pentagon. EADS had yet to truly prove itself as a reliable defense contractor, whereas NGC had no such handicap. By the time Round Three commenced, EADS North America, led by Ralph Crosby, a former senior NGC execu-

the meantime, Boeing, having benefitted from the USAF debrief and having more experience with the disastrous KC-767 International program, made major changes to its offering. A revised (but as-yet paper) version of the KC-767 was conceived. It kept the revisions secret from the media and the public domain, but renderings showed the 767 having winglets, which added 3.5 percent in fuel efficiency. A long time later, it emerged that Boeing created another "minor variant" of the 767-200ER, called the 767-2C. It is a combination of the 767-200ER fuselage, the -300ER wing and the glass cockpit of the 767-400. No winglets would make it into the final design.

Boeing re-ran the anti-Airbus campaign, telling Congress and the media what was wrong with the A330 and that Airbus benefitted from illegal subsidies, repeating most of the arguments from Round Two. But the subsidies issue was the dominant argument advanced by Boeing and its supporters. Boeing spent more time talking about how bad Airbus was, rather than talking about the attributes of its airplane, which once again raised suspicions that Boeing had an inferiority complex about its tanker.

By law, the USAF couldn't consider the WTO actions on the U.S. Trade Representative complaint about Airbus's subsidies (which, indeed, were found to be illegal in several respects, as were Boeing's). Military programs are exempt from this consideration. But the second- and third-round competitions were as much or more about the politics of the contract award than about the merits of the two airplanes. Although Congress isn't supposed to influence procurement, in the end it controls the purse strings, so members meddle with the process as much as they can.

Boeing and its surrogates gave short shrift to the advantages that should have been communicated: its experienced workforce, a mature manufacturing site and long experience in maintaining tankers. As a smaller airplane, the 767 was less expensive to operate, though not nearly as much as Boeing claimed.[99]

---

tive, had successfully delivered on several Defense contracts, and the Pentagon said it was comfortable with EADS North America taking the lead as the prime contractor.

99. In Round Three of the competition, the turning point for Boeing was when U.S. Rep. Norm Dicks (D-WA), now retired, virtually compelled the USAF to consider the useful life of the tanker as 40 years, instead of the initially presumed 25. It was a fair point. The KC-135 tanker (and even the newer McDonnell Douglas KC-10) certainly proved this. By adding 15 years to the assumption, the delta between the operating cost of the larger KC-330 and the smaller KC-767 increased to a point where this made a real difference in the analysis. Indeed, some KC-135s will be more than 50 years old by the time they are retired. Although under TALP the award eventually came down to price, the operating cost projections were a significant factor that EADS/Airbus could never win.

Gregoire, governor of Washington, naturally wanted Boeing to win the contract and joined with other Boeing-leaning governors—and a coalition of Washington state interests—in a public relations campaign in support of the tanker. But she was far more astute than the Washington State Congressional delegation. Gregoire focused on the message Boeing should have advanced rather than bashing Airbus. Why?

Washington's tax breaks to Boeing for the 787 were subject to an EU complaint about illegalities in the counter-case before the WTO. The WTO already found Airbus to have benefitted from illegal subsidies. The A330 became the focus of Boeing's anti-Airbus, illegal subsidies campaign. Any objective analysis about those Washington state tax breaks concluded that the WTO would identify these as illegal under their rules, too. It would have been awkward for Gregoire to bash Airbus tax breaks, only to have the state's found to be illegal, which is exactly what happened.[100]

Just as the world was shocked when Northrop/EADS won the competition the first time, the interested parties were all shocked that Boeing was selected in Round Three in 2011. The pricing wasn't even close—Boeing's winning bid was 10 percent less than EADS. Airbus's extra capabilities played no role.

McCain's tanking the 2002 lease deal, thereby forcing competition, was key to the win for the taxpayer. However, the senator, it turned out, had former EADS employees on his staff. A few suggested there was an improper connection between McCain and his support for EADS entering the competition (although there also was a whispering campaign), but appearances matter—and having the ear of the senator certainly didn't hurt EADS.

Many months later, there was a rumor that the USAF awarded Northrop the contract in part to send Boeing a message. It fully expected Boeing to "shape up" for another round of competition. This seems a little conspiratorial, but this is Washington, D.C., after all, so it can't be ruled out.

The Third Round of competition provided for the eventual purchase of 179 KC-46A tankers, as the 767-based entry would be named by the USAF. First came the development of four tankers to serve as the test airplanes. The entire contract was a fixed price rather than cost-plus, meaning that if Boeing experienced cost overruns, it would be on the hook.

For Boeing, it was a sweet win, coming nearly 10 years after it first pro-

---

[100]. Boeing and the U.S. Trade Representative would appeal the ruling. The appeal was rejected. In 2020, to head off tariffs, Boeing asked the Washington Legislature to void the tax breaks. Whether the WTO finds this acceptable remains to be seen. But the issues are moot, at least for now. In 2021, the EU and U.S. agreed to a five-year standstill while they joined forces to look at how China subsidizes its aerospace industry.

posed the lease deal. But through 2020, Boeing took forward losses on the initial contracts of more than $5 billion. The balance of the contracts, also fixed-price, make it clear it will be decades before Boeing sees any profits.

The USAF's frustration reached the point where officials floated the idea of reopening procurement to Airbus for future tanker purchases. In 2019, Lockheed Martin and Airbus proposed a venture to offer KC-330 MRTTs to the USAF via, of all things, a leasing arrangement.[101]

Losing the contract was a bitter pill for Airbus—and for the state of Alabama and the city of Mobile. As part of the Northrop-EADS proposal, Airbus said it would build an FAL in Mobile. When the award was overturned by the General Accounting Office and after Northrop withdrew from Round Three, Airbus reaffirmed its commitment to building the FAL should it be re-awarded the contract.

After Boeing won, Mobile's hopes for an aircraft FAL were dashed. Little did anyone know that the idea would be resurrected by Enders to build an A320 FAL, eventually followed by the FAL for the A220, née-Bombardier C Series. Talk about making a silk purse out of a sow's ear.

As much as Boeing denigrated Airbus and its lack of experience in building tankers—and (eventually) promoted its own experience—the Airbus tanker won every competition in the rest of the world except Japan (which has a special relationship with Boeing and bought four of those KC-767 tanker dogs). Despite some teething issues with its own refueling boom, Airbus's KC-330 is in service and performing missions, while Boeing, in 2021, is still sorting out problems with its KC-46.

AIRBUS'S BRIBERY SCANDAL

While the tanker competitions were rooted in Boeing's leasing scandal and the USAF's bungling of the second-round competition, Airbus had a scandal of its own that was brewing.

In the vast international arena of commercial aviation, murky deals were not unusual over the decades. Even airlines engaged in questionable tactics. For example, the exploits of Pan Am and its founder, Trippe, are recounted in many histories of the airline. He used guile, power and, according to lore, even toppled governments to win route authorities.

In his excellent chronicle of the demise of Braniff International Airways, *Splash of Colors,* author John Nance detailed how Braniff's history in Latin America included off-the-books ticket sales, a thinly disguised slush fund airline agents used to curry favor with local travel agents and offi-

---

101. https://www.defensenews.com/air/2018/12/05/lockheed-airbus-venture-ups-the-pressure-on-boeing-to-deliver-its-us-air-force-tankers/

cials. During the early 1970s, Lockheed was caught having bribed Japanese government officials to win an order from ANA for the L-1011. McDonnell Douglas had been awarded the contract for DC-10s—but ANA wound up buying the TriStar instead.

Bribery, in the form or "commissions" or even more overt black bags full of money, was not uncommon in the third world in the '70s and even the '80s. These practices were simply the way of doing business in certain parts of the world.

Retaining local business partners, agents or lobbyists was not unusual for Boeing, Airbus or the engine manufacturers in third world countries. They provided local knowledge and connections. They spoke the local language and could help tailor a sales campaign to local needs. The vast majority were, and are, honest and above board. Some, unfortunately, were not, as Airbus was to discover.

By the year 2000, companies in Europe and the U.S. were required to carefully vet and provide appropriate "due diligence" before engaging a business partner. International companies built compliance organizations and enhanced their legal oversight of commercial activities, particularly those conducted by business partners.

In 2000, EADS established a JV with French interests, based in Paris, called the Strategy and Marketing Organization, or SMO. (The JV was dissolved in 2003 with EADS becoming the sole owner.) As with the use of any sales consultant, the purpose of SMO was to engage someone with local connections. However, the EADS SMO operated independently of Airbus. It made for an odd arrangement.

It wasn't until 2012 that things began to fall apart with a German police raid.[102] Ironically, Airbus had an internal compliance process that won an award for its policies. But as events unfolded, Airbus's own legal department uncovered questionable transactions involving commissions paid to consultants via an EADS company set up in Paris. When the Airbus finance department looked into the questions, it discovered that the compliance procedures weren't as good as it thought. Airbus failed to disclose some deals involving export credit financing and including the involvement of consultants, which needed to be clearly disclosed. In other cases, consultants' names were mixed up.

Airbus disclosed the problems to the U.K. Export Finance, which suspended further financial support pending investigation. The Serious Fraud Office

---

102. A 2017 article in the German publication Der Spiegel outlines the Airbus scandal, including the police raid. https://www.spiegel.de/international/business/airbus-corruption-scandal-threatens-ceo-tom-enders-a-1171533.html. See also https://www.mofo.com/resources/insights/180214-airbus-corruption.html.

(SFO) was called in. From there, the emerging scandal blew up out of control. Prosecutors in France and Germany launched their own probes. German prosecutors raided an Airbus office and seized documents. Authorities in Austria launched their own investigation into a military deal via EADS. Eventually, the U.S. Justice Department became involved over violations of export of hardware that dealt with dual uses between military and commercial airplanes. Print media across three continents jumped on the story.

After the German police raided Airbus offices in 2012, Airbus began a deep-dive look into the consultant arrangements. A rat's nest of sloppy paper trails by the SMO—or, in some cases, no paper trails at all—was uncovered. Commissions that were paid for military and commercial deals sometimes had little or no back-up paper. One former Airbus official told this author that, in some cases, consultants were identified on U.K. Export credit documents who, in fact, were not a part of a particular deal. On others, the name or names that should have been included were not.

The internal investigation took four years to complete. As the scandal unfolded, one European-based aerospace reporter observed, "You won't recognize Airbus in 18 months." As it turned out, the full impact wouldn't be seen for nearly five years. Otherwise, the reporter was right.

The scandal eventually swept almost the entire Airbus leadership from office. Scores of lower-ranking officers and sales employees also were pushed out, whether guilty or not. It seems most were not guilty. Many people were just in the wrong place at the wrong time. Nevertheless, appearances mattered to the Airbus board and their legal advisors.

The U.K.'s SFO outlined the actions of EADS and Airbus in its "Statement of Facts" contained in the 2019 DPA settling the case.[103,104] "Airbus SE did not prevent, or have in place at the material times, adequate procedures designed to prevent those persons associated with Airbus SE from carrying out such conduct," the SFO found.

Airbus was faced with the disastrous prospect of possible criminal charges for the company, its executives and board, as well as possibly being barred in Europe and in the U.S. from defense contracts. The company

---

103. See https://www.sfo.gov.uk/2020/01/31/sfo-enters-into-e991m-deferred-prosecution-agreement-with-airbus-as-part-of-a-e3-6bn-global-resolution/ and https://www.sfo.gov.uk/download/airbus-se-deferred-prosecution-agreement-statement-of-facts/.

104. A Deferred Prosecution Agreement, or DPA, whether for Airbus or Boeing, is not a finding of guilt by a court of law but rather a deferral of prosecution upon a payment of a large fine and agreement by the company to make significant structural changes to procedures and personnel. This sometimes involves hiring an outside monitor to be sure the changes are implemented.

decided full cooperation with the authorities was the best course of action. The company cooperated fully with the British, who had become the lead investigators through the SFO. The French followed. The U.S. DOJ became involved. Austrian and German authorities continued their probe into the fighter deal.

In 2019, Airbus finally reached a DPA with Britain, France and the U.S. (the Austrian-German probe was settled earlier). The fine was a whopping $3.9 billion. The German fine for the Eurofighter scandal was $99 million. At the time, this was the largest corporate fine ever. These numbers compare with the $898 million Rolls-Royce paid in 2017 for its own bribery scandal, and the $615 million Boeing paid in 2006 (equal to $732.9 million in 2020) for a trade secrets theft and the tanker scandals.

Airbus's commercial and defense units were found in violation. "In principle," the SFO wrote in its DPA, "SMO International was supposed to ensure the Business Partners were independent of Airbus's customers and was responsible for compiling and appraising applications from potential and existing BPs for the purposes of a compliance risk assessment."

Airbus officials were confident their compliance program was robust, the DPA noted. "In late 2012, Airbus commissioned the audit and certification services of a private company to review its compliance program. A few months later, that company awarded Airbus an anti-corruption compliance certificate for the design of its anti-bribery compliance program." But the 2014 audit found "significant" violations of compliance policies, concluding that most of the projects from the SMO "performed poorly and questioned whether BPs helped create viable businesses."

In the DPA with the U.S. DOJ, it was revealed that Airbus violated U.S. International Traffic in Arms Regulations, known as ITAR. These guidelines restrict the export of U.S. defense and military technologies. The U.S. DPA didn't detail what the violations were, but the KC-330 aerial tanker has U.S. content for which ITAR probably applies.[105] There are also dual-use applications of technology on civilian aircraft. Boeing shipped one such part to China between 2000 and 2003 for use on 737s, inadvertently violating ITAR.[106]

The Airbus board of directors, following the advice of outside advisors, demanded a broad housecleaning, even as the probes were underway. Actual guilt or innocence took a back seat to appearance. Some 100 people were let go, many in the SMO and others throughout Airbus. Just as the

---

105. Jim McNerney, CEO of Boeing during the bitter fight to win a contract from the USAF for the KC-X tanker program, once suggested Airbus was violating ITAR. Airbus indignantly denied the allegation.

106. http://www.barnesrichardson.com/?t=40&an=7213&format=xml&p=3734

tanker scandal cost Boeing CEO Condit his job—because he was the CEO and the buck stopped with him—Enders and Airbus CFO Harald Wilhelm left even though they initiated internal investigations and reported findings to authorities.[107]

Airbus must monitor and report its actions for three years (to 2023), but the full effects of the wholesale housecleaning won't be really understood for years. (The coronavirus further muddies these waters.) The Airbus DPA, agreed to in 2019, was finalized in 2020 in the midst of Boeing's MAX grounding.

BOEING'S MAX SCANDAL

The MAX accidents were tragic and raised questions about the design of the MCAS. These questions were embarrassing enough for Boeing. But investigations by Congress, the FAA, the Department of Transportation Inspector General (DOT is the FAA's parent agency) and the U.S. DOJ revealed alarming lapses and scandalous actions by Boeing as well. Emails from and between two Boeing test pilots were especially damning. The FAA's own actions were roundly criticized for ceding too much oversight and authority to Boeing.

The DOT's investigation largely cleared the FAA of any wrongdoing, an outcome that surprised few. But in January 2021, in the final days of the Trump administration, Boeing and the U.S. DOJ announced they reached a DPA.[108] This DPA was quickly and widely criticized. The two test pilots were singled out as wrong doers. The DPA essentially exonerated the leadership and executives. The penalties, as described in Chapter 24, were mostly for the money Boeing already agreed to pay customers in compensation. There was a boost in the victims' fund, but the criminal penalty was a paltry $244 million. The DPA agreed that there was only one criminal count of fraud filed against Boeing.

"The [U.S. DOJ] Fraud Section determined that an independent compliance monitor was unnecessary, based on the following factors, among others: (i) the misconduct was neither pervasive across the organization, nor undertaken by a large number of employees, nor facilitated by senior management; (ii) although two of the Company's 737 MAX Flight Technical

---

107. At Airbus, authorities reviewed 30.5 million documents from more than 200 people. Interviews were conducted across Airbus. Airbus legal and investigative fees were reportedly more than $600 million.

108. https://www.justice.gov/opa/pr/boeing-charged-737-max-fraud-conspiracy-and-agrees-pay-over-25-billion and https://www.justice.gov/opa/press-release/file/1351336/download.

CHAPTER 25   **SCANDALS**

Pilots deceived the FAA ... about MCAS by way of misleading statements, half-truths and omissions, others in the Company disclosed MCAS's expanded operational scope to different FAA personnel who were responsible for determining whether the 737 MAX met U.S. federal airworthiness standards," the DPA states.

Like the Airbus DPA, Boeing's has a three-year monitoring provision, but this could be terminated early. (Families of the victims of the two fatal crashes were outraged at the DPA's terms and conditions, especially when the DPA revealed Boeing initially failed to cooperate with the probe.) Again, like Airbus, the full impact of the MAX crisis and the DPA won't be fully known for years; the coronavirus muddies the waters.

One of the responses Boeing made to the unfolding scandal was the creation of a board-level aviation safety committee. At the time, just how effective the creation of a board-level safety committee, an executive-level safety manager and other reforms remained the question. None of the safety committee members had aerospace experience. None was an airline pilot. None was an aerospace engineer or had experience in designing and producing airplanes. It wasn't until 2021 that the board appointed a new member who had 30 years of experience as a pilot on Boeing airplanes for United. She became a member of this committee.

Previous attempts at addressing ethics and safety violations didn't seem to have a lasting effect. The DPA noted that Boeing's corporate integrity and commitment to safety were subjects of previous government enforcement. "The Company's prior history of misconduct includes a criminal conviction from 1989 for an employee illegally obtaining confidential military planning documents, and a criminal non-prosecution agreement from 2006 for an employee engaging in procurement fraud. The Company's history also includes a civil FAA settlement agreement from 2015, related to safety and quality issues concerning the Company's Boeing Commercial Airplanes business unit," the DPA stated.

McNerney made a priority of improving Boeing's ethics after the tanker scandal. Calhoun started anew in the middle of the MAX crisis. His successor, whomever this may be, must continue the task.

26

Coronavirus

"We're bleeding cash at an unprecedented speed, which may threaten the very existence of our company."

—**GUILLAUME FAURY,** AIRBUS CEO, IN A MESSAGE TO EMPLOYEES

WHEN CALHOUN ASSUMED THE LEADERSHIP OF BOEING IN 2020, the company already had written off billions of dollars in costs, charges and customer compensation for the MAX grounding. Billions more would come. Calhoun also faced stagnant demand for the 777X. Boeing originally expected the 777-9 would enter service in early 2020, or maybe in the late fourth quarter of 2019. Development of the ultra long-range 777-8 was to follow by two years and the 777-8F two years after that. But EIS slipped a year when the giant GE9X engine ran into technical issues. Those already received for the test airplanes had to be shipped back to Cincinnati, GE's headquarters, for fixes.

Clark's Emirates had 150 on order, by far the largest number of any customer. He was already unhappy over engines for his A380 fleet, which included those produced by the GE-P&W JV Engine Alliance and Rolls-Royce. Clark told Boeing—and everyone else who would listen, including the press—he expected Boeing to do a 16-month flight test program to be sure the engines were okay before delivery.

The Trump administration's trade war with China affected sales. Boeing counted on China to become a solid customer for the 777X, but no new orders of any kind from China had been placed since 2017. None could be expected.

Then there was the impact of the certification controversy over the MAX. The 777X was next up on the FAA's certification plate after the MAX 7 and MAX 10. Everyone expected the FAA to take its sweet, meticulous time with the 777X after the MAX experience. Boeing initially professed there wouldn't be an FAA-induced delay for EIS, but few accepted these assurances. Calhoun finally acknowledged the obvious in the 2020 third quarter earnings call.

Calhoun had scores of unhappy MAX customers to appease. The USAF was also unhappy because Boeing Defense couldn't get the remote-controlled refueling boom to work properly. Ultimately, Boeing threw in the towel and said its supplier would design a new one. Plus, the USAF was unhappy with BCA because the USAF kept finding foreign object debris (FOD) in the wing tanks. Delivery of the KC-46A tankers was stopped twice while Boeing sorted this problem out.

FOD also was discovered in the wing tanks on the newly produced and stored MAXes. All 450-plus MAXes had to be inspected by Boeing. At one point, FOD was found in about half of those inspected. The 387 MAXes that were in service when the global fleet was grounded March 10 to 13 also had to be inspected. News broke over the summer about more FOD and quality-control issues with the Charleston-built 787s. This was a persistent problem at Charleston since the plant began assembling airplanes.

The FOD-QC (quality control) issues were deeply embarrassing for Boeing and went straight to the perception that Boeing had become a sloppy, lax company. Deal now had another problem to handle. Calhoun made one quick decision upon taking office: He all but killed the NMA. Officially, Calhoun suspended further R&D on the NMA, while a broad review of BCA's product line and future options was undertaken. This was a logical thing for any new CEO to do, he said.

There certainly was truth to this statement. However, unless Calhoun served on the Boeing board in sequestration, he was privy to whatever BCA leaders briefed the board about the NMA and alternatives. Rather, a Wall Street analyst who had been briefed by Chicago told a reporter that Calhoun had been against the NMA for a long time. "Killing" the airplane (not "suspending" it) only carried out Calhoun's long-held wishes. The executive was quick to say that suspending the NMA didn't mean Boeing wasn't going to pursue a new airplane program.

What was clear all along, even under Muilenburg, was that Boeing wasn't about to launch a new airplane while the MAX and its all-important cashflow were grounded—not until cash flow and profits resumed. Cynics said it wouldn't be until after shareholder value stock buybacks resumed, either. The lack of anticipated cash flow from deliveries of the 777X exacerbated matters. Calhoun also had a decision to make about the proposed JV with Embraer.

Of the 10 regulators that had to pass judgment on the anti-trust ramifications of the JV, nine cleared the deal. Only the EU held back. Slattery was livid. Despite assurances otherwise, he was convinced the EU was holding the JV hostage in the trade wars between the U.S. and the EU initiated by the Trump administration. Given the transaction history the EU was reviewing—20 years—and the hundreds of thousands of documents it demanded, it was hard to conclude otherwise.

Boeing and Embraer originally hoped the JV would pass regulatory approval by the end of 2017. But 2017 became 2018 and after multiple delays, Slattery hoped for final approval by the end of 2018. This wasn't to be, either, as 2018 turned into 2019. Then the MAX grounding happened, and Boeing's cash flow dried up.

During the year, Boeing issued $4.5 billion in new debt, earmarked to pay for the purchase price of ECA. Yet, as the MAX grounding dragged on and on and on, rumblings emerged that it made no sense for Boeing to spend this money when cash was pouring out the door.

Embraer's stock price had been sliding throughout 2018 and 2019. Sales of the fuel-efficient E2 jet were slow. The family's smallest member, the E175-E2 (intended for the U.S. market), was too heavy to comply with labor contract Scope Clause restrictions. Unless there was Scope relief—a dead issue, as far as the unions were concerned—the 175-E2 was a dead duck. The U.S. market was by far the largest for the E2 family. Without it, there was no way the E2 program could be profitable in the foreseeable future. Slattery's repeated promises of 175-E2 sales outside the U.S. were never fulfilled.

This shot a big hole in the business case and valuation of acquiring ECA. Embraer's market value declined for this, and other reasons, to one-fourth of the agreed acquisition price. Why pay $4.2 billion for something with a market value of $1.25 billion?

Slattery suggested that keeping Embraer out of the hands of a replacement party and Boeing competitor, was worth the premium. But there was more to it than just the E2. Acquiring the E2 was the last of four reasons for Boeing to do the deal. First was access to Embraer's young engineering force to replace Boeing's aging engineers. These would be assigned to the NMA.

The MOU creating the JV specified that Embraer would be responsible for developing a new airplane in the 100- to 150-seat sector. Embraer was also to become a major supplier for the NMA. But without the NMA, there was no need for the engineers or a new 100- to 150-seat airplane, at least not in the near- to-mid-term.

While Boeing was weighing these factors, it also faced a rising number of canceled orders for the MAX. Several lessors, including some in the U.S., canceled or swapped MAX orders. Still, even before the MAX grounding, there was a supply-demand imbalance for lessors trying to find homes for MAXes. In many cases, lease rates for the new, fuel-efficient airplane were below those for the 737NG, the older design. And the MAX lease rates were lower than for the A320neo. It was an upside-down situation. When the MAX was grounded and 12 months rolled by, some lessors saw an opportunity to get out.

Notably, neither accident carrier, Lion Air nor Ethiopian, canceled their orders for the MAX as of this writing, although each threatened to do so.

Some at Boeing believed Airbus was using its influence with EASA to stall recertification of the MAX to pave the way for A320 sales. Airbus denied it. The denials had the ring of truth about them. Airbus wants simultaneous certification reciprocity between EASA and the FAA. Sequential certification only delays EIS. The A321LR and A330-800 certifications were then on the near horizon. The A321XLR certification would be needed in 2023. Getting in the middle of an international certification dispute and tit-for-tat retaliation didn't work in its interest. By March 2020, there was no end in sight regarding when the MAX would be recertified. Calhoun and Boeing faced only dark days ahead, while Airbus was on the ascent. And then the world fell in.

In late 2019, a mysterious, deadly virus broke out in Wuhan, China. The government enacted a strict lockdown, but information was scant outside China. Dubbed the coronavirus, or COVID-19, outbreaks soon appeared in Europe and the U.S. The rest of the world eventually became infected. Hospitals were overwhelmed and deaths began to soar. It soon became clear the world was entering a pandemic stage.

By mid-March, the pandemic exploded across the globe. Air travel plunged by up to 90 percent or more. Airlines grounded increasing numbers of their fleets: first 25 percent, then 50 percent, then up to 90 percent. Even with this drastic reduction, load factors (the percentage of seats on an airplane) were running 10 percent. Many countries across the globe closed their borders, rendering international flights moot.

Airbus quickly suspended production to sanitize assembly plants. Boeing, already reeling from a year's grounding of the MAX, was much slower. Although the IAM 751 complained that its members on the FALs were at risk, Boeing didn't shut the Everett plant until after a worker died. Charleston followed a short time later.

Deliveries of virtually all commercial airliners ground to a halt at Airbus, Boeing and Embraer. For Boeing, already crippled by the MAX grounding and a laggard 777X program, seeing the 787 deliveries plunge all but rendered BCA impotent. Finally, on April 25, Calhoun pulled the plug on the Embraer JV.

"Boeing has worked diligently over more than two years to finalize its transaction with Embraer. Over the past several months, we had productive but ultimately unsuccessful negotiations about unsatisfied MTA [Master Transaction Agreement] conditions. We all aimed to resolve those by the initial termination date, but it didn't happen," said Marc Allen, president of Embraer Partnership & Group Operations. "It is deeply disappointing. But we have reached a point where continued negotiation within the framework of the MTA is not going to resolve the outstanding issues."

Embraer was furious. Brazilians are known for their friendly, laid-back culture. The executives uncharacteristically minced no words. "Embraer believes strongly that Boeing has wrongfully terminated the MTA, that it has manufactured false claims as a pretext to seek to avoid its commitments to close the transaction and pay Embraer the US$4.2 billion purchase price," it said in a statement. "We believe Boeing has engaged in a systematic pattern of delay and repeated violations of the MTA, because of its unwillingness to complete the transaction in light of its own financial condition, and 737 MAX and other business and reputational problems. Embraer believes it is in full compliance with its obligations under the MTA and that it has satisfied all conditions required to be accomplished by April 24, 2020."

The companies moved to arbitration as provided in the JV agreement. For Boeing, the move saved a commitment of $4.2 billion. Boeing's claim that it canceled the JV for cause saved a $100 million break-up fee. For Embraer, the $130 million it spent carving out Commercial Aviation from the larger corporation was money down the drain. During the long period awaiting regulatory approval, Slattery said potential sales were sidelined as customers waited to see what Boeing would do with Embraer. Development of the turboprop had been delayed. Embraer was back in a position of competing on its own against Airbus for the lower end of the 100- to 150-seat sector. Future roles on new Boeing airplanes, whatever they were, were gone. And now Embraer had to face the COVID crisis alone. One executive admitted that Embraer's survival was at stake.

Four days after Boeing walked, it reported its first quarter earnings. On the earnings call, Calhoun was straightforward about the impact of COVID-19. "The COVID-19 pandemic is a global crisis like no other," Calhoun began. "To preserve the long-term competitiveness of our company, as well as our industry, we are intensely focused on ensuring liquidity through the immediate crisis."

In addition to BCA taking a big hit from the virus crisis, BGS also took a pounding. At least half of BGS's revenues came from the airline industry. With airlines essentially grounded, revenue to BGS dropped dramatically. Boeing immediately drew down its credit lines, initially telling Washington that the aerospace industry needed $60 billion in immediate government aid. Boeing's ask for its share was never specifically highlighted, but news reports later pegged it as $17 billion.[109]

Calhoun announced a voluntary layoff plan to cut 10 percent of the company-wide workforce, with mandatory layoffs, if necessary, to meet this goal. Most of the reduction was to come from BCA. Over the course of the next few months, the reductions doubled, again hitting BCA harder than Defense of BGS.

From Washington state's perspective, most of these layoffs came from here. The impact wasn't just with Boeing, however. For each direct job at

---

109. However, when the Department of Treasury said terms and conditions would include a requirement to grant stock or warrants to the government as a condition of loans, Boeing said, "No thanks." Instead, Boeing went to the bond markets and raised $25 billion. Treasury bought billions of dollars of these bonds.

CHAPTER 26 **CORONAVIRUS**

the giant, three to four indirect jobs in Washington were affected at suppliers, all the way down to restaurants, coffee shops and janitors.

Symbolically, the biggest blow to Washington came in October when Boeing announced it was consolidating production of the 787 into Charleston. The FAL in Everett was shutting down in 2021. Calhoun telegraphed the blow on the second quarter earnings call July 29 when he said Boeing would reduce production to six per month and study consolidation. While he took pains to say no decision had been made, few believed this. *The Seattle Times, Leeham News*, several other news outlets, and just about every observer and analyst who was asked said there was no question the sole FAL would be in Charleston.

In fact, once Boeing decided in October 2009 that the second FAL would be in Charleston, most concluded that when the inevitable day came that market demand lowered production, Charleston would be the sole 787 producer. Labor costs were lower. Environmental regulations were looser. The cost of doing business was lower. And once Boeing decided that the 787-10 would be produced only in Charleston, the writing was on the wall for the long-term future.

The corollary was that a new Boeing airplane, presumably what became the NMA, would have free space in Everett. But this, too, was put on hold when Calhoun killed this airplane and suspended R&D for any new one in the required cost-cutting move. As part of cost reduction, Boeing later announced that it would reduce its real estate footprint by 30 percent. BCA's Renton headquarters would be sold. BCA executives might be relocated to excess space at Renton Airport or Everett, and a "floating BCA CEO" was contemplated to be closer to production. Even Boeing's lease of the expensive Chicago headquarters was being reconsidered.

Selling the Renton headquarters would be a major, symbolic loss to Washington—and perhaps a harbinger of eventually relocating BCA headquarters outside the state. Boeing's cost cutting even extended to selling its $13 million yacht, the "Daedalus," in November 2020. Long a highly valued perk for BCA sales and executives to entertain customers and international visitors, it was something Airbus lacked. One former insider said selling the yacht showed just how bad things really were. The Boeing yacht had survived previous recessions, depressions, production shutdowns and even 9/11.

One must stretch very hard to find anything good coming out of the pandemic, but the crisis gave Boeing executives the ability to go after sacred cows and clean house in ways that never would have been possible otherwise. For decades, outsiders and many insiders complained that Boeing was bloated and filled with deadwood, sustaining a self-protective personnel infrastructure with a history of moving incompetents around rather than firing them.

Boeing's customer airlines, having grounded most of their fleets at the start of the pandemic, didn't want to take delivery of airplanes. Lessors faced the same issue with their lessees. In turn, the lessors didn't want new airplanes from Boeing, either. The MAX grounding allowed some customers the ability to cancel airplanes without penalty.[110] For customers who ordered the 787 or the 777 Classic (mostly freighters), deferrals rather than cancelations were typically sought.

At Airbus, Faury was quick to say the company's very survival was now at stake. "Our challenge at Airbus is to adapt to this new reality as fast as possible and limit the scale of the damage," Faury wrote in a message to employees. "We're bleeding cash at an unprecedented speed, which may threaten the very existence of our company."[111]

Airbus immediately raised €15 billion (approximately US$17.6 billion) to bolster its liquidity. It cut A320 production from 60 per month to 40. A350 rates were slashed from 10 to six and A330 rates were cut down to two. The A380, already on its way out, was left alone to build its last five aircraft. Many wondered why Airbus didn't cut rates even more, especially for the A320. This rate, Airbus explained, was needed to preserve the health of the supply chain.

Unlike Boeing, which can act freely to expand or contract, constrained only by "WARN" requirements (60- day warning notices to employees in advance of layoffs), Airbus has strict labor laws in Europe to contend with. It's not free to lay off at will. This is the main reason why Airbus tries to maintain steady workforces and production through economic cycles.

When the pandemic hit, Airbus announced employment reduction of 15,000 people. But French law especially required negotiations with the unions, who, despite the obvious need for cost cutting, objected. Nevertheless, Airbus proceeded with production reductions as negotiations began. Officials said R&D spending, except for the A321XLR, was suspended. However, as the nine-month reports for BCA and Airbus Commercial show, each company was still spending a fair amount on R&D.

---

110. The contracts have complicated provisions which allow cancelations under tightly defined circumstances. One provision concerns delayed deliveries, with the trigger typically tied to six or 12 months. Even these are restricted by excusable and non-excusable reasons for the delays; even these sometimes get caught up in legal interpretations by lawyers for the OEM and the customer. In the case of the MAX groundings that ultimately stretched 21 months (or more, in the case of China), customers were able to cancel orders without penalty. In the case of developmental delays, as with the 787 and now the 777X, customers can cancel, but it may be on a rolling, airplane-by-airplane basis rather than the entire order book.

111. https://www.reuters.com/article/health-coronavirus-airbus-text/text-airbus-ceos-survival-at-stake-memo-to-employees-idUSL5N2CF5EA

Airbus cut production shortly after the pandemic took hold. Officials said they would revisit the rates the following August or September. These months came and went without a new announcement. In October, news leaked that Airbus was alerting the supply chain to prepare to increase production of the A320 from 40 to 47 per month in the second half of 2021. Most were skeptical that demand would support the higher rate. Once more, Airbus explained, the health of the supply chain was paramount.

By the end of June, Airbus produced 145 A320s that were parked in Hamburg and Toulouse, awaiting delivery to customers. A smaller number, but not insignificant considering the values, of widebodies were also parked. Remarkably, by the end of the third quarter, Airbus delivered enough airplanes to stem the cash bleeding.

"After nine months of 2020 we now see the progress made on adapting our business to the new COVID-19 market environment," Faury said. "Despite the slower air travel recovery than anticipated, we converged commercial aircraft production and deliveries in the third quarter, and we stopped cash consumption in line with our ambition. Furthermore, the restructuring provision booked shows our discussions with social partners and stakeholders have advanced well. Our ability to stabilize the cash flow in the quarter gives us confidence to issue a free cash flow guidance for the fourth quarter."

As 2020 slid into 2021, however, signs of hope emerged. Despite worrying spikes in coronavirus infections and deaths in Europe, Japan and the U.S.—and the slow rollout of vaccines—at least the world was fighting back.

At Boeing, the FAA recertified the MAX in November. Brazil's regulator, which oversees Embraer, followed a few days later. Transport Canada and EASA telegraphed their recertification would follow in January. Brazil's GOL, Aeromexico and American were the first carriers to put the MAX back in service. United, Southwest and Canada's WestJet were next. Ryanair ordered 75 MAX 8-200s. Alaska Airlines added to its previous order for the MAX 9.

Airbus ended 2020 with more than 500 deliveries and more than 300 orders—both deemed fantasies as the pandemic unfolded. Recovery for Airbus, Boeing, Embraer and the entire commercial aerospace industry depends on how quickly airlines recover. And recovery from the pandemic controls all.

Airbus was free of the unique circumstances impacting Boeing with the MAX, the development/certification delays for the 777X and later, new production issues that emerged with the 787. Its customers were no less interested in deferrals or cancellations, but this time—in contrast to the 9/11 era—Airbus's leadership took a tougher stance. CEO Faury and the top salesman, Scherer (Leahy's deputy in the 9/11 era), played hardball.

The WSJ outlined the strategy in an article entitled "Airbus Soars Past Boeing by Showing Little Mercy to Struggling Customers."[112]

"The aircraft giant established itself ahead of its longtime rival by making airlines honor contracts, despite the pandemic," *The WSJ* wrote. "Mr. Faury spent the bulk of the pandemic trying to force his biggest and most loyal customers, some of whom were teetering on the brink, to live up to their ironclad contractual obligations. That gamble, which bucked industry convention, has helped lift Airbus into the strongest competitive position in its history against rival Boeing Co."

Airbus plans to return production of the A320 to 63 per month by 2023. It alerted the supply chain to plan for additional rate hikes to 70 and even 75 A320s a month by 2025. Boeing, meantime, hopes to boost 737 production to 31 a month in 2022 and return to 52 a month, the rate the MAX was at when it was grounded in March 2019, a few years later. At the time of the grounding, Boeing was prepared to take the 737 production rate to 57 a month by the end of 2019. Wide-body rates for both companies are expected to remain suppressed until at least 2025.

For Leahy, as well as Enders, Carson, Albaugh and Conner—even for Muilenburg, Calhoun and the hundreds of thousands employees at Airbus and Boeing—the "air wars" since 1984 brought triumphs, disappointments, scandals, tragedies and brutal global combat.

The next 35 years will offer similar challenges, but it's unlikely there will be another Leahy for Airbus or another Conner for Boeing—whom Leahy called his toughest competitor—that will have the same level of influence.

---

112. https://www.wsj.com/articles/airbus-boeing-rivals-max-11626189853

27

Retirement

"That's why we bought you a first-class seat. So you can sleep on the airplane. You can have a Sheraton the next time."

—**JOHN LEAHY** TO TOM WILLIAMS ON THE LACK OF HOTELS ON A ROUND-THE-WORLD TRIP

JIM McNERNEY RETIRED AS CEO IN 2015, following 10 tumultuous years as CEO of The Boeing Co. He never did hit the board target of $200 a share. It was said the board was increasingly unhappy with McNerney and forced Dennis Muilenburg on him when Muilenburg was named president and COO in December 2013.

Although this was the story floating around the aerospace analyst community, it was never confirmed by Boeing. Regardless, Muilenburg was clearly the CEO-in-waiting. Boeing announced in February 2016 that Muilenburg would succeed McNerney as chairman, too. The move was effective the next month—the same month the MAX flight testing began, as it turned out, though the timing was coincidental. McNerney left the board.

With Muilenburg's ascension, the president and COO title reverted to one man again, combined with the chairman and CEO position. It would remain thus until the board stripped Muilenburg of the chairman's title in the wake of the MAX crisis.

Ray Conner, the lifer who began his Boeing career on the shop floor and rose to become vice chairman of The Boeing Co. and CEO of BCA, retired in November 2016. He didn't formally leave the company until December 2017, serving in an advisory and transitionary role to his successor. Kevin McAllister, from GE Services, replaced him. Stan Deal left BCA to become CEO of BGS. John Wojick, who headed BCA's sales, retired in early 2017. He was replaced by Ihssane Mounir as vice-president of sales and marketing. Mounir, just 44 at the time, had been the head of sales for North Asia and China.

Over at Airbus, John Leahy was tired. He would be 67 in August 2017. He was overweight. He had health issues, and he was no longer the famously energetic globetrotter of his younger years. Leahy couldn't chase the time zones anymore for maximum efficiencies. In his younger days, he could hop on an airplane to Singapore, work a full day, get on the next flight back to Toulouse via Paris and work a full day on arrival.

When the industrial wiring problems on the A380 emerged in 2006, resulting in what would ultimately be a two-year delivery delay, Leahy and Tom Williams embarked on a customer situation update and hand-holding trek. Leahy was 55 at the time; Williams was 53. "The wheels were off the bus at this point," Leahy recalled. "The situation with the 380 was dire. It was showing all sorts of problems, and a lot of work needed to be done to get things sorted out. Tom Williams and I went around the world to explain this to the launch customers and existing customers of the A380. We met with Tim Clark first up in London. In an hour-long meeting, where we got in about two minutes worth of talking, Tim lectured us about the fiasco with the 380 and the chaos it had cost to his airline and asked what we going to do about it.

"We then flew around the world seeing the CEOs and top management of 380 launch customers. Although they were upset and shocked, as you could well imagine, they were all staying with the program. They clearly had the right to cancel, walk away, get their deposit back, even get some damages. They all decided to stay with the program," Leahy added.

The trip and its pace were grueling. The slightly younger Williams vowed never to do a trip like that again with Leahy. "Why?" the latter asked. "We had beautiful hotel rooms. We had fine dinners and everything. We flew first class around the world."

Williams said, "We may have had the beautiful hotel rooms, but we hardly ever used them. In a 10-day period, I got to sleep in a real bed two nights." He complained that the nights were spent sleeping on a plane. "I was just so annoyed because, by the time I came back, I was like a bent toy, I was so exhausted. You go away for a week, and you look at the itinerary and see there are no hotel rooms for overnight sleeping. 'That's why we bought your first-class seat,' John would say. 'You can sleep on the airplane. You can have a Sheraton the next time,'" Williams said. "We went one trip like that right around the world in a week. We went from Europe, down into Middle East, to Asia, Japan and back to the States. I got home on a Sunday, and I needed four days to recover. John went off on another trip [the] next week. It was just incredible."

In the early days when Leahy took the Concorde, he'd make his staff work during the flight. After all, the trip was only a few hours long. "The flight's pretty short on the Concorde," recalled Leahy. "On an international trip on other planes, the fact that people would just sit back, get a bottle of wine and put their feet up and watch a couple of movies was a little bit frustrating."

Leahy said he wanted his team to use the time on fine-tuning the presentations. "Let's review our numbers. Let's see what the competition is up

CHAPTER 27 **RETIREMENT**

to, so when they hear what we're claiming, what might they say in reply. We needed to be ready. You want to use some of that time productively. It doesn't mean I'm this ogre that doesn't let the guys have a few glasses of wine, but it's not an eight- or 10-hour party on the airplane either. We've got to get some work done."

Still, Kiran Rao, who worked for Leahy for 25 years, said beneath the gruff exterior and exacting demands, Leahy was just a "pussycat." He cared about his team. Leahy fought for them internally, especially when it came time for annual bonuses.

Leahy's ambition and chutzpah were always on display. It's already been noted that he wanted to be hired by Alan Boyd as sales manager, coming from Piper where he never actually sold an airplane. Steve Hazy's good-natured, if somewhat biting characterization of Leahy as a marketing apprentice, may understate Leahy's experience at Piper. When he left for Airbus in 1984, he was Piper's director of marketing with a staff of about 25.

Dana Lockhart once saw a business plan Leahy created while at Airbus North America in which Leahy named himself chairman of the unit. He never got that job, but it didn't stop his upward ascent. Leahy was a pilot; he wasn't an aeronautical engineer. His MBA was in finance and transportation, but he was a quick study and was never reluctant to weigh in on product strategy, Lockhart said. The A300B4 and A310 were designed principally for European use. They did what they did reasonably well but were unable to be used or were inferior for transatlantic operations. Leahy brought an important U.S. and global perspective that Airbus needed.

"Jean Pierson trusted John and John had Pierson's ear" in those early days, Lockhart said. Pierson, the "bear of the Pyrenees" as he was known, by sheer force of will drove the leadership and the partners to approve decisions, approve deals and approve ways forward, some of which came out from North America and Leahy.

"It was that essential link, and it was John's brilliance in the early days to put himself in that unique communication role with Pierson," Lockhart said. "He got to educate Pierson about what the North American market was really like. Pierson was a factory guy. He didn't understand commerce." But Pierson was shrewd. He had an innate ability to focus on deals that needed to be won.

On paper, Leahy reported to Alan Boyd and later Jim Bryan. But each served more as door openers than as active salesmen. "It is my belief that John had both engineered an organization chart that favored him getting ahead, and also [that he] benefited from. I would have to call it benign neglect, Jim Bryan as his boss. Even though John was brash, and Alan Boyd could find fault with him, Alan thought John was a brilliant salesman, and he was delivering results. That's this side of the pond," Lockhart said.

"On the other side of the pond, by controlling the communication link between North America and Toulouse, John to Pierson, Pierson to John, Pierson depended on John's inherent veracity to not position Pierson in a way that would embarrass him. I think they had a level of confidence and mutual trust that allowed Leahy to explain things to Jean in a way that allowed Jean to go use his force of will to get things approved, transactions and ways forward."

If Leahy failed to have either one of those, or if Bryan had wanted to be more involved, it would have stepped on Leahy's toes. If Pierson hadn't trusted Leahy as much as he ultimately did, Leahy would have faced serious trouble when many of the North American deals soured.

"Let's face it," Lockhart said, "John was delivering deals, but some of the deals turned into fertilizer. Airlines were going bankrupt, and airplanes were never going to be delivered. The headlines in the late '80s and early '90s, before John moved to Toulouse, were a litany of one disaster after another, one bankruptcy after another, after another, after another."

When the airlines went through bankruptcies, a few failed but most successfully reorganized, and Airbus benefitted in the end. United came out of bankruptcy. US Airways came out of two bankruptcies. America West came out of bankruptcy and bought US Airways, and US Airways bought American. American went into bankruptcy but reconfirmed the historic A320neo deal.

"Admittedly, the Airbus leadership changed over the years, but in the early days, what Pierson knew and understood about the North American market, he knew and understood via John," Lockhart said.

Leahy says he often stepped back to let his sales team pursue the deals, consulting and making decisions in the background, but he didn't hesitate to become directly involved when needed, either. "When you are out with John on a campaign, you just watch him in action. He was a closer," recalled Williams. "He was a guy, like lots of great people, who could make wonderful marketing presentations and could dazzle you with slides. But in terms of closing, getting a deal done, no one can hold a candle to John."

ILFC was one of Leahy's biggest customers. John Plueger said the lessor did several "Hallmark" deals with Leahy. Some of them didn't turn out as Leahy or ILFC expected. One of ILFC's early Hallmark deals was the A380. The company was the only lessor to sign up for the giant airplane: five passenger models and five freighters.

"The first problem that turned out was that the A380 was not going to be that great of a freighter," Plueger said. "Airbus first came to us and said, 'Well, look, it's not going to happen for the freighter.' Suffice to say that we made a big deal out of it and said, 'Well, that was part of our balance of our A380 platform to minimize our risk.' And we ended up getting a big concession for not having the freighter."

There were only three customers that had signed up for the A380 freight-

CHAPTER 27 RETIREMENT

er: FedEx, UPS and ILFC. "After consultation with the two other customers, we all came to the realization that loading that upper deck in high-wind conditions with a forklift became extremely problematic," Plueger said. "All of us reached the conclusion—the cargo A380 was just not really something that made a lot of sense," added Steven Udvar-Hazy. "To get us out of the deals, Airbus had to buy their way out of it to make it work," explained Hazy. Airbus was supposed to have a certain number of customers committed by a certain date. There were milestones that were in the purchase agreement, and Airbus was reaching none of those, he concluded.

"One of those milestones is that they had to get at least one customer in the Western Hemisphere—an airline customer," Plueger said. "That goal was never reached. They never got an airline either in North or South America. So that gave us the automatic right to say, 'Bye.' And that cost Airbus again more money because they had to channel funds to other contracts we had with Airbus and other products."

And then there was the industrial fiasco, the wiring bundles. Top executives from ILFC and its parent, AIG, went to Toulouse to inspect the airplanes. "It was like a bomb went off in there," Hazy said. "It was awful. The chairman of AIG looked at us and asks, 'Do all airplanes look like this?' The Airbus chief engineer was almost bragging that there are 90 miles of wiring, spaghetti wiring, in the interior, and it was almost a nightmare. The AIG chairman made a comment, 'I wouldn't want to fly on this thing.'"

ILFC canceled the order. ILFC received an additional concession amount, which ultimately went to buy other Airbus planes. ILFC was one of the shrewdest buyers of airplanes. Hazy said that nevertheless, ILFC made three "major mistakes" with Leahy. Two of them were made "because Leahy was a very powerful sales guy."

One was the A380, which ended up in a positive way because compensation was applied to other aircraft. The second one was an order for 30 A318s with the P&W 6000 engine. The engine was a disaster and ILFC canceled, receiving $30 million in compensation from P&W. "That was the best airplane deal we never did," Plueger said.

"The third mistake, and that's where John Leahy won and we lost, was when he talked us into buying A340s," Hazy said. "The first one was the A340-300, with Airbus advocating that a four-engine plane over intercontinental routes was much better than the 777. Later on, we bought the A340-600. We had customers for all of these aircraft. At the time, the lease rates we got were actually defensible; they were not bad. But I think where we missed the mark was projecting the residual value."

Residual value is important to lessors. A chunk of profits comes from selling the planes early in their life cycles—typically five to 12 years—and the values are assumed at certain points in the future when the lessor first acquires the airplane. In simple terms, residual value is what a consumer pays at the end of a car lease if he wants to buy the car, or the assumed value at the end of the lease, based on assumed ending mileage.

The A340's residual value assumptions never lived up to expectations. The airplane quickly became outdated by long range, twin-engine airplanes like the 777 and Airbus's own A330. Unfortunately, the A340's performance initially failed to live up to its promises. The Rolls-Royce engines on the A340-500 and -600 were also very expensive to maintain. "We would crucify John about that, and we would hold it against him with every subsequent negotiation," stated Plueger.

Leahy is known for his biting sense of humor, and he is a master of one-liners. But he also had an image of a staid, buttoned-down guy. Tony Fernandes, the CEO of AirAsia, demanded Leahy dance with his flight attendants at a Paris night club before he would sign a contract for a huge order after the clock struck midnight. When Leahy balked, Tom Enders—a German with a keen, subtle sense of humor who was already dancing with a tie wrapped around his head—ordered Leahy to comply. It's a very funny story that Enders, Fernandes, the CFM salesman and others told. His corporate communications team says Leahy really hates it.

Which makes the story of the time he and Hazy got into a prankish shoving match over dinner (that saw both of them going into a swimming pool at a fancy Hawaiian hotel) seem out of character. Airbus held its annual customer event at the Four Seasons Hotel in Maui, Hawaii. Customers could bring their wives. Business meetings occurred in the mornings with socializing and golf, thereafter.

ILFC was in a contentious negotiation with Leahy. One morning, ILFC announced an order for 50 737-800s from Boeing. The deal made the front page of *The WSJ*. Hazy and Plueger made sure a copy made its way, indirectly, to Leahy. The timing was deliberate.

"Good morning, John. How are you?" Plueger asked when he saw Leahy a short time later. "And he goes, 'Well, not so good this morning.'" Hazy added, "We wanted to kind of give John a little knifing because he was being very stubborn on some other items. Sure enough, Leahy had a very bad day."

"Around the time the A330-200 was introduced, we had such a time with John," recalled Plueger. "He was beating the crap out of us, and we were beating the crap out of him. It was really, really tough, and we are duking it out. One night, right after dinner, we [ILFC] all sort of had it. We are walking toward the pool. Steve, me and a couple of other big guys from ILFC hit on this plan that we were going to throw Leahy in the pool."

After dinner, the ILFC crew was ready to execute its "Dunk Leahy" plan. But, Plueger said, somehow Leahy had gotten wind of it. So he beat them to the punch and pushed Hazy into the pool. Plueger and a big ILFC employee, Marty Olson, immediately pushed Leahy into the pool, who managed to pull them in as he went.

CHAPTER 27 **RETIREMENT**

"All of a sudden, people started going into the pool, and hotel security came running down," Plueger said. "Everybody starts scattering to the winds because they think it's going to be a mess pulling people from the pool." Everyone was dressed for dinner, Hazy noted. Such tomfoolery, however, was few and far between.

In 2015, the year he turned 65, Leahy, after some serious hesitation, extended his contract by two years. Chasing the deals simply didn't have the appeal that it once did. By January 2018, it was finally time for Leahy to pack it in. He enjoyed taking cruises with Grace and other members of his family. Although he lived in Miami, he divided his time between two homes along the East Coast of the U.S.. He enjoyed visiting Dublin, where his son, Robert, lives with his family and works for a lessor. He has a daughter in Australia and another in Washington, D.C., and grandchildren on three continents.

Leahy's 33 years at Airbus were filled with successes, failures and controversies. His successes are clear. Taking Airbus from a low global market share to 50 percent or more is the most obvious success. Establishing the A320/A321 as the dominant single-aisle family is another. But Leahy points out that he failed the other 50 percent of the time—or 47 percent or 40 percent, depending on the given point of measurement. He also says that if Boeing got too low a share of the market, it might force them to take a product development risk, which would force Airbus to respond before it was ready to develop a new airplane. This was always part of the equation in considering what Boeing would do in response to the A320neo and later, when Boeing debated whether to launch the NMA. When Leahy moved to Toulouse in 1994, he vowed to the Airbus executive board that the company could grow to at least 50 percent of the market by 2000. He had a little over five years to go from low double digits to this lofty goal.

The Airbus executive board initially laughed at him, Leahy recalled. But his goal was key to Airbus's future. "I said we need to be in a band of 40 percent to 60 percent. I remember going to the executive board meeting, which was the CEOs of the manufacturers that owned us: Aerospatiale, Deutsche Aerospace, British Aerospace and CASA. They listened to my presentation in January [1995] and why this was so important," Leahy recalls. "They said, 'That sounds very motivating for your sales team, but we want to know what is the real and realistic goal for market share that we should be aiming for.' I paused, and I said 50 percent. That's what we need to do. They started laughing. Somebody said, 'You can't be serious. Twenty-five percent, maybe 30 percent, would be a more reasonable, more sustainable target.'" A genuine debate ensued about whether 50 percent was ever attainable under any circumstances, Leahy added.

The first year of Leahy's new position (1995) ended with Airbus at an 18 percent market share. He speculated that, in an American corporation, the executive board would have concluded he didn't do well and would have booted him out, or at the very least, given him one more year. When Leahy went to the board meeting in January 1996, "there was none of that. I thought that I'd be heavily criticized. But they wanted to know what was happening in the market, what was Boeing doing and their pricing strategies against us. Everybody seemed quite comfortable that this was a long-term strategy." Leahy credits the long-term view in European companies as one of the reasons for the success of Airbus. Leahy cultivated stability in his sales teams. He emphasized constant customer contact, local knowledge and "boots on the ground."

By 1997, McDonnell Douglas was down to about a seven percent market share in commercial aviation. Boeing and MDC merged. Through the early 2000s, Boeing—following MDC strategy, critics said—focused on derivatives instead of investing in new airplanes. Boeing came under a lot of criticism during this period, particularly by noted consultant Richard Aboulafia, for starving spending for R&D. Aboulafia routinely pointed to Boeing's stingy R&D spending and the larger funding at Airbus as one of Boeing's strategic mistakes.

But to some degree, it's not this simple. Boeing, Airbus and others pursue derivatives following costly new airplane programs because this is where the profits are. The question was whether Boeing made a strategic mistake in producing the 757-300, 767-400 and 737-900 (standard), none of which sold well, or that Boeing tried the proverbial push to a bridge too far. "I hate to go into whether Boeing got it right or wrong," Leahy says. "We've got enough strategic mistakes that we've made at Airbus. I focus on those more than my competitor's strategic mistakes."

PRICE, MARKET SHARE WAR

Pressed, Leahy said, "If you go back to mistake number one, is why did we have 18 percent market share in 1995? I think Ron Woodard [then president of BCA] and his management team were absolutely appalled at this concept that Airbus would even dream of the possibility of having a 50 percent market share by 2000. They were determined that they were going to crush us."

Woodard believed Boeing had an "enormous industrial might" and Europe didn't, allowing Boeing to go into the market and cut prices ("which he was doing in 1995"), based on high volume, lower production costs and the ability to pass through lower prices. "He also offered very early delivery slots," Leahy recalled. Woodard offered airplanes the next year or in 18 months. "He knew we couldn't."

The result was a disaster for Boeing. Leahy said Boeing probably could have sustained the low pricing, and it did. But as Woodard upped produc-

CHAPTER 27 **RETIREMENT**

tion of the 737, everything fell apart. The supply chain couldn't keep up with a dramatic increase in the production rate (from 21 737s a month to 27, at the time an unprecedented rate). Production lines fell behind, quality control suffered and deliveries were late. Boeing took the unprecedented step of shutting down the 737 line for 30 days to catch up. The company reported its first loss in 40 years. Woodard lost his job over the snafu. "I think that set Boeing back quite a few years," Leahy observes. "That would be the first strategic mistake, at least during my career, that I think they made." (It set Boeing back two years, said Gary Scott.)

Breaking the Boeing dominance or monopolies at airlines throughout the world were also key successes for Leahy. Gambling on the A320neo was a very big win. Proceeding with the A330neo, not so much. The A380 program, which a few critics charged was a Leahy ego project, was a sales bust. Misreading the threat of the 787 also was a miscue. Correctly identifying the potential of lessors and low-cost carriers were big successes, each of which helped drive Airbus's growth and success.

Claims by Faury, in May 2019, that the A380 was a success is pure revisionist history. While it is certainly true Airbus benefitted from lessons learned, this approach was hardly the business model put forth for the executive board and governments to approve the program.

The A330neo, on the other hand, was never viewed internally as the prospective success external public relations suggested. A low-cost effort, Airbus didn't need a large number of airplanes sold to make money—500 was the internal sales target, Rao said. Airbus was hard-pressed to meet this target even before COVID-19 tanked the market. Delivering 300 A330neos may be a stretch, given the poor customer quality of the skyline. (In 2020, Leahy characterized the A330neo as an "opportunistic" airplane.) But, if looked at from the objective to continue to put pricing pressure on the 787, there's little question this goal was achieved. While McNerney consistently denied there was pricing pressure between the 330neo and 787, the market was clear that this was the case.

As Leahy prepared to retire, whoever would replace him couldn't possibly fill his shoes. His personality, his drive and his legend simply could not be matched. Initially, Enders chose Rao, Leahy's deputy and protégé of 25 years. He was highly regarded throughout Airbus and the customer base. Rao's appointment was announced, but then he got caught up in the negative halo effect of the SMO scandal. Although Rao never was part of the SMO, the board-mandated clean-sweep prompted Enders to rescind the appointment. Even those within Airbus thought Rao got a raw deal.

Disappointed and disillusioned, Rao later left Airbus. He became a consultant to the Indian airline IndiGo, becoming the point man when the carrier studied whether to order the MAX and diversify its reliance on Airbus. Media reporting suggested management was leaning toward a MAX order when regulators grounded the airplane. IndiGo re-ordered the A320neo. The irony of Airbus having to pitch Rao for IndiGo's order was not lost on those in Toulouse. Rao was later cleared of any wrongdoing by the SFO, the lead agency in the probe.

Enders' eventual choice to succeed the retiring Leahy was an odd one. The contenders were Scherer, at the time the CEO of ATR in which Airbus owned a 50 percent share, and Eric Schulz of Rolls-Royce. Scherer was legacy Airbus. His father had been one of the original Airbus employees, and Scherer followed in his footsteps into the company. Among the positions he held were sales and strategy before being named to the CEO position at ATR. Before that, Scherer had worked for Leahy both in the U.S. and Toulouse. In fact, he previously held Rao's job as deputy to Leahy for many years until finally moving to strategy.

Enders named Eric Schulz to Leahy's job. At the time, the buzz was that the board of directors didn't want Scherer because of the "appearance" issue as a long-time insider, including during some of the period in question. They wanted an outsider.

If appearance was a criterion, then Schulz's selection was hard to explain. Rolls-Royce had just been fined a record amount for its own bribery scandal. There was no hint that Schulz was any way involved, but if appearances mattered....

There was another reason Schulz's selection was strange. At the time, Rolls-Royce was in hot water with airlines around the world that were operating the Rolls-Royce-powered Boeing 787. The Trent 1000 engine suffered technical problems, which appeared years after entering service. Upward of 50 787s were grounded across the globe and many would be for years as Rolls-Royce worked through the problems to repair or replace them. The A330neo, A350 and A380 all had Rolls-Royce engines. The A330neo's Trent 7000 was merely a Trent 1000 with bleed air—essentially the same engine as on the 787. Appointing a former Rolls-Royce salesman to the top sales job at Airbus didn't seem likely to soothe upset customers who had 787s on the ground—and it wasn't. Airlines and leasing companies complained.

In any event, Schulz didn't last a year. In a power play to gain more authority, Enders didn't bite. Schulz quit. This time, Enders named Scherer to the job he should have gotten the first go around.

In October 2015, two months after Leahy's 65th birthday and after he extended his contract with Airbus for two more years, the Wings Club honored him. The prestigious group holds a black-tie annual event every October in New York to recognize an industry leader for his contributions. At the dinner, McNerney offered congratulations to Leahy in a very funny video. The clip starts as McNerney is getting his microphone and being lint-brushed. The blue screen behind him has an outdoor scene.

CHAPTER 27 RETIREMENT

MCNERNEY: What's next? What am I? [*Puzzled.*] Who am I doing this for?

VOICE OFF CAMERA: It's the Leahy tribute video.

MCNERNEY: [*Appalled.*] John Leahy? Of Airbus? Really?

VOICE OFF CAMERA: Sir, your mike is still on.

MCNERNEY: Oh. Oooh. Sorry. Uh, make sure you cut that out of the video. Thank you.

VOICE OFF CAMERA: Okay, I think we're ready. Action.

The audience was rolling in laughter. So was Leahy.

The blue screen background changes to a 787 on take-off at the Farnborough Air Show. While McNerney talks, the 787 goes through a series of aerobatic moves that demonstrate the impressive flying ability of the airplane.

MCNERNEY [*Enthusiastically*]: John! My good friend. It's great to see you. We've known each other for close to a quarter century, going back to my GE Engines days. Over the years, you have been my valued customer, my ferocious competitor and everything in between. As everyone will attest, you have contributed immensely to the success of Airbus, and added color and energy to our industry for more than 30 years, and that's an understatement. And you've sold a hell of a lot of airplanes, too. So, on behalf of your friends at Boeing, congratulations on this well-earned recognition.

VOICE OFF CAMERA: Okay, we got it. Cut.

MCNERNEY: Is the mike off?

An employee in a shirt adorned with "BOEING Builds it BETTER" moves in to remove the mike.

MCNERNEY shakes his head [*Exasperated*]: Don't ever make me do that again, please.

It was hilarious. The audience of more than 1,000 loved it. It demonstrated a rare show of magnanimity and humor on the part of the staid, buttoned-down McNerney and Boeing. Unfortunately, Boeing insisted that the video not be released into the public domain.

Leahy and his commercial team booked more than 15,000 net orders with a list price of more than $2 trillion from his first year as commercial director in Toulouse through January 2018, when he finally retired.

Leahy more than made good on his promise to the Airbus board in 1995. By the time he retired in January 2018, Airbus consistently outsold Boeing. It had a market share of 55 to 57 percent in the single-aisle sector and, depending on the year, slightly more than 50 percent of the market in wide-body sales.

While Boeing tended to rotate its chief salesman every few years, Airbus's super-salesman reported to seven CEOs during his 23 years in Toulouse as commercial director of Airbus: Jean Pierson, Noel Forgeard, Gustav Humbert, Christian Streiff, Louis Gallois, Tom Enders and Fabrice Bregier. In all, Leahy spent 33 years at Airbus. In terms of personal achievement—and company stability in sales—Leahy's tenure and achievement remain unmatched.

AIR WARS

240 AIR WARS

ENTRY INTO SERVICE (EIS) DATES FOR MAJOR AIRPLANE MODELS

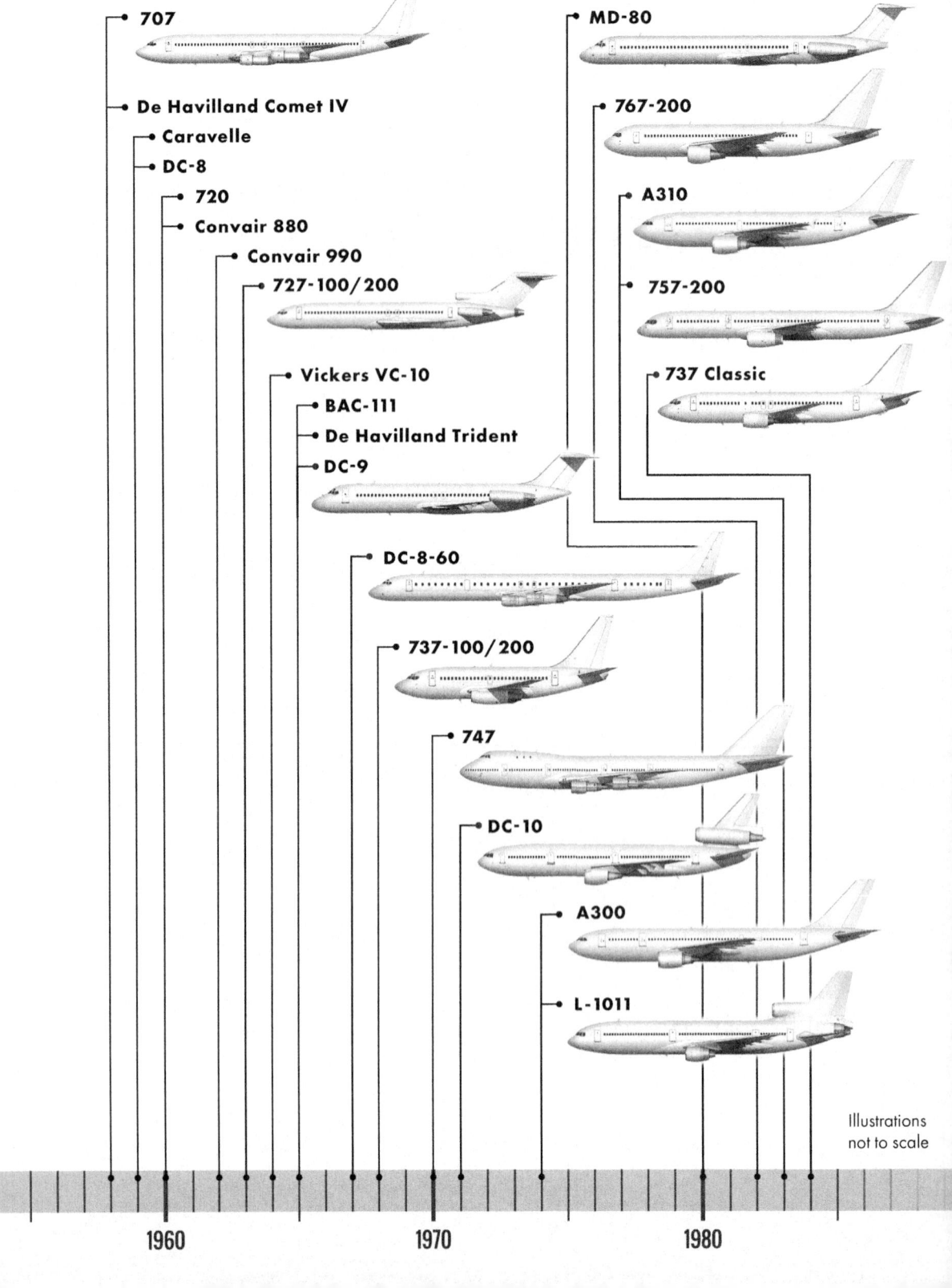

Illustrations not to scale

APPENDIX

ENTRY INTO SERVICE (EIS) DATES FOR MAJOR AIRPLANE MODELS

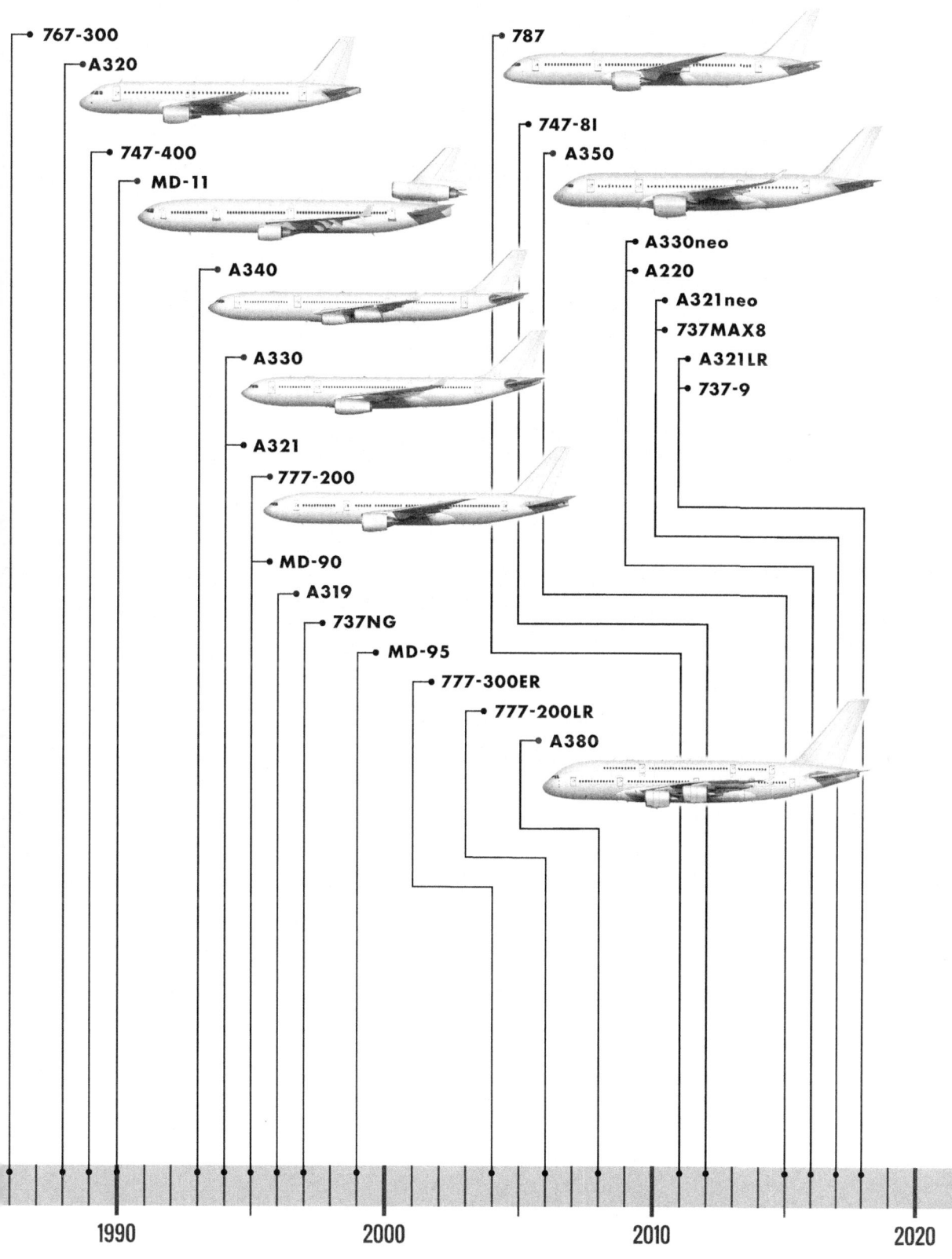

Acknowledgments

FIRST AND FOREMOST, I must acknowledge Gail Twelves. She encouraged this project for years before I finally got off the dime. As stipulated in the "Author's Note," I originally encouraged Leahy to write his memoirs. From the start, Gail said I should write the book.

Writing a book requires countless hours. This one took nearly three years with current events, work and other issues interrupting the flow. A non-fiction book also requires the help and forbearance of everyone who is interviewed. These people sit through what may be hours of discussion, repeated phone calls and endless questions.

I've covered Boeing directly since 1992. I've had a contentious relationship with Boeing for probably about half this time, mostly since development of the 787 from the delays beginning in 2007. Thus, when it came time to reach out to former Boeing employees and executives, I had little reason to believe they would cooperate or offer candid answers. Boeing declined to answer questions, or to make Calhoun or Smith available for interviews. Except for one former employee, who declined after asking Boeing for permission to speak with me, which was denied, every current or former Boeing person I approached cooperated and did so freely. Some required anonymity, but that was okay.

I'm especially grateful that three former CEOs of BCA, Scott Carson, Jim Albaugh and Ray Conner, talked with me. All were forthcoming about their tenures at BCA. They provided rich stories and perspective about the competition with Airbus and combatting Leahy.

The executives and others at Airbus were generous with their time and stories. Tom Enders, John Leahy, Christian Scherer, Robert Lange, Kiran Rao, Rafael Alonso and Tom Williams all agreed to speak on the record. Leahy and I spent hours on the phone and in person, talking about his 33 years at Airbus.

Industry officials, such as Steven Udvar-Hazy and John Plueger from Air Lease Corp/ILFC, provided wonderful stories about their long relationship with Leahy. Nico Buchholz's career spanned Airbus, Lufthansa and Bombardier. The list goes on.

There are many sources who remain anonymous. They provided candid observations and important information to the stories of Airbus and Boeing.

Interviews I conducted over the years, stories I wrote for *Leeham News* and other publications, and my own archival information provided invaluable information now included in *Air Wars*. Transcripts of Boeing executive employee meetings and earnings calls, also from my own files, were key sources of contemporary events.

I thank the following for their assistance:

Richard Aboulafia, Jim Albaugh, Rafael Alonso, Laurence Barron, Toby Bright, Nico Buchholz, Scott Carson, Richard Cherney, Charles Cleaver, Mike Conway, Bob Crandall, Barry Eccleston, Tom Enders, John Feren, John Leahy, Dana Lockhart, Clay McConnell, Bob Lange, Terry Maxon, Rainer Ohler, Adam Pilarski, John Plueger, Robert Priddy, Kiran Rao, Dan Reed, Judson Rollins, Stefan Schaffrath, Christian Scherer, Gary Scott, Nick Tomassetti, Steven Udvar-Hazy, Steve Vella and Tom Williams.

I am also indebted to many others whose names are unfortunately not possible to include here. I had enough material for a 650-page book with a lot left over. I had to whittle this down to a manageable size. I apologize to those who gave me great stories that didn't make it into this published version.

Finally, I extend my thanks to editors Susan O'Meara and Michael Brady, Dan Reed, Trudy White, Miki Mullor, Hugh Saffel and Eric Nord, all of whom contributed to this effort in various supporting roles.

SCOTT HAMILTON
August 2021

Index

9/11 attacks, 81, 84, 105, 111, 176, 204–7, 225

A

Aboulafia, Richard, 38, 74, 234
Aero Mechanic, 114, 134
Aeromexico, 43, 95, 225
Aerospatiale, 93, 233
AIG, 33–34, 205, 231
AirAsia, 44, 130
Air Baltic, 152
Airbus Industries
    American relationship, 4–9, 184–85
    America West relationship, 26
    Asia relationship, 43–44
    Bombardier relationship, 120, 123, 157–60, 163–64, 167
    bribery scandal, 168, 202–203, 212–16
    Chinese relationship, 35–40
    coronavirus effects, 221–26
    financial risks, 29–35
    Latin America relationship, 40–43
    Northwest relationship, 22–23
    Pan-Am relationship, 22–23, 27
    safety, 138–39
    structure, 87–92
    Toulouse headquarters, 10, 29, 32, 37, 87, 90–91, 231
    trade complaint, 74, 76–77
    USAF relationship, 206–212
    VLA forecasts, 75–76
Airbus Beijing Engineering Centre (ABEC), 37
Air Canada, 65, 76, 86, 96, 152–53
aircraft
    Airbus
        A220, 161–63, 212
        A220-100, 162

A220-300, 162–63
A300, 4–6, 21–22, 29, 31, 39–40, 43, 45, 53, 57, 75–77, 83
A300-600, 22, 200, 37
A300-600R, 4–5, 30, 150
A300-800neo, 179
A300B4, 21, 229
A310, 21, 23, 27, 29–30, 32–33, 36, 39, 47, 76–77, 83, 229
A310-300, 26–27, 30
A318, 69, 118, 231
A319, 1–2, 60, 69, 118, 120, 124, 126–27
A319ceo, 134, 158
A319neo, 134, 158, 162
A319RE, 130
A320, 1–5, 26, 29, 33–34, 37–42, 44–46, 48, 65–66, 120, 124–28, 130, 158, 212, 220, 224–26, 233
A320neo, 4, 7–9, 120–21, 126, 135, 141, 152, 162–63, 165, 168, 183, 220, 230, 233, 235–36
A320RE, 3–4, 130
A321, 1, 67, 126, 128, 176, 180–81, 198, 233
A321ceo, 67, 134, 155, 179
A321neo, 67, 134, 155–56, 163, 178–81, 183, 185–86
A321LR, 149, 179, 185, 221
A321RE, 130
A321XLR, 64, 67, 149, 185, 221, 224
A330, 1, 29, 31, 34, 38, 45–47, 51–54, 74–75, 83, 87, 94–95, 99, 124, 141–42, 172, 180, 207–11, 224, 232
A330F, 150
A330-20, 52–53, 150, 207, 232
A330-200ceo, 179–80
A330-300, 23, 47, 53, 76, 173

A330-800, 179–80, 186, 221
A330-800neo, 179–80
A330-900F, 150
A330ceo, 149
A330 MRTT, 93, 150, 206
A330neo, 141–42, 159, 171, 177, 180, 234–36
A340, 29, 43, 45–52, 54, 74–77, 87, 120, 232
A340-200, 47–48
A340-300, 46, 50
A340-500, 47, 50, 52, 232
A340-600, 50, 52, 89, 98, 231
A350, 1, 37, 44, 52, 64, 88, 91–92, 94–101, 124, 139, 149, 168, 171–73, 224
A350F, 150
A350-800, 94, 97
A350-900, 98, 171
A350-900ULR, 98
A350-1000, 97, 143–44, 148
A350-2000, 148–49
A350 XWB, 89, 96, 139, 143
A380, 1–2, 55, 70–77, 83, 87–94, 103, 142, 149–50, 168–73, 224, 228, 230–31, 235–36
A3XX, 70, 74
A400M, 1, 91–94, 97, 124, 159
Boeing
  707, 20, 30, 35, 53, 56, 93, 100, 102, 206
  717, 59, 81, 102, 153
  720, 56
  727, 37, 53, 56, 100, 125, 175
  727-200, 65, 102, 175
  737, 1–4, 8–10, 27, 34, 37, 40–42, 46, 59, 63–66, 68–69, 74, 111–12, 115, 121, 125–30, 132–36, 154, 164, 175–78, 184–85, 188–90, 205, 226, 234–35
  737-7, 121–22, 153–54, 157–58, 162, 183
  737-8, 134, 154, 158, 162
  737-9, 177, 185
  737-10, 155, 177
  737-200, 69
  737-300, 65–66, 69, 126
  737-400, 65–66, 127
  737-500, 58, 128
  737-600, 58, 63, 67, 118, 128
  737-700, 1–2, 63, 66–67, 118, 121–22, 126–27, 152–54, 157, 161, 183
  737-700RE, 130
  737-800, 1–2, 8, 65–67, 127, 130, 132, 134, 154, 158, 161, 175–76, 232
  737-900, 66, 126, 128, 234
  737-900ER, 1, 67, 126, 130, 155, 176
  737 MAX, 9, 135–36, 149, 152–53, 155–58, 161–62, 168, 175–77, 180–84, 186–91, 193–203, 216–218, 220–21, 225–26
  737NG, 3–5, 8, 60, 66–67, 127–29, 154, 185, 190–91, 220
  737RE, 3–4, 8–9, 129–31, 133, 135–36
  747, 20–21, 34, 55, 68, 73–76, 112, 139, 143, 149–50, 173–74, 198, 205
  747-8, 2, 100, 117, 142–43, 149–50, 168, 173
  747-8F, 1, 135, 150, 173
  747-8I, 135, 173
  747-100, 101
  747-300, 50
  747-400, 1, 70, 72
  747–500, 70, 72, 74, 78–79, 83
  747-600, 83
  747-X, 83
  757, 34, 53, 63–64, 74, 100, 102, 112, 118, 175–77, 179, 182, 184, 205
  757-200, 175–76
  757-300, 81, 184, 234
  767, 21–23, 29–30, 34, 45, 47, 53–54, 57, 63–64, 74–75, 78–81, 172, 177, 182–84, 205–210
  767-2C, 210
  767-200, 53, 183
  767-200ER, 23, 205–10
  767-300ER, 53, 63–64, 206, 208
  767-300ERF, 53, 151
  767-400, 81, 208, 210, 234
  777, 45, 47–54, 75, 81, 112, 115, 143–44, 147–50, 153, 172, 205, 224
  777-8, 76, 98–99, 218, 148–50
  777-8F, 150–51, 218
  777-8P, 150–51
  777-9, 76, 98–99, 148–50, 169, 218
  777-200, 46, 48, 50, 54, 63–64
  777-200ER, 49–50, 52, 54, 74, 97–98
  777-200LR, 149, 173
  777-200LRF, 1, 150–51
  777-200X, 54

INDEX

777-300, 50
777-300ER, 1, 50, 52, 55, 76, 97–98, 143, 150, 153, 169, 173
777-300X, 54
777X, 40, 48, 76, 98, 143–51, 153, 169, 181, 195, 218–19
787, 1–2, 37–39, 53–54, 59–60, 73–75, 78, 80–87, 93–97, 99–112, 114–17, 133–45, 149, 153, 180, 211, 219, 223–25, 235–37
787-3, 104, 184
787-8, 54, 98–99, 104, 138, 140–41, 176–77
787-9, 97–99, 141, 176–77
787-10, 104, 171, 223
797-7, 178–80
7E7, 78, 81–83, 109–10
B-47, 207
B-52, 207
Dreamlifter, 107
Dreamliner, 100, 104, 138, 177
KC-46, 53, 143, 193, 211–12, 219
KC-135, 203, 205, 207
KC-330, 206, 208–209, 212, 215
KC-767, 84, 206–208, 210, 212
MQ-25, 178, 182
NMA-5, 185
NMA-6, 184–85
NMA-7, 186, 177, 179–80, 182
Sonic Cruiser, 78–83, 173
Stratocruiser, 56
Super Sonic Transport, 78
T-X, 178, 182
Bombardier
 CRJ, 2, 119–23, 152, 158
 CS100, 2, 118, 120, 122, 152–54
 CS300, 2, 118, 120–22, 152–54, 163
 CS500, 120
 Q400, 121–23, 152, 166
Douglas/McDonnell/McDonnell Douglas
 C-17, 93
 C-54, 56
 D-80, 4–5, 8, 30, 36, 39, 61, 125
 DC-2, 56
 DC-3, 56
 DC-4, 56
 DC-6, 56
 DC-7, 56
 DC-8, 20, 22, 30, 40, 56

DC-8-60, 125
DC-8-62, 149
DC-9, 23, 30, 40, 56
DC-9 Super 80, 30
DC-10, 40–41, 47–48, 57–58, 65, 109, 140, 206, 213
DC-10-30, 74
DC-10-40, 22
MD-11, 45–46, 58–59, 61, 63, 65, 74–75
MD-80, 4–5, 8, 30, 36, 39, 61, 63, 125
MD-90, 36, 39, 61, 63
MD-95, 58–60, 63, 81, 102, 105–106
MDF-100, 58
Embraer
 E175-E2, 162, 220
 E190-E1, 152, 153, 163
 E190-E2, 162–63, 166
 E195-E2, 153, 162–63, 166
 KC-390, 161–62
Others
 Aerospatiale/BAC Concorde, 207, 228
 ATR 42, 166
 ATR 72, 166
 Avro RJ100, 120
 Beechcraft 18, 12, 14
 Braniff BAC-111, 23–24
 COMAC ARJ21, 38–39, 146
 COMAC C919, 38, 156
 COMAC CR929, 38
 Convair 990, 40
 Convair CV-880, 40
 Eurofighter Typhoon, 215
 Fokker 100, 41
 Learjet 85, 123
 Lockheed Constellation (Connie), 56
 Lockheed C-130, 93
 Lockheed Martin C-130J Super Hercules, 93
 Lockheed L-1011, 40, 57–58, 213
 Lockheed Tristars, 47, 58
 Sud Aviation Caravelle, 22
Air Data Inertial Reference Unit (ADIRU), 191
Air Deccan, 44
Airfinance Journal (AFJ), 25
Air Mauritius, 52
Air Transport World (ATW), 96

Albaugh, James, 9, 62, 73, 121–22, 128, 132–37, 143–44, 152, 186
Alenia, 93, 103, 106–7
all-electric airplane, 82, 101, 124
Allen, Ron, 26–28, 30
All Nippon Airways (ANA), 83, 85, 105, 135, 138–40, 190, 213
Alonso, Rafael, 40–43
American Airlines, 4–10, 15, 24–27, 30–31, 63–64, 67–68, 80, 127, 132–35, 175–76, 184, 190, 201, 225, 230
America West, 25–26, 30–31, 65, 176, 230
Arpey, Gerard, 5–6, 8–9, 68
ATR, 166, 236
aviation accidents, 4–5, 60–61, 139–40, 164, 182, 187–94, 197–202
AVIC (Aviation Industry Corporation of China), 37
Azul Airlines, 166

B

Bair, Mike, 128–32
bankruptcy, 5, 8, 24–26, 28, 31–32, 81, 112, 154, 230
Barron, Laurence, 36–40, 169–70
Bell, James, 129
Bellemare, Alain, 158–59
Bethune, Gordon, 23
BIA-COR, 24–25
Boeing Brasil-Commercial (BBC), 161, 164–65
Boeing Capital Corp., 61
Boeing Commercial Airplanes (BCA)
    American relationship, 4–9, 67–69, 176
    Bombardier relationship, 121–22
    company structure, 179, 205
    coronavirus effects, 218–26
    Everett plant, 38, 102, 112–16, 118, 144–45, 148, 205, 221, 223
    FAA review, 193–194
    lessors relationship, 34
    market share, 57–58, 81, 181, 233–35
    MAX scandal, 187–201, 216–17
    NMA development, 182–86
    price-dumping trade complaint, 154–56
    public relations, 35, 193–202
    Renton headquarters, 37, 68, 118, 135–36, 176, 205, 223
    sales force, 84–85
    subsonic aircraft, 78–80
    supplier management, 106–108
    tanker scandal, 203–212
    unions, 106–107, 110–116
    USAF relationship, 205, 219
    VLA forecast, 75–76
Boeing Defense, Space and Security (BDS), 161, 179
Boeing-Embraer Joint Venture, 161–167
Boeing Global Services (BGS), 179, 222
Boeing Integrated Defense Systems (IDS), 205
Boeing-McDonnell Douglas merger, 63–64, 69, 74
Bombardier Commercial Airplanes, 2, 117–23, 127, 152–60, 163–67
Bonderman, David, 26
Boyd, Alan, 18, 229
Braniff Inc. (Braniff II), 24–26, 31
Braniff International Airways (BI), 24, 212
Bregier, Fabrice, 91, 141, 166, 238
Bright, Toby, 35, 47, 50–51, 65–66, 73, 79, 81, 84–85, 135
British Aerospace, 93, 233
British Airways, 40, 85, 127, 201
British Caledonian, 40
Bryan, Jim, 229–30
Buchholz, Nico, 48–49, 119–120
Burlington Northern Air Freight, 12–13

C

CAAC (Civil Aviation Administration of China), 36, 190
CASA, 93, 233
Calhoun, David, 185, 195–99, 217–19, 221–23, 226
Carey, Daniel, 201
Carson, Scott, 80, 84–86, 104, 108, 226
Cathay Pacific Airways, 149
Cebu Pacific Air, 76
CFM International, 2, 46
Champion, Charles, 88, 90
Cherney, Richard, 6, 67–68
China Southern, 169
Chodorow, Jeffrey, 24
Clark, Tim, 96, 98, 149, 169–71, 218, 228
Cleaver, Charles, 25–26
Cohen, Arthur, 24

INDEX

Colodny, Ed, 23
COMAC (Commercial Aircraft Corporation of China), 38
Commercial Aviation Report (CAR), 25
Condit, Bill, 60, 67, 70, 74, 76, 78, 81, 83, 206, 215–16
Condor Airlines, 175
Conner, Ray, 35, 70–73, 78–80, 85–86, 105–10, 115, 133–37, 139–40, 144–46, 154–58, 161–63, 176, 181, 183–84, 194, 226–27
Continental Airlines, 4–5, 25, 31, 63–65, 176
Convair, 40
Conway, Mike, 25–26
Coupron, Henri, 159
COVID-19, 37, 142, 149–50, 204, 216–18, 221–25, 235
Crandall, Robert, 6–7, 15, 27, 31, 63, 67–68

D

Dailey, Marlin, 9, 184
Davies, David, 32
Deal, Stan, 179, 196, 219, 227
de Castlebajac, Patrick, 159
Deferred Prosecution Agreement (DPA), 202–203, 214–17
de Havilland, 118
Delta, 4–5, 26–28, 30, 49, 63–64, 121, 123, 127, 152–56, 158, 176
Department of Transportation, 193–94, 216
Deutsche Aerospace, 233
Dickson, Steve, 197
Douglas Aircraft Co., 7, 21–22, 40, 56–63, 109
Druyun, Darleen, 206
Dubai Air Show, 148, 170–71

E

EADS (European Aeronautic Defence and Space Company), 38, 87–88, 90, 207–214
Eccleston, Barry, 5–10, 124, 126–27, 159
E-Jet family, 2, 119, 158, 161–65
Emergency Airworthiness Directive (AD), 139, 189
Emirates Airline (EK), 55, 96, 98–99, 143, 148–49, 156, 169–71, 218
Enders, Tom, 3, 9, 38, 73, 76, 88–94, 123, 126, 159–60, 169–72, 179, 212, 216, 226, 232, 235–36, 238
Engine Alliance, 83, 169–71, 218
engines
　CFM International LEAP, 2, 183
　CFM LEAP-X, 129
　CFM56, 46, 48, 120, 125
　CFM56-5C, 46
　Engine Alliance GP7200, 169
　GE90, 50–52
　GE CF34, 119
　GEnx, 94, 100
　GE-Pratt Engine Alliance GP7000, 83
　IAE SuperFan, 45–47
　IAE V2500, 45–46, 120
　PW180, 93
　P&W 6000, 231
　P&W Geared Turbofan (GTF), 2–3, 45, 119–20, 124, 129, 156, 168, 183
　P&W JT3D, 35–36
　RR Trent 900, 83, 169
　RR Trent 1000, 180, 183, 236
　RR Trent 7000, 180, 236
　Snecma M88, 93
Ethiopian Airlines, 189, 202
Etihad Airways, 98–99, 148–50, 156
ETOPS (Extended-Range Twin-Engine Operations Performance), 52, 54, 175, 179
Euroflag, 93
European Union (EU), 7, 63–64, 74–75, 119, 163, 165–66, 172, 187, 207, 211, 219
European Union Aviation Safety Agency (EASA), 190, 220, 225
Everett Herald, 95, 103–104, 115, 173
Evrard, Didier, 91
exclusive deals, 4, 8–10, 63–65, 67–68, 120

F

Farnborough Air Show, 119–20, 122, 164, 168, 177, 179
Faury, Guillaume, 91, 171–73, 224–26, 235
Federal Aviation Administration (FAA), 139–40, 188–90, 193–197, 199–202, 204, 216–218, 220
FedEx, 17, 102, 230–31
Feith, Greg, 199–202

Feren, John, 41–42, 47, 61–62, 83–84
Fernandes, Tony, 44, 232
Flight Global, 173
Florida Express, 24
Fokker, 41, 58
Forgeard, Noel, 70–71, 88, 90, 238
four-engine aircraft, 29, 45, 51, 52, 54, 231
Franke, Bill, 26
freighters, 50, 52, 54, 74–76, 224, 230
Frontier Airlines, 69, 120
Future International Military Airlifter (FIMA), 93

G

Gallois, Louis, 88–90, 92, 238
General Aviation (GA), 16–17
General Electric (GE), 46, 48, 51–52, 83, 95, 102, 126, 147, 153, 183, 218
General Electric Capital Aviation Services (GECAS), 34, 95, 205
Gillette, Walt, 105
Global Aeronautica, 103, 107
Go Air, 44
Gogolia, John, 199
GOL, 43, 225
Great Financial Crisis of 2008, 2, 5, 112, 123, 172
Greenberg, Hank, 204–205
Gregoire, Christine, 113–16, 211

H

Hamlin, George, 74
Hart-Smith, Dr. L. J., 109
Hazy, Steven, 18–19, 33–34, 95–96, 204–205, 229, 231–33
Healy, Tim, 115–16
Horton, Tom, 5–9, 184
Humbert, Gustav, 88, 90, 238

I

IAM 751, 38, 105, 111, 113–14, 116, 134–36, 144, 194, 221
ICAO (International Civil Aviation Organization), 151
Ilyushin Aircraft Finance, 122
Indian Airlines, 44
IndiGo, 44, 121, 130, 171, 235–36
industrial footprint, 36, 39
intellectual property (IP), 38–39
Interjet, 43

International Aero Engines (IAE), 3, 24–25, 43, 45–46, 48, 63, 120
International Lease Finance Corp. (ILFC), 33–34, 95, 204–205, 230–32
International Trade Commission (ITC), 157
Iraq Air, 122

J

Japan Air Lines (JAL), 85, 138–40, 190, 198
JetBlue, 69, 158, 163
Jet Capital Co., 25
Joyce, David, 126

K

Keating, Tim, 115
Kelleher, Herb, 69
Kellner, Larry, 197
Kelly, Gary, 196
Kenya Airways, 33
Kight, Doug, 115
King, Jim, 25–26
Kingfisher, 44
KLM, 41
Korean Air Lines, 122, 158
Krauthamer, Gary, 18–19
KSSU, 41–42

L

LAN Chile, 41–43
Lange, Robert, 70, 94
LATAM, 43
Leahy, John
  A320 re-engine, 3–4, 120–21, 124–30
  A340/777 campaign, 48–51
  A380 launch, 70–74, 78, 83, 93, 109–110
  AIG merger, 34
  American relationship, 4–9, 31, 68
  Asian deals, 43–44
  Bombardier relationship, 2
  Chinese sales, 35–39
  early life, 10–11
  Emirates deal, 170–71
  flying career, 11–14
  Latin American sales, 40–43
  "Leahy Tracking," 85
  MDC job offers, 61–62, 90
  Pan-Am relationship, 21–27, 32
  Piper career, 15–19
  post-9/11, 84, 204–5

reputation, 226–32
retirement, 227–238
United relationship, 65–66
Learjet, 123, 152
Leeham News, 51, 98, 115, 155, 157, 162, 173, 223
Lehman Brothers, 21, 103, 112, 123
Leverkuhn, Keith, 194
Lion Air Group, 182, 187–89, 191–92, 194, 198–202, 220
Lockhart, Dana, 26, 30–33, 229–30
Lockheed Co., 21, 40, 56–58, 93, 213
Lockheed Martin, 212
Lorenzo, Frank, 20, 25
low-cost carrier (LCC), 33, 43–44, 235
Lufthansa Group, 45, 47, 51, 119–20, 122, 148–50, 152

M

Malindo Air, 168, 187
Maneuvering Characteristics Augmentation System (MCAS), 188–94, 199–201, 216–17
McAllister, Kevin, 227, 196, 198–99
McCain, John, 206–207, 211
McDonnell Corp., 56
McDonnell Douglas Corp. (MDC), 4, 22, 29–30, 35–36, 39, 41, 45, 53, 56–65, 74, 81, 93, 101, 109, 125, 207, 213, 234
McDonnell, John, 61–62
McNerney, James, 38, 81, 86, 102, 108–10, 112–13, 115–16, 135–137, 144, 148, 175, 179, 184, 217, 227, 235–37
ME3, 148–150
Messerschmitt-Bölkow-Blohm, 93
Mexicana, 43
middle of the market (MOM), 141, 176, 178–81, 186
Mohawk Airlines, 23
Mounir, Ihssane, 227
Muilenburg, Dennis, 155–56, 178–81, 186, 189–90, 193–99, 201, 219, 226–27
Mulally, Alan, 79, 81, 85, 108

N

Nadol, Joe, 101, 103–104
narrow-body aircraft, 1–3, 29–30, 41–43, 54, 57, 64–66, 124, 126, 129, 132–33, 153, 175–78, 182–84, 237. *See also* single-aisle aircraft

National Airlines, 20
National Labor Relations Board (NLRB), 114, 116, 136
National Transportation Safety Board (NTSB), 5, 140, 192, 199
Neeleman, David, 69
New Lite Twin (NLT), 176, 178
New Midmarket Aircraft (NMA), 64, 75, 132–35, 162–65, 172, 176–86, 195, 219–20, 223, 233
Norris, Guy, 54
Northrop Grumman Corp. (NGC), 74–75, 135, 207–209, 211–12
Northwest Airlines, 4, 23
NSA (New Small Airplane), 127, 132–33, 161, 176

O

Odyssey Airlines, 122
Omega Air, 102, 206
Open Skies, 47, 73
outsourcing, 81, 106–107, 109, 111, 113–15

P

Pan Am, 20–28, 30, 32, 35, 65, 212
Paris Air Show, 38, 47, 98, 101, 130, 170, 179, 184
Performance Improvement Packages (PIPs), 99, 170–71
Pierson, Jean, 23, 29–31, 35–36, 43, 46, 62, 229–230, 238
Pilarski, Adam, 56–58
Piper Aircraft, 10, 16–19, 229
Piedmont Airlines, 20, 23–24, 69
Plueger, John, 33–34, 220–33
Power 8, 89–90, 94
Pratt & Whitney (P&W), 2, 25, 35–36, 45–46, 48, 56, 63, 75, 83, 93, 129, 156, 175, 183, 218, 231
Priddy, Robert, 60
Project Gemini, 114

Q

QC2, 72
Qantas, 96
Qatar Airways, 96, 99, 148–49, 156

R

Rao, Kiran, 3–4, 43–44, 49–50, 52, 96, 98, 121, 125, 141–42, 166, 235–36
regional jet, 2, 117, 121
Republic Airways Holdings, 120
Rolls-Royce, 46, 48–50, 63, 72, 75–76, 83, 129, 141, 169–71, 175, 183, 215, 218, 232, 236
Rowe, Brian, 51
Royal Air Force, 206
Ryanair, 225

S

SabreTech, 61
Safran, 46
SAS, 41, 58–59
Scherer, Christian, 3, 125–26, 204, 225, 236
Schulz, Eric, 236
Scope Clause, 162, 166, 220
Scott, Gary, 68, 118–19, 122–23, 155
Sears, Mike, 206
Seattle Times, 104, 134, 136, 147, 223
Securities and Exchange Commission (SEC) filings, 25, 27–28, 173
Shrontz, Frank, 23
Singapore Airlines, 50, 70, 79
single-aisle aircraft, 1–3, 22, 29–30, 33–34, 41–43, 54, 57, 64–66, 124, 126, 129, 132–33, 153, 175–78, 182–84, 233, 237
Sinnett, Mike, 190–92
SkyWest, 166
Slattery, John, 153, 161–67, 219–20, 222
Smith, Greg, 182, 185, 197
Snecma, 46, 93
Society of Professional Engineering Employees in Aerospace (SPEEA), 106–107, 111, 113–15, 163–64
South African Airways (SAA), 49–50
Southwest Airlines, 4, 8, 27, 63, 66, 69, 122, 133, 154, 190, 196, 201, 225
Speed Trim System, 190–92
Spencer, Scot, 24
Spirit Aerosystems, 112, 159
Stagecoach Airlines, 12
Strategy and Marketing Organization (SMO), 213–15, 235
Stonecipher, Harry, 53, 59–60, 76, 81–86, 108–109, 206

Streiff, Christian, 88–90
Swissair, 41, 58

T

Taca Airlines (TACA), 40–42
TAM Airlines, 41–43
tankers, 53, 58, 116, 135, 143, 150, 205–12, 218–19
Terrible Teens, 105, 144
Texaco, 27–28
Texas Air Corp. (TAC), 20, 25
Texas International Airlines, 25
Thomas, Geoffrey, 96
Thornton, Dean, 65–66
Tomassetti, Nicolas, 45–46, 59–60, 63
Transcontinental and Western Airline (TWA), 30–31, 35, 63, 65
Transport Canada, 190, 225
Trippe, Juan, 20, 212
Trump administration, 40, 154, 157, 165, 172, 190, 216, 218–19
turboprop engines, 2, 222, 93, 163–66
twin-aisle aircraft, 1–3, 29, 31, 57, 75, 129, 132, 134, 176–77, 182–85
twin-engine aircraft, 29, 47, 52, 54, 57, 99, 172–73, 175, 232

U

ultra-long-range (ULR) airplane, 98
unions, 13, 28, 37–38, 81, 106, 110–16, 135–37, 144–48, 162–63, 190, 194–95, 201, 220, 224
United Airlines, 4–5, 26–27, 43, 48, 63–69, 121, 127, 133, 138–39, 153, 156–58, 176, 190, 225, 230
U.S. Air Force (USAF), 58, 81, 93, 116, 135, 143, 203, 205–12, 218–19
US Airways, 5, 30, 95, 230
U.S. Court of International Trade (CIT), 158
U.S. Department of Justice (US-DOJ), 193, 202, 215–16
U.S. Export-Import Bank, 156
U.S. Navy, 206
U.S. Trade Representative, 119, 155, 207, 210
UTA, 41

V

ValuJet, 60–61, 63

VASP, 42
Vella, Steven, 53, 244
Very Large Aircraft (VLA), 75–76
Virgin America, 69, 130
VivaAerobus, 43
Volaris, 43
Vought, 103, 106–7

W

WestJet, 69, 225
wide-body aircraft, 1, 3, 22, 29, 43, 54, 57, 75–76, 86, 95, 132–34, 149, 176–78, 182, 184–85, 226. *See also* twin-aisle aircraft.
Widerøe, 166
Wilhelm, Harald, 216
Williams, Tom, 2, 87, 91, 120
Wojick, John, 177, 227
Wolf, John, 61
Wood, Heidi, 135
Woodard, Ron, 7, 68–69, 234–35
World Trade Organization (WTO), 76–77, 100, 118, 144, 155–56, 172, 207, 210–11
World War II, 20, 56, 69, 93, 111, 207
Wroblewski, Tom, 116, 145, 148

Y

Yeager, Chuck, 19

Printed in Great Britain
by Amazon